MW00617521

MY FATHER'S HOUSE

MY FATHER'S HOUSE

TEMPLE WORSHIP AND SYMBOLISM IN THE NEW TESTAMENT

RICHARD NEITZEL HOLZAPFEL
DAVID ROLPH SEELY

BOOKCRAFT
Salt Lake City, Utah

Library of Congress Catalog Card Number: 94-73430
ISBN 0-88494-954-0

First Printing, 1994

Printed in the United States of America

For Nathan

For Jo Ann, Rachel, Joseph, and Kathryn

Contents

Acknowledgments................................. ix

Prologue: My Father's House 1

1   The Temple as the Pathway to Eternal Life 11

2   The Temples of Ancient Israel 21

3   Temple Worship at the Time of Christ 55

4   Luke and the Presence of God in the Temple 81

5   The Early Church and the Temple in Acts 119

6   Jesus and the Temple in the Gospel of John 141

7   Matthew and the Destruction of the Temple 171

8   The Temple Made Without Hands in Hebrews 183

9   The Body-as-Temple and the Temple-Church 195

10   Promises to the Faithful in John's Revelation 207

Epilogue: My House 251

Notes.. 257

Bibliography.................................. 267

Illustration Credits 275

Index....................................... 281

Acknowledgments

We thank our publisher, Bookcraft, especially Cory Maxwell, Jana Erickson, and Garry Garff. We also thank Richard Draper, Frank Judd, Jennifer Hammond, Jeni Broberg Holzapfel, Nathan Holzapfel, Susannah Broberg Langenheim, Michael Lyon, Matthew Moore, Veneese Nelson, D. Kelly Ogden, Bruce Pearson, John Pendlebury, Julie Place, Jo Ann H. Seely, and Ted D. Stoddard for their help in making this effort better than it would have been without their contributions.

We have also utilized the works of many scholars, whose publications are noted in our bibliography. We alone, however, are responsible for the content, organization, and interpretations of this book.

PROLOGUE

My Father's House

*And [Jesus] said unto them that sold doves, Take these
things hence; make not my Father's house an house of
merchandise.*

—John 2:16

A small company follows him from a fishing village on the
northwest shore of the Sea of Galilee in the springtime. They
walk to Jerusalem in the mountains more than one hundred
miles south from where they begin their journey. It is a de-
manding trip, not just in terms of distance but also in terms of
the ascent in elevation from six hundred feet below sea level to
more than twenty-five hundred feet above the Mediterranean
Sea. Traveling along dusty footpaths and ancient roads, the

◄ The Lord commanded the children of Israel to "appear before him" three
times a year at the great feasts—Passover, Festival of Weeks, and Feast of
Tabernacles—and at these times large numbers of Jews made their way to
Jerusalem (see Ex. 23:14–17). The temple, that was the pilgrims' goal. To see it,
to walk in its courtyards, to bring sacrifices and pray—these were what brought
them from all over the Mediterranean world. As they approached they sang
from the book of Psalms: "I was glad when they said unto me, Let us go into the
house of the Lord. Our feet shall stand within thy gates, O Jerusalem. Jerusalem
is builded as a city that is compact together: whither the tribes go up, the tribes
of the Lord, unto the testimony of Israel, to give thanks unto the name of the
Lord." (Ps. 122:1–4.)

group joins others making their way to the Holy City for the most solemn of Jewish holidays—the Passover.

The group leaves Capernaum and travels south on a journey lasting several days through the monotonous landscape of the Jordan River valley. Eventually, the dreary landscape gives way to a lush palm tree oasis—Jericho, the ancient city eight hundred fifty feet below the Mediterranean. From Jericho, they travel on a Roman road—a steep thoroughfare rising sharply through limestone ridges of the bleak Judean desert. They ascend some three thousand five hundred feet in just seventeen miles to Jerusalem. The countryside changes from the wilderness to cultivated fields, vineyards, and groves of olive trees as they reach the top of the Mount of Olives.

Here they crest the nearest of the ridges of hills that help to protect Jerusalem on the east. From the summit, they catch their first glimpse of Jerusalem, a thrilling and long-awaited sight. The group naturally and instinctively looks beyond the walls of the city to the Temple Mount—known as *Har Habayit,* the "Mountain of the House [of God]." The enormous raised platform, with its huge retaining walls to bear the weight of the fill and of the structures built above, is nearly 172,000 square yards, making it the largest site of its kind in the ancient world.[1] On this spacious site is the jewel and heart of Jerusalem and of the Jewish nation—the holy temple. Radiant on the Temple Mount, it stands isolated from the city by a large courtyard. Its brilliant white stones and gold-covered facade reflect the sunlight directly into the travelers' eyes—creating a sense of awe and wonder among these religious pilgrims.

After a brief stop to relax from the tedious trip and to contemplate the sights before them, the group continues on its way. The company crosses the Kidron Brook in the eastern valley below Jerusalem and sings from the book of Psalms: "O give thanks unto the Lord; for he is good: for his mercy endureth for ever" (Ps. 136:1).[2] Their pace increases, so that many are joyously dancing as they walk toward King David's hilltop stronghold, now dominated by the magnificent temple built by Herod. The happy procession enters through one of the massive gates.

They stop again to satisfy their thirst from one of the many wells or springs. Now, with their faces set toward the Temple Mount—a forty-acre area at the time—they ascend the stepped street paved with large limestone slabs.

The houses of the lower city are spread out before them like the crescent of the moon; higher up, on their left, they can see the magnificent palaces of the nobility in the upper city. As they ascend, their eyes focusing on the glittering gold spikes of the temple in the distance (spikes which keep birds from landing on the temple), they move forward through the oldest part of the city, established long ago by King David and Solomon. All along the street the merchants of the lower market are transacting business in their stalls. The travelers are jostled by the farmers and traders who have come to buy and sell, as well as by their beasts of burden.

They soon cross one of the many busy intersections within the city walls and continue moving toward the monumental staircase leading up to the Double Gate of the Temple Mount. Here they stop one more time. Passing the Double Gate to the east, they come to a bathhouse where they ritually purify themselves before entering the Temple Mount. The pools are deep enough to allow total immersion. Here they wash themselves and remove their shoes from their feet, heightening the sense of holiness of this place. Finally, they pass through a dark tunnel and emerge into the blinding sunlight to behold the grandeur of the holy place. The architectural glories of this temple far surpass even Solomon's famous temple that once stood on the same site.

Standing on the ground of sacred past events in the outer court, the Court of the Gentiles, the group is surrounded by majestic colonnades thirty-seven feet high. They are not the only ones who have come to this place to celebrate Passover, as literally thousands pass through the gates of the Temple Mount—they have become part of the great throng who have come to worship at the "house of the Lord." As many as three million people arrive in Jerusalem to celebrate Passover, many before Nisan 1, the day the half-shekel temple tax is due. Some dress in luxurious clothing, and others wear the only garment they own. Most of the men wear a prayer shawl and their *tefillin* (phylacteries)—little boxes containing Bible tracts. The Levites and priests pass through the area to prepare for their duties in the temple.

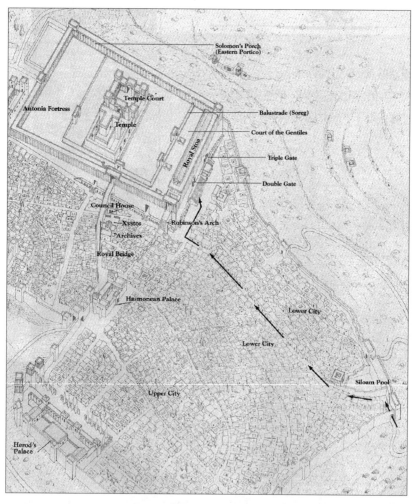

Herod's Temple Mount was nearly twice the size of the platform of Solomon's temple—thirty acres larger than Temple Square in Salt Lake City, or roughly the size of thirteen football fields. It was one of the most massive sites of its kind in the ancient world. Those who visited the temple ritually washed themselves and removed their shoes, many dressing in white, before entering through the right side of the Double Gate. While on the Temple Mount they were careful not to turn their backs to the temple except when they exited through the left side of the same Double Gate.

Here in the Court of the Gentiles, even non-Jews are allowed to enter and purchase offerings to be sacrificed by the priests at the great altar. The temple is also a tourist attraction; foreign monarchs, merchants, and servants alike visit the Court of the Gentiles and gaze in wonder at the building about which has been written, "He who has not seen the Temple in its full construction has never seen a glorious building in his life."[3]

Jews and Gentiles gather together in one place, but most are descendants of father Abraham and mother Sarah. Some come from Jerusalem and from Judea and Galilee. Others have traveled long distances to be here on the solemn occasion—these are the Jews of the Diaspora (the Dispersion). No matter what language they speak or how they dress, the Jews gather to the court to exchange their Roman and Greek coins for a kind of coin accepted at the temple, a coin known as the "Holy Shekel," and to buy animals and birds for sacrifice. The bleating of sheep, the lowing of cattle, and the cooing of doves and pigeons mix with the noise of people talking and moving from place to place.

The sounds of diverse accents and foreign tongues amid the hustle and bustle of throngs of people, coupled with the very strong smells of penned animals and of burnt sacrifices, create a singular impression of something unusual. Yet those who have followed him from Capernaum are unaware of what is about to happen. As they wander among the mass of people and business, they are conscious of the conspicuous presence of Roman soldiers standing watch from the looming Antonia fortress overlooking the temple grounds. They approach the balustrade, also known as the *Soreg,* a wall or barrier beyond which Gentiles were not allowed on penalty of death. On the other side is the sanctuary area itself, a place reserved for ritually pure Jews. But the newly arrived group does not enter this area now.

Their leader, without warning, turns away from them and the balustrade and pushes through the crowds. He takes some cords he has found along the way and purposely and pensively fashions a small whip. Then again, seemingly without warning, he begins to drive the caged animals from their pens, turning over tables laden with coinage and commanding the merchants, especially

the money changers, to leave the Temple Mount with their be-
longings. The disciples stand amazed, trying to make sense of
what they see Jesus do in this most sacred and holy spot.

All the Gospels agree that Jesus came to Jerusalem at
Passover and cleansed the ancient temple precincts—taking possession of his Father's house (see Matt. 21; Mark 11; Luke 19;
and John 2).[4] John records this particular episode: "And [Jesus]
found in the temple those that sold oxen and sheep and doves,
and the changers of money sitting: and when he had made a
scourge [whip] of small cords, he drove them all out of the
temple, and the sheep, and the oxen; and poured out the
changers' money, and overthrew the tables; and said unto them
that sold doves, Take these things hence; make not my Father's
house an house of merchandise" (John 2:14–16).

It was fairly common for Jews to make frequent pilgrimages
to the ancient city of Jerusalem for the great festivals that punc-
tuated the calendar of ancient Israel. Even poor peasants, like
those who followed Jesus from Galilee, made their way to the
Holy City to fulfill the commandment given to their fathers at
Sinai. John points out one small but important detail regarding
the cleansing of the temple—Jesus made a small whip. The
scriptures suggest that he effectively drove the animals out of the
precincts with it, causing chaos among the money changers, and
finally ordered out the pigeon dealers with their caged birds.

Jesus' statement made during this astonishing instance alludes to the words found in the Old Testament book of
Zechariah: "And in that day there shall be no more *the Canaanite*
in the house of the Lord of hosts" (Zech.14:21, emphasis
added). Zechariah's reference to Canaanites can also be translated "merchants," or "traders," since the Hebrew word *qana'* has
both meanings.[5] Zechariah is therefore prophesying of a future
day when merchants will not be present in the temple. Thus the
Galilean peasant is fulfilling prophecy by this sudden deed.

Jesus' surprising actions on this occasion also highlight his
close relationship with his Father when he declares that the
temple is "my Father's house." The disciples, following a moment of reflection, also interpret their Master's act in light of a

passage found in the book of Psalms: "For the zeal of thine house hath eaten me up; and the reproaches of them that reproached thee are fallen upon me" (Ps. 69:9; see John 2:17).

The subject of this particular psalm is that of a righteous sufferer: even his personal devotion and dedication toward the temple are held against him by his enemies. And now, in fulfillment of messianic prophecy, Jesus' love for his Father's house and his action of cleansing it cause the temple priests to confront and challenge his authority (see John 2:18–22). For the disciples who witnessed this extraordinary event, however, Jesus' actions fit perfectly the biblical words of prophetic writers who spoke of this day.

Jesus' life and ministry were bound up in the temple and its important holidays and celebrations. Simeon and Anna found him there when he was just an infant. At twelve, he remained in the temple to talk with the Jewish scholars, as his friends and family made their way home to Nazareth. Later, during his public ministry, he visited the holy site on several occasions, and taught daily within its hallowed walls during his last week of life.

Following Jesus' suffering, death, and resurrection, the disciples, some of whom were with him on that pivotal Passover visit, continued praising God in the temple and declaring the good news to anyone who would listen. Both Peter and Paul alluded to ancient temples and temple worship as they wrote to the early Christian Saints. The book of Revelation is also full of temple imagery. Many of the stories and expressions found in the New Testament are better understood within the context of ancient temple worship and symbolism as revealed through the Hebrew scriptures—the Old Testament.

We do, however, recognize that the New Testament is not a textbook on temple worship or symbolism. The mortal Messiah dominates the four Gospels, and the risen and exalted Jesus Christ dominates the remaining portion of this wonderful book. We believe it passionately—the New Testament was written and preserved so that we "might believe that Jesus is the Christ, the Son of God; and that believing [we] might have life through his

name" (John 20:31). Everything else is of secondary importance
to the overall message and purpose of the "new covenant"
record.

Yet, one of the great misunderstandings among many people
who accept the New Testament as sacred scripture is the place
the temple held in the hearts of the early Apostles and Christian
Saints. Not only did God command the Israelites to build sacred
structures (the tabernacle and the temple), but he manifested his
divine favor in these places of worship on many occasions (see,
for example, 1 Kgs. 8:10–13). Anyone familiar with the Old
Testament knows that Jerusalem was not the only place the Lord
was worshipped in righteousness. Recent archaeological evi-
dences support the fact that sacred buildings and sites dedicated
to the Lord were spread throughout Israel at different times.[6]

Further, the primary function in the temple at Jerusalem was
not sacrifice. The Old Testament prophets and the Lord himself
stated that it was a "house of prayer" par excellence (see Isa. 56:7;
cf. Matt. 21:13). This appears to be the overriding theme of
temple worship both ancient and modern. The rituals and ordinances performed in the temple were not secret, but sacred.
Only members of the house of Israel were permitted to enter
and participate in the "washings and anointings" and other ceremonies connected with the house of God. The book of Exodus
clearly outlines the Lord's commandment regarding these sacred
practices performed in his holy sanctuary, far away from the
gaze of the world (see Ex. 28–29, for example).

These ordinances were shadows of heavenly realities, yet
even following the death of Jesus Christ, the early Apostles and
Saints continued to praise God in the temple (see Luke 24:53).
These faithful followers of the Lord did not build a new temple,
because they already had one in their midst and they participated in its worship services (see Acts 22:17–21).

The rending of the veil at the time of the Crucifixion did not
signal the end of temple worship. The very disciples of Jesus who
described in detail this event continued to attend the temple and
participate in divinely sanctioned worship. The rending of the
veil may in fact have a completely different meaning than what is

generally understood. (See Luke 23:44–49.) Since the main function of the temple was not to be a place of sacrifice but to be a house of prayer, it continued to play a significant role in the early Church (see, for example, Acts 3:1).

The New Testament does speak metaphorically about our bodies being temples, and also speaks of the Church in those terms. This nevertheless does not diminish the role of a man-made structure dedicated to God as part of proper worship. Even Moses, Solomon, and the prophets knew that the temple on earth was but a counterpart to the eternal temple made without hands. Yet, in the holy sanctuary the power and presence of God were manifested in both the Old and New Testament periods (see Ex. 40:34–38). The Israelites and the early Christian Saints knew that God could be worshipped anywhere—including a temple made with hands. Many Jews and Christians still take Ezekiel's vision of the reconstructed temple seriously and literally (see Ezek. 40–44). Temple worship and symbolism can be discovered throughout the New Testament.

John's vision of the eternal temple in heaven and the worship performed there by the Lord's Saints prepares us for what lies ahead in a better world to come—temple worship before the face of God and his Son Jesus Christ as we return to their presence. By looking forward we come to realize and understand that temple worship is in reality an eternal blessing of the righteous. The awe-inspiring promises given to the faithful in the book of Revelation by him who stood among the candlesticks, dressed in the robes of the priesthood, confirm that the Lord will "suddenly come to his temple" again (see Mal. 3:1).

ONE

The Temple as the
Pathway to Eternal Life

*For behold, this is my work and my glory—to bring to
pass the immortality and eternal life of man.*

—Moses 1:39

*These shall dwell in the presence of God and his Christ
forever and ever.*

—D&C 76:62

The blessing of eternal life means to enter into the presence
of the Eternal Father and to enjoy life with him and to live the
kind of life he lives. Paradoxically, the attainment of eternal life
involves leaving the presence of God for a time. Mortality is a
period of probation wherein Heavenly Father tests his children
"to see if they will do all things whatsoever the Lord their God
shall command them" (Abr. 3:25). Being out of the presence of
God is essential to this probationary period, giving mortals a
chance to exercise agency, develop faith, and repent of their
sins. As "all mankind, by the fall of Adam being cut off from the

◄ After the Fall, Adam and Eve were cast out of the Garden of Eden where they
had enjoyed the presence of God. Once removed from the presence of God,
they could learn to exercise faith in the Lord and be tested as to their obedience.

presence of the Lord, are considered as dead," so "the resurrection of Christ redeemeth mankind, yea, even all mankind, and bringeth them back into the presence of the Lord" (Hel. 14:16, 17). Thus, the Atonement completely reverses the effects of the fall of Adam for everyone in that all overcome death and all are brought back into the presence of God. But only those who have prepared themselves through mortality and have kept their "second estate" (Abr. 3:26) are allowed to enjoy the presence of the Father. At the Day of Judgment, those who have not been faithful are sent to other degrees of glory which do not enjoy the fulness of the Father. Life is a journey back into the presence of our Father in Heaven, and the plan of redemption teaches us how to be prepared to regain his presence and enjoy eternal life with him. Those who inherit the celestial kingdom are promised the "fulness of the Father" (D&C 76:71), and "these shall dwell in the presence of God and his Christ forever and ever" (D&C 76:62).

After the Fall, Adam and Eve "called upon the name of the Lord, and they heard the voice of the Lord from the way toward the Garden of Eden, speaking unto them, and they saw him not; for they were shut out from his presence" (Moses 5:4). Although they no longer enjoyed walking and talking with God, the Lord heard their prayer and responded by teaching them the gospel, which contained all that Adam and Eve would need to know and those things they must do in order to go back into the presence of the Father and enjoy eternal life. Even though mortals are cut off from the presence of God because of the Fall, the Lord has provided many means of communication, beginning with prayer and the Spirit and extending to the Lord's messengers both mortal and divine. The Lord gave Adam and Eve commandments "that they should worship the Lord their God, and should offer the firstlings of their flocks," an offering they made, an angel told Adam, in "similitude of the sacrifice of the Only Begotten of the Father." The angel further instructed: "Thou shalt do all that thou doest in the name of the Son, and thou shalt repent and call upon God in the name of the Son forevermore." (Moses 5:5, 7–8.) In these commandments we find the essence of ancient temple worship: to worship the Lord God; to offer blood sacrifice in similitude of the future sacrifice of Jesus Christ; to make covenants in the name of the Son; to repent; and to call upon the Father in the name of the Son.

The Lord, in turn, promised redemption, "that as thou hast fallen thou mayest be redeemed" (Moses 5:9), and Adam and Eve rejoiced to know that in this life they might find many blessings—

Adam: "Blessed be the name of God, for because of my transgression my eyes are opened, and in this life I shall have joy, and again in the flesh I shall see God" (Moses 5:10).

Eve: "Were it not for our transgression we never should have had seed, and never should have known good and evil, and the joy of our redemption, and the eternal life which God giveth unto all the obedient" (Moses 5:11).

From the beginning, the Lord instituted the principles of temple worship to prepare his children—through instruction, covenants, and great endowments of blessings and power—to return to him. In short, the temple is a model of mortality, providing on many different levels the eternal perspective and knowledge necessary to fulfill the measure of our creation. Much of the symbolism of temples focuses on regaining the presence of God. Both Adam and Eve recognized the joy that can be found in mortality by obedience to the gospel, and acknowledged their ability, through the atonement of the Only Begotten, to "see God" and attain "the eternal life which God giveth unto all the obedient."

In fact, the presence of the Lord, in varying degrees, can be enjoyed by the faithful while in mortality. There are many occasions preserved in scripture when the Lord has revealed himself to his children. For example, the Lord appeared to the brother of Jared on a mountain (see Ether 3), to Moses also on a mountain (see Moses 1), to Paul on the road to Damascus (see Acts 9), and to Joseph Smith in the Sacred Grove (see JS-H 1:11–19). The Lord taught his ancient disciples, "If a man love me, he will keep my words: and my Father will love him, and we will come unto him, and make our abode with him" (John 14:23).

Similarly he has spoken to the Latter-day Saints, "Every soul who forsaketh his sins and cometh unto me, and calleth on my name, and obeyeth my voice, and keepeth my commandments, shall see my face and know that I am" (D&C 93:1).

Throughout the ages temples have served as concrete reminders of the Lord's promise to dwell in our minds if we are faithful and of the promise of eternal life—that through our faithfulness we can return to live with him once more. In the Old Testament the terminology used for the temple emphasizes the fact that it was a building where the Lord dwelt. The tabernacle, forerunner of the temple, was called the "dwelling place" (Heb. *mishkan*) or "tent" (Heb. *'ohel*). The English word *temple* is most often a translation of the Hebrew word *hekal,* meaning "a large house or palace." The temple is frequently referred to in the scriptures as the "house of the Lord" (Heb. *beth Jehovah*) or the "house of God" (Heb. *beth Elohim*). In the New Testament the temple is referred to as the *naos,* a Greek word meaning "the dwelling of a god." Jesus referred to the temple as "my Father's house" (John 2:16) or as "my house" (Matt. 21:13).

The temple, as a dwelling place of God, serves as a link between heaven and earth, and functions as the center of religious life for the covenant people. Above all, the house of the Lord was "holy," an English translation of the Hebrew word *qodesh,* which means "to be set apart," referring to the division between that which is sacred and that which is mundane or profane. "Holiness" is the essential attribute of God, and on numerous occasions the Lord invites his people to be holy like him: "Ye shall be holy: for I the Lord your God am holy" (Lev. 19:2; see also 11:44). Thus, entering the temple was the model of leaving behind those aspects of mortality, both spiritual and temporal, that keep us from being holy. The Lord speaks of this process as "overcoming the world" (see D&C 64:2) and becoming "sons and daughters" in his kingdom (D&C 25:1). The temple is where mortals are invited to learn what holiness is and how to become holy, and is a graphic reminder that to enter into the presence of God one has to become holy, even as he is.

The entire law of Moses was devoted to directing all men to

Christ and to making Israel into a holy nation, as they were commanded by the Lord to be "a kingdom of priests, and an holy nation" (Ex. 19:6; 22:31). In the New Testament Peter reiterated: "Ye are a chosen generation, a royal priesthood, an holy nation" (1 Pet. 2:9). The scriptures identify the process of becoming holy like God as sanctification. In fact, the English word *sanctification* means "to become holy," from the Latin *sanctus* ("holy") and *facere* ("to make"). The Lord commanded Adam to teach his children the plan of salvation, including the following principles which describe the process of becoming holy and gaining eternal life as a second birth:

> That by reason of transgression cometh the fall, which fall bringeth death, and inasmuch as ye were born into the world by water, and blood, and the spirit, which I have made, and so became of dust a living soul, even so ye must be born again into the kingdom of heaven, of water, and of the Spirit, and be cleansed by blood, even the blood of mine Only Begotten; that ye might be sanctified from all sin, and enjoy the words of eternal life in this world, and eternal life in the world to come, even immortal glory;
>
> For by the water ye keep the commandment; by the Spirit ye are justified, and by the blood ye are sanctified (Moses 6:59–60).

The second birth is brought about by three important elements: water, Spirit, and blood. These become important symbols in the gospel, and especially in temple worship, both under the higher law and under the law of Moses. The water coincides with baptism and refers to the cleansing process which can occur through faith on the Lord Jesus Christ and repentance in his name. Water represents cleansing both from the world and from sin. In addition to its association with baptism, water is a prominent symbol in the many washings prescribed by the law of Moses.

The Spirit coincides with the gift of the Holy Ghost, the agent which actually purifies us from sin as with fire, and gives to us truth, life, light, and comfort. It is through the Spirit that we can overcome sin and the propensity to sin. In the Old Testament the Holy Ghost is often closely related to the anointing with olive oil (see 1 Sam. 16:13–14; Isa. 61:1).[1] The Doctrine and Covenants identifies the Holy Ghost with the olive oil in the lamps in the parable of the ten virgins (see D&C 45:56–57). Olive oil was a prominent symbol in the law of Moses, both as it related to the various anointings of prophets, priests, and kings and as it pertained to the candelabrum which burned in the holy place of the tabernacle and the temple.

The blood refers to the sacrifice of the Savior. Blood represents the life of Jesus which he gave on our behalf. It also represents his suffering in the Garden of Gethsemane by which, in some unfathomable way, he took upon himself the sins of the world. The sacrificial system given to Adam and the patriarchs, and later the law of Moses, contained many rituals in which blood was an important symbol.

The ordinances represented by these symbols are eternal. The first man, Adam, received the ordinance of baptism, after which "the Spirit of God descended upon him, and thus he was born of the Spirit, and became quickened in the inner man" (Moses 6:65). Joseph Smith explained that baptism was practiced from the beginning[2] and that there can be no baptism without the Holy Ghost.[3] The Lord explained, "This is the plan of salvation unto all men, through the blood of mine Only Begotten, who shall come in the meridian of time" (Moses 6:62).

The same symbols which taught the process of sanctification to those living under the law of Moses are central to temple worship in the dispensation of the fulness of times. The prominence of these three elements—water, Spirit, and blood—in temple worship is designed to remind us of Christ and his sacrifice and to teach us how, through the Atonement, we too can become holy, like him. It is worth considering the value of these symbols as manifested in the temples of ancient Israel. A study of ancient temple worship can help us to better understand and appreciate temple worship in our own day.

The focus of this book is the temple at the time of the Savior. While it was the most prominent symbol of the presence of God among his covenant people, when God himself, Jesus Christ, came to earth, many of those who regularly worshipped there were not able to recognize or accept him as the fulfillment of all of the symbols of the centuries and centuries of temple worship. The Savior worshipped there and fulfilled all of his temple obligations under the law of Moses. He regularly taught in the confines of the temple and performed many miracles in its shadow. Perhaps most important, he used the well-known symbols of the temple and its worship to teach the covenant people that he had come as the Only Begotten, as the Messiah, and as the Lamb of God, to fulfill the conditions of the plan of redemption and provide the way for all to return to the presence of God, and for the faithful, through him, to regain their place in his Father's house. Some who heard him understood these symbolic teachings, accepted him, and received their temple blessings.

Overleaf, pp. 18–19. *Fig. 1:* Adam and Eve were created on the "mountain of God" (see Ezek. 28:16). Eastward in Eden the Lord planted a garden—containing both the tree of life and the tree of the knowledge of good and evil—where he placed Adam and Eve (see Gen. 2:8). As a result of the Fall, they were expelled to the east from the garden, and the Lord placed cherubim and a flaming sword to prevent their reentering the garden in their fallen state to partake of the tree of life. In biblical Hebrew, one oriented oneself by facing east. Thus, the movement into mortality, away from God's presence, was a movement forward—to the east. After their expulsion, Adam and Eve were taught the gospel. They repented of their sins, received the ordinances of baptism and the gift of the Holy Ghost, and offered sacrifice to the Lord, learning through the three elements of water, Spirit, and blood how through the Atonement they might regain God's presence.

Fig. 2: The tabernacle was built at the foot of Mt. Sinai, the "mountain of the Lord," where the people entered into the covenant with the Lord. Eventually the tabernacle was moved to the "mountain of the Lord" in Jerusalem, where the temple would be erected. Once a year, on the Day of Atonement, the eastward expulsion of Adam and Eve away from God's presence was symbolically reversed. The high priest, representing all of Israel, went to the tabernacle in the simple white priestly robes. He ritually washed himself, offered sacrifice on the altar, and entered the tabernacle from the east through the outer veil, which bore the embroidered figures of cherubim. He progressed westward through the Holy Place, lit by the menorah, to the inner veil, which also bore the figures of cherubim. He passed through the veil, carrying with him incense, hot coals, and the blood of the animal sacrificed on the altar. Once in the Holy of Holies, he burnt the incense, and sprinkled the blood on the mercy seat on top of the ark of the covenant, symbolically cleansing the people from their sins. Thus through water, Spirit, and blood, the high priest directed Israel how through the Atonement they might once again enter into the Lord's presence.

Fig. 1

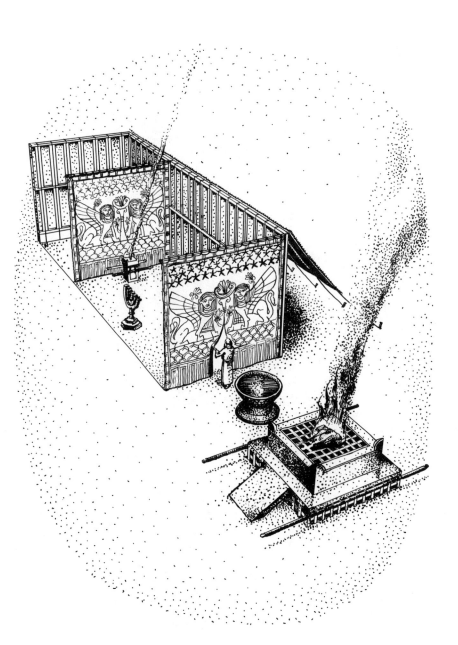

Fig. 2

TWO

The Temples of
Ancient Israel

*And let them make me a sanctuary; that I may dwell
among them.*

—Exodus 25:8

Sacred Places and the Patriarchs

On numerous occasions the Lord revealed himself to
Abraham and made a covenant with him: "And the Lord appeared unto Abram, and said, Unto thy seed will I give this land:
and there builded he an altar unto the Lord, who appeared unto
him" (Gen. 12:7). Each time this happened Abraham built an
altar, offered sacrifice, and "called upon the name of the Lord"
(Gen. 12:8). This occurred at Haran, at Jershon, at Sechem on
the plain of Moreh, east of Bethel, on the plain of Mamre near
Hebron, at Beer-sheba, and on Mount Moriah.[1] Many of these
places, because of these sacred events, continued as important
centers of worship throughout biblical times.

◄ Thousands of Israelites labored seven years to build Solomon's temple. The
stones were precisely fitted together without mortar, and cedar beams were
placed at intervals for strength. Though not a fragment of the building remains
today, it stood for four hundred years on a hill overlooking the city of Jerusalem.

At Haran the Lord revealed his name with a promise: "My name is Jehovah, and I know the end from the beginning; therefore my hand shall be over thee" (Abr. 2:8). After the battle with the kings from Mesopotamia, Abraham met Melchizedek, the king of Salem, with whom he ate a sacred meal of bread and wine, to whom he paid his tithing, and from whom he received his ordination to the Melchizedek Priesthood (see D&C 84:14). Josephus, a Jewish historian living shortly after Christ, preserves a tradition that this Melchizedek was the " 'Righteous King'; for such indeed he was. In virtue thereof he was the first to officiate as priest of God and, being the first to build the temple, gave the city, previously called Solyma [Salem], the name of Jerusalem."[2] Although there is no scriptural record, it is possible that there were temples among the covenant people before the time of Solomon. In any case, it is certain that sacred ordinances were anciently performed in appropriate places in order to fulfill the plan of redemption among the sons and daughters of God.

Similarly, the Lord appeared to Isaac at Gerar (see Gen. 26:2–5) and at Beer-sheba (see Gen. 26:23–25), and later to Jacob at Bethel (see Gen. 28:10–22) and at Peniel (see Gen. 32:24–32) to renew with them the Abrahamic covenant. Isaac in turn "builded an altar there [at Beer-sheba], and called upon the name of the Lord" (Gen. 26:25). Jacob erected a pillar in commemoration of his experience at Bethel. At a place not designated in scripture the Lord also revealed himself to Joseph to make these same promises and to bless him with a look into the future of the fulfillment of the Abrahamic covenant (see JST, Gen. 50:24–38). These places became sacred for the descendants of the patriarchs as reminders of the Abrahamic covenant, of which they were a part, and of the reality of the Lord, who would manifest himself to those who were proven worthy.

Following the pattern by which the gospel was taught to Adam and Eve, sacred places of worship were established where the Lord revealed himself to his children. At these places the patriarchs and their families worshipped the Lord, offered sacrifice in similitude of the Only Begotten, made covenants in the name of the Son, and called upon the name of the Lord.

Moses on Mount Sinai

The Lord revealed himself to Moses on Mount Sinai; there he called Moses to be a prophet (see Ex. 3–4). On an unidentified high mountain, the Lord also unfolded to Moses an astounding vision of the eternities (see Moses 1). A high mountain is an appropriate place to meet with the Lord: it is usually a quiet and solitary place, and it provides a place to gain perspective both in a geographical as well as a spiritual sense. In addition, it symbolizes the effort of man to meet God. Man must ascend as far as he is able and then the Lord can descend to meet with him. All of these are important echoes of temple worship.

On Mount Sinai, Moses was instructed to take the shoes from his feet as he entered the presence of the Lord, "And [God] said, Draw not nigh hither: put off thy shoes from off thy feet, for the place whereon thou standest is holy ground" (Ex. 3:5), a reminder of the separation from the world which is characteristic of temple worship. Entering into the presence of God requires a mortal to leave behind earthly entanglements and concerns, here symbolized by Moses' shoes.

The Lord commanded Moses to deliver the children of Israel from bondage in Egypt and to bring them to Mount Sinai so that they too could enter into the presence of the Lord (see Ex. 3:12). Moses brought Israel out of Egypt and presented them before the Lord at the foot of the holy mountain to prepare them to meet with the Lord (see Ex. 19:17). Just as Moses took off his shoes to enter the presence of God, so too the people sanctified themselves (see Ex. 19:10). Moses went up to the Lord to receive the covenant and the law. While Moses was on the mountain the children of Israel desecrated themselves by making a golden idol in the form of a calf which many began to worship with a riotous party (see Ex. 32:1–6). At the same time that the Lord upon Sinai was delivering the higher law upon the tablets of stone (see Ex. 32:15–16), the people were down below breaking the very commandments being revealed to their representative before the Lord. When Moses returned and saw the apostasy of his people he broke the tablets in his anger (see Ex. 32:19).

Moses intervened on his people's behalf, and the Lord gave Israel another set of tablets containing the law and the covenant (see Ex. 34:1–2). This time, however, the Lord gave them the lower rather than the higher law. As explained in the Joseph Smith Translation of Exodus, the lower law differed from the higher law in two important respects: "But it shall not be according to the first, for *I will take away the priesthood out of their midst;* therefore my holy order, and the ordinances thereof, shall not go before them; for my presence shall not go up in their midst, lest I destroy them. But I will give unto them the law as at the first, but it shall be *after the law of a carnal commandment.*" (JST, Ex. 34:1–2, emphasis added.) The Lord took the Melchizedek Priesthood away from the congregation of Israel as a whole and added to the lower law the carnal commandments. We must remember that Melchizedek Priesthood was preserved among individuals and small groups in ancient Israel. For example, Joseph Smith taught that "all the prophets had the Melchizedek Priesthood."[3] Certainly Lehi and his worthy sons had the Melchizedek Priesthood. Alma 13 speaks of Nephite priesthood as the "high priesthood" and says that those who received it were "after the order of the Son, the Only Begotten of the Father" (Alma 13:8–9). More specifically, Alma speaks of his priesthood authority as "according to the holy order of God, which is in Christ Jesus" (Alma 5:44).

Among the majority of Israel, however, the Lord allowed only Aaronic Priesthood. In addition, priesthood, under the lower law, was not held by all worthy males in Israel but was confined to the descendants of the tribe of Levi, to which Moses and Aaron belonged. This had a marked impact on temple worship in ancient Israel. First of all, the priesthood at the temple was Aaronic rather than Melchizedek. Second, priesthood was passed along from father to son, regardless of personal righteousness, and was not enjoyed by all worthy males. Without priesthood, the members of the congregation could not enter the tabernacle or the temple themselves, but were represented before the Lord inside the sanctuary by the priests. Third, and perhaps most notable, the law of Moses was characterized by a whole series of carnal commandments which Paul called the "schoolmaster to bring us unto Christ" (Gal. 3:24). The carnal commandments consisted of a host of laws respecting that which was holy and unholy, ceremonies, rituals, symbols, festivals, and a complex series of sacrifices, all of which were centered around the tabernacle and later the temple. The purpose of the law of Moses was to teach the people about the atonement of Christ and to help them to become holy, even as the Lord God is holy (see Lev. 11:44; 19:2). In order to understand the temple at the time of Christ, familiarity with the law of Moses is essential, since Jesus taught people already familiar with it.

At Sinai the people entered into a covenant with the Lord to live the gospel through obedience to the commandments of the Mosaic law (see Ex. 24). The covenant ceremony was sealed when Moses took of the blood of the sacrifice and "sprinkled it on the people, and said, Behold the blood of the covenant, which the Lord hath made with you concerning all these words" (Ex. 24:8). The Lord promised them great blessings of prosperity and protection and eternal life if they were obedient. As Moses told his people, "The Lord shall establish thee an holy people unto himself, as he hath sworn unto thee, if thou shalt keep the commandments of the Lord thy God, and walk in his ways" (Deut. 28:9). On the other hand, the Lord promised that disobedience to the covenant would result in plague, drought, and destruction. The presence of the Lord would be taken from his covenant people, and, Moses explained, "the Lord shall scatter thee among all people, from the one end of the earth even unto the other" (Deut. 28:64).

The Tabernacle

In connection with the law of Moses, the Lord commanded the children of Israel to make a tabernacle representing the dwelling place of God among his covenant people: "And let them make me a sanctuary; that I may dwell among them" (Ex. 25:8). Modern revelation offers insight into the function of the tabernacle: "For, for this cause I commanded Moses that he should build a tabernacle, that they should bear it with them in the wilderness, and to build a house in the land of promise, *that those ordinances might be revealed which had been hid from before the world was*" (D&C 124:38, emphasis added). Thus, the function of the tabernacle was the same as that connected with sacred places all the way back to Adam. It was to be a place where the covenant people could receive the sacred ordinances of salvation, and a place where they could meet with God to worship, offer sacrifice, make covenants, and seek the Lord through prayer.

The Lord revealed the plan and furnishings of the tabernacle as recorded in Exodus 25–30, and the revealed rituals, ceremonies, and festivals to be performed at the tabernacle are recorded throughout the books of Exodus, Leviticus, Numbers, and Deuteronomy. Many of the features and objects of the tabernacle have important symbolic value. The meaning of some of these symbols the Lord has revealed, some are obvious, and some we can only guess at. The chastened and repentant children of Israel built and outfitted the tabernacle at the base of Mount Sinai exactly as the Lord commanded (see Ex. 35–40), and took it with them in their forty years of wandering in the wilderness. The word *tabernacle* in Hebrew is *mishkan* ("dwelling place") or *'ohel* ("tent"), and represents the fact that just as the children of Israel lived in tents, so did their God; when they moved he would move with them and would always be present in the center of their camp.

Thus the tabernacle was erected in the center of the camp of Israel, symbolizing the presence of God in their midst and the significance of maintaining him central in their lives. It was built of the finest materials available (see Ex. 25:1–7), representing the willingness of the Israelites to sacrifice for their God. Sacrifice has been a hallmark of temple building from the beginning. Addressing the Lord in the dedicatory prayer for the Kirtland Temple, Joseph Smith said of the Saints there, "For thou knowest that we have done this work through great tribulation; and out of our poverty we have given of our substance to build a house to thy name, that the Son of Man might have a place to manifest himself to his people" (D&C 109:5).

The children of Israel, men and women, were all invited to enter into the presence of the Lord in varying degrees. All Israelites, in a state of ethical and ritual purity, could enter the gate of the courtyard and proceed to a line just before the altar, where they could present themselves "before the Lord" and worship him through sacrifice, prayer, and song. (In the scriptures the phrase "before the Lord" often refers to people presenting themselves at the tabernacle or the temple.[4]) From this vantage point, the Israelites could observe the sacrifices being performed on the altar on their behalf. Only the priests could enter into the tent itself, and only the high priest, once a year on the Day of Atonement, could go into the Holy of Holies to sprinkle the blood of the sacrifice on the mercy seat of the ark of the covenant.

The dimensions of the tabernacle complex and its furnishings are described with some detail in Exodus 25–31 and 35–40. (Throughout the scriptures, measurements are most often given in cubits. There were two different cubits used in the biblical world, the more ancient short cubit and the more recent long cubit. The short cubit was probably about 18 inches, the long cubit about 21 inches. For the sake of simplicity, measurements in this book will be given in feet, with those given for the tabernacle and Solomon's temple being based on the short cubit of about 18 inches, and those given for the temple of Herod on the longer cubit of about 21 inches.[5]) The tabernacle itself was a rectangular tent measuring 45 by 15 feet and was erected facing east at the western end of a courtyard. It was 15 feet high. The courtyard around the tabernacle measured 150 by 75 feet and was surrounded by a screen with a gate at the eastern end. In the courtyard, between the door of the tabernacle and the gate into the courtyard, there was a large bronze altar for the many sacrifices and offerings prescribed by the Mosaic law. The altar was 8 feet square and 5 feet tall and was approached by the priest from a ramp on the south side. Between the altar and the door of the tabernacle was a bronze laver full of water for the ritual washing and cleansing of the priests. The dimensions of the laver are not given.

The Tabernacle

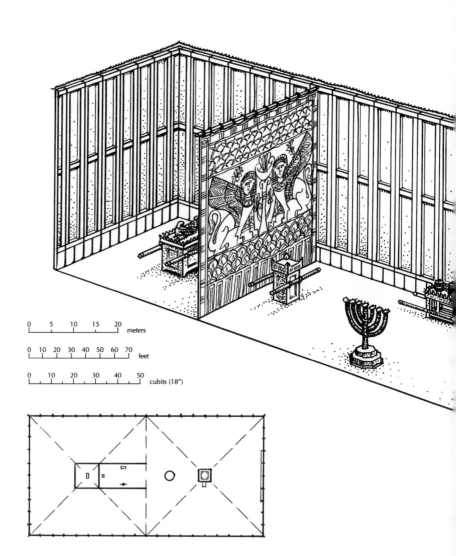

0 5 10 15 20
meters

0 10 20 30 40 50 60 70
feet

0 10 20 30 40 50
cubits (18")

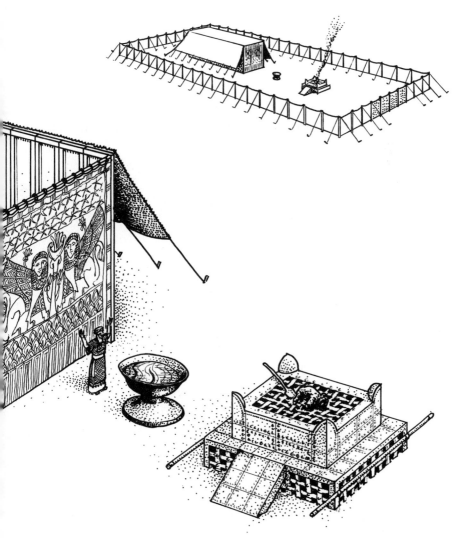

The tabernacle complex used sacred space to teach the Israelites the need for
purity and the power of the priesthood in order to enter into the presence of the
Lord. His perfection was symbolized by a series of square courts and cubes,
climaxing in the Holy of Holies, which contained the ark of the covenant and
the tablets of the law.

The tabernacle was divided into two rooms: the Holy Place, measuring 30 by 15 feet, and the "Most Holy Place," or "Holy of Holies," which was a perfect cube, measuring 15 by 15 by 15 feet. This inner room is called in Hebrew *qodesh qodeshim,* literally "holy of holies."[6] The priest would enter the tabernacle from the east. As he entered the Holy Place he would see three objects. To his left, on the south side, was a seven-branched candlestick (Heb. *menorah*) made of pure gold. The King James Version term *candlestick* can be misleading. The candlestick can more accurately be called the lampstand. The lamps were oil lamps, seven bowls of oil with a wick in each to hold a flame. The children of Israel were commanded to bring "pure oil olive beaten for the light, to cause the lamp to burn always" (Ex. 27:20). In the scriptures light represents the presence of God, as well as knowledge, truth, and understanding.

To the right, on the north side, was the table with the shewbread (pronounced shōbred). The term *shewbread* (Heb. *lehem happanim*) literally means "bread before the face" or "bread of the presence," signifying the bread placed before the Lord. Each week the priests offered twelve loaves of bread, representing each of the twelve tribes, before the presence of the Lord. In this way all of Israel was represented before the Lord. At the end of the week the priests ate the loaves, perhaps symbolic of a communal meal shared between the Lord and his people, the priests eating the bread on behalf of the twelve tribes. Right in front of the veil that separated the Holy Place from the Holy of Holies was an altar made of shittim wood and covered with gold upon which the priests daily burned incense to the Lord. In the scriptures, burning incense, with the smoke ascending to heaven, is symbolic of prayer (see Ps. 141:2; Rev. 5:8; 8:3).

A veil of fine-twined blue, purple, and scarlet linen divided the Holy Place from the Holy of Holies, "and the vail shall divide unto you between the holy place and the most holy" (Ex. 26:33). Embroidered upon the veil were cherubim. Naturally a veil represents the final division between man and God. The innermost room was called the "Most Holy Place," or the "Holy of Holies." Inside was the ark of the covenant, a box made of shittim wood covered with gold which measured 4 feet by 2½ feet by 2½ feet. The box had rings with staves passed through them so that it was easily carried when the tabernacle was moved or when it was used to accompany Israel into battle. The ark contained the tablets of the law written by the finger of the Lord on Sinai (see Ex. 25:16, 21; 40:20; Deut. 10:1–5) and represented the covenant relationship—the promises made by God and man—which Israel had entered into at Sinai. Also in the ark were relics reminding the people of the intervention of God in their behalf, items such as a cup of manna and Aaron's rod (see Heb. 9:4–5).

On top of the ark was a gold slab called the mercy seat, with a gold cherub at each end, which represented the throne of God. In the Bible the Lord is often designated as the one who "dwellest" or "sitteth between the cherubims" (Ps. 80:1; 99:1; Isa. 37:16). Cherubim are attested in the ancient Near East as guardians of the throne, and thus the mercy seat represents the throne of Jehovah. It was from above the mercy seat that the Lord promised to meet with men (see Num. 7:89). The Hebrew word for "mercy seat" is *kapporeth,* which means "to cover," from a verb meaning "to cover one's sins" or "to atone," and is from the same root as *Yom Kippur,* meaning "Day of Atonement." The Greek equivalent in the New Testament is *hilasterion,* meaning a "place or object of propitiation," which is applied to Jesus Christ in Romans 3:25: "Whom God hath set forth to be a propitiation through faith in his blood."

The priest would enter the Holy of Holies once a year on the Day of Atonement and sprinkle the mercy seat with blood from the sacrifice, representing the power of the atonement of Christ to "cover" or "cover over" our sins so that we might achieve "at-one-ment" with God—that we might be able, through repentance, to enter again into his presence. The high priest who officiated at the tabernacle wore on his forehead a gold plate inscribed with "Holiness to the Lord" (see Ex. 28:36; 39:30). This signified that the tabernacle, as the domain of God, was declared holy. The priests were also consecrated to the sanctuary and thus were dedicated to being "holy." Because they represented Israel

before the Lord, the "Holiness to the Lord" applied to all of
Israel as well.

The three symbols of sanctification were prominently displayed. The ritual washings taught the need to be purified before one participated in the sacred ordinances of the priesthood
and entered into the presence of the Lord. The olive oil which
was burned in the lamps may have been associated with the
Holy Ghost and the light and truth which guides and directs
(see D&C 45:56–57). Blood was a part of most of the sacrifices,
and reminded the people that only through the sacrificial shed-
ding of blood could they be cleansed from their sins, these sacrifices being types of and therefore ultimately pointing to the
atonement of Christ.

When the people had completed building the tabernacle and
all of its furnishings, they presented it to the Lord. The scriptures report that "a cloud covered the tent of the congregation,
and the glory of the Lord filled the tabernacle" (Ex. 40:34). The
Lord then signaled his acceptance of the tabernacle with dramatic signs. After the priests had been washed, anointed, and
consecrated and had offered the first sacrifice on the altar, "there
came a fire out from before the Lord, and consumed upon the
altar the burnt offering and the fat: which when all the people
saw, they shouted, and fell on their faces" (Lev. 9:24). The book
of Exodus ends with the tabernacle set up. The Lord's presence
with his people was symbolized, as mentioned above, by the
cloud which "covered the tent of the congregation" and by the
glory of the Lord which "filled the tabernacle" (Ex. 40:34). A
similar symbol of divine acceptance, "a bright light like a pillar
of fire," was witnessed in the latter days at the dedication of the
Kirtland Temple.[7]

When the tribes conquered Canaan and entered the
promised land, the tabernacle was brought into the land at Gilgal
and then to Shiloh, where a building was apparently built either
in conjunction with the tabernacle or to contain it. The story of
Hannah in 1 Samuel speaks of "the house of the Lord" (1 Sam.
1:7) and the "post of the temple" (1 Sam. 1:9). Temples, or sacred
places that served as temples, existed at one time or another at

Shiloh, Dan, Bethel, Gilgal, Mizpah, Hebron, Bethlehem, Nob, the hill-country of Ephraim, Ophrah, Gibeah, and Arad.[8]

The tabernacle and the ark of the covenant were located at Shiloh, then Nob, Gibeon, and finally Kirjath-jearim. David became king and succeeded in uniting the tribes into a mighty empire. He established his capital in Jerusalem and moved the tabernacle there: "So David went and brought up the ark of God from the house of Obed-edom into the city of David with gladness" (2 Sam. 6:12). Eventually David purchased a threshing floor on the top of a high hill, the traditional site of Mount Moriah, where Abraham went to sacrifice Isaac (see 2 Chr. 3:1). There David built an altar and offered sacrifices to the Lord (see 2 Sam. 24:18–25). David desired to build a temple for the Lord, but the Lord deemed it more appropriate that his son Solomon would build it, since David was a man of blood and war (see 1 Kgs. 5:3; 1 Chr. 22:8). The Lord, in response to David's wish to build Him a "house," promised to build for David a "house," a royal dynasty (see 2 Sam. 7).

On this occasion the Lord made a covenant with David—a covenant of mercy, in which he promised David that kingship would remain in his house forever. The Lord told him, "Thy throne shall be established for ever" (2 Sam. 7:16), a promise which would be fulfilled when Jesus Christ, the king of heaven and earth, would be born the Son of David, the king of the Jews (see Matt. 2:2). Although David was not permitted to build the temple, passages in 1 Chronicles record that David received by revelation the plans for the future temple and that he was instrumental in obtaining many of the materials which would be used (see 1 Chr. 22; 28:11–21).

Solomon's Temple: The First Temple

The Lord had ordained Solomon to build His temple. Solomon began to build the house of the Lord in the fourth year of his reign (see 1 Kgs. 6:1). Solomon's temple was a magnificent building of stone, cedar, and precious metals and stones. It housed the ark of the covenant, and the tabernacle was apparently folded up and stored somewhere inside (see 1 Kgs. 8:4).

The Temple of Solomon

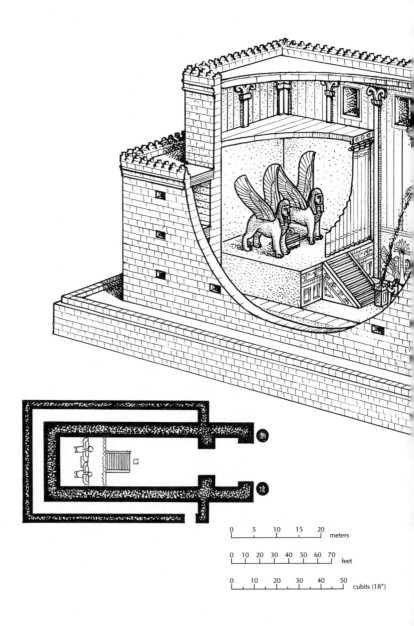

0 5 10 15 20 meters

0 10 20 30 40 50 60 70 feet

0 10 20 30 40 50 cubits (18")

Solomon's temple had a large courtyard containing the altar for the sacrifices and a great bronze basin called the "sea" for the ritual washings of priests. The temple was divided into three rooms. The porch was empty and served as a transition room between the outside world and the temple proper. The Holy Place contained the menorah, the table of shewbread, and the altar of incense. In the Holy of Holies, the gold-covered wings of two olive-wood cherubim overshadowed the ark of the covenant from the tabernacle.

The temple of Solomon seems to have been modeled after the tabernacle complex, but its dimensions were larger than those of the tabernacle. The temple's dimensions and furnishings are described in 1 Kings 6–7.[9] The temple was a rectangular building which faced east and measured 150 feet long and 75 feet wide, excluding auxiliary courts and storehouses on either of the long sides of the temple. It was built of the finest cedar and of costly hewed stones, and it was lavishly adorned with gold. Overall the temple had the same two-to-one dimensions as the tabernacle. In front of the temple was a huge altar which was 15 feet high and 30 feet square. Between the altar and the gates of the temple was the bronze basin called the "sea"—15 feet in diameter and $7\frac{1}{2}$ feet tall—which rested on the backs of twelve bronze oxen, three facing each of the cardinal directions, representing the twelve tribes of Israel. In addition, there were ten smaller portable bronze water basins, mounted on wheels, whose water was used for washing and purification of the priests.

The temple was divided into three rooms rather than two like the tabernacle: the "porch" (Heb. *'ulam*); the Holy Place, or "palace" (Heb. *hekal*); and the Holy of Holies, or "inner sanctuary" (Heb. *debir*). At either side of the huge entrance doors of the temple were two large pillars of bronze called Jachin and Boaz, each 27 feet high. They have been variously interpreted as incense altars, representations of the tree of life, or as standing stone pillars such as those erected by the patriarchs.[10] Their significance is a matter of debate. Some scholars argue they represented the divinely ordained kingship bestowed on David and Solomon.[11]

The porch was 30 feet long and 30 feet wide. It appears to have been empty space and served as a transitional room from the gate to the house of the Lord. The second room, the Holy Place, was set up much like the Holy Place in the tabernacle, only the furnishings were on a much grander scale. It was the largest of the rooms, measuring 60 feet long by 30 feet wide and 45 feet high. First of all, there were ten large wooden lampstands, overlaid with gold, five on the north side and five on the south. It is not clear whether they had seven arms or more or less. There was also a table for the shewbread offerings. Just before the door, or veil, to the inner sanctuary was a small cedar altar, also covered with gold, for the incense offering.

The inner sanctuary, or Holy of Holies, was a cube of 30 feet. The Hebrew name *debir* is generally thought to come from the verb "to speak" and to refer to the fact that it was here that the Lord would speak to those who inquired of him (see Num. 7:89). In this room were found two cherubs (the Hebrew plural is *cherubim*), 15 feet high with 15-foot wing spans, sheltering the ark of the covenant.

We learn much about the significance of this building in antiquity from Solomon's dedicatory prayer and from the many psalms preserved in the Bible which were used in worship at Solomon's temple. The dedication of Solomon's temple took place at the Feast of Tabernacles, as recorded in 1 Kings 8. Solomon summarized the significance of the temple for Israel: "Then spake Solomon, . . . I have surely built thee an house to dwell in, a settled place for thee to abide in for ever" (1 Kgs. 8:12–13). In preparation for the dedication of the temple the priests brought up the tabernacle and all of its sacred furnishings, offered many sacrifices, and installed the ark of the covenant into the "Most Holy Place." The ark contained the "two tables of stone" representing the covenant which the Lord made with the children of Israel. As a sign of his acceptance of the temple, the Lord, just as at the dedication of the tabernacle, filled the house with a cloud of glory: "The cloud filled the house of the Lord, . . . for the glory of the Lord had filled the house of the Lord" (1 Kgs. 8:10–11). Thus, the temple, the house of the Lord, is a house of sacrifice, covenant, and glory.

In order to dedicate the temple, Solomon fell to his knees and stretched forth his hands to heaven (see 2 Chr. 6:13). First, he blessed the people, and then he blessed the Lord, "who keepest covenant and mercy," whose name shall be found in the temple. Solomon prayed that the Lord would hearken unto the prayers of his people and respond with forgiveness; that the Lord would hearken to condemn the wicked and justify the righteous; that, in response to the people's repentance and prayers, the Lord would deliver them from their enemies and from famine, pestilence, and sickness; and that he would hearken to the supplications of the stranger who came to worship the one and only true God. (See 1 Kgs. 8:23–53.) The temple, as the dwelling place of God, is described as a house of prayer, of repentance and forgiveness, of the covenant and mercy. As a symbol of the covenant of mercy, it represented the Davidic covenant, that the throne of David "shall be established for ever" (2 Sam. 7:16), a covenant that was only fulfilled with the coming of the Messiah. It also represented the covenantal blessings of the Mosaic covenant, including those of prosperity, protection, and missionary work.

The Psalms reveal the significance of the temple as the house of the Lord to which the Lord invites his children that they might enter his presence:

To see thy power and thy glory,
    so as I have seen thee in the sanctuary (Psalm 63:2).

Elsewhere the Psalms reveal the requirements of entering into the house of the Lord:

Who shall ascend into the hill of the Lord?
    or who shall stand in his holy place?
He that hath clean hands,
    and a pure heart;
who hath not lifted up his soul unto vanity,
    nor sworn deceitfully. (Psalm 24:3–4.)*

But Israel through the centuries did not live up to their covenants symbolized by the temple. In 587 B.C., on the ninth day of the month of Ab, the temple of Solomon was captured and burned by Nebuchadnezzar and the Babylonians, and many of the vessels were taken to Babylon (see 2 Kgs. 25; Jer. 52). Rather than the promised blessings, recorded in Deuteronomy 27–28, of prosperity, protection, and eternal life, they had reaped the promised curses of devastation, death, and destruction.

Occasionally in this book a passage of biblical poetry is rendered in its poetic lines to help the reader better appreciate its form and content.

Zerubbabel's Temple: The Second Temple

A mere fifty years later, Babylon was itself sacked and burned. In 539 the Lord raised up Cyrus, the Persian, and invited the children of Israel to return to the promised land in order to rebuild their temple (see Ezra). The people were led back to their land by Zerubbabel, the crown prince and descendant of David, who immediately erected an altar and began the series of sacrifices as ordained by the Mosaic law. The dedication of the altar (see Ezra 2:2–4), like the dedication of Solomon's temple, was celebrated in conjunction with the Feast of Tabernacles. Because of opposition in the land and difficult financial conditions, the people were unable to finish the temple for many years. Finally, in response to the admonitions of the prophets Haggai and Zechariah, the people finished the temple, known to historians as the second temple, or Zerubbabel's temple, since he was one of the motivators of its rebuilding. In 515 B.C. the Israelites rededicated it: "And this house was finished on the third day of the month Adar, which was in the sixth year of the reign of Darius the king. And the children of Israel, the priests, and the Levites, and the rest of the children of the captivity, kept the dedication of this house of God with joy." (Ezra 6:15–16.) On this occasion the dedication was celebrated along with Passover and the Feast of Unleavened Bread (see Ezra 6:20, 22).

There are virtually no descriptions of Zerubbabel's temple in the Bible, though there is an ancient document, the Letter of Aristeas, which contains a description of this temple and the vestments of the high priest.[12] It was undoubtedly modeled after Solomon's temple in its location and dimensions. Perhaps it was not as splendid or as costly in its materials. Many of the vessels from Solomon's temple had been preserved in Babylon and returned with the exiles (see Ezra 1:7–11), which certainly added to the splendor of the rebuilt house. But much had been lost and destroyed. The ark of the covenant was gone and the Holy of Holies was empty. It is recorded that when the foundation was laid for the second temple, those present who remembered Solomon's temple wept at the contrast between the two (see Ezra 3:12).

Israel would not have another Davidic king until the coming of Christ. Under Persian rule they were under the jurisdiction of a Persian governor. Nevertheless, they were free to practice their religion as they saw fit. From 539 through 332 B.C. there was calm in the land, and temple worship was carried out unimpeded. Then Alexander the Great put an end to the Persian Empire.

The Maccabees: Rededication of the Temple

The years from 200 B.C. to the coming of Christ were turbulent ones. After the death of Alexander the Great his empire was divided among several of his warring generals. Ptolemy got control of Egypt, and Seleucus got Syria. Palestine, at first, was a part of the Ptolemaic empire, which continued the Persian tradition of tolerance for the various local religions under its jurisdiction. The Jews continued to practice their religion, centered at the temple, just as they had before. In 198 B.C. a battle was fought between the Seleucids and the Ptolemies in which the Seleucids took control of Palestine. In contrast to the Ptolemaic kings, the Seleucid kings considered the religion of Israel to be a threat to their empire. Therefore, under the direction of King Antiochus IV (Epiphanes), Judaism was declared illegal, and penalties were imposed for reading the Torah and for circumcision. The temple in Jerusalem was defiled by the introduction of pagan sacrifices to Zeus and to the emperor, including the sacrificing of pigs, which were unclean under the law of Moses.

Under the direction of a priestly family called the Hasmoneans, or the Maccabees, the Jews revolted in 168 B.C., and against overwhelming odds they were miraculously successful in defeating the mighty Syrian armies. In 165 B.C. the Maccabees cleansed and rededicated the temple in a festival called the Feast of Dedication or Lights (Heb. *Hanukkah*). They set up an independent kingdom of Judah—with one of their own descendants on the throne—and eventually displaced the legitimate Aaronite high priest with a member of their own family. This caused a problem because according to the scriptures, kingship was established in Israel only through the house of David, and the office of high priest was open only to descendants of Aaron.

The Hasmonean, or Maccabean, dynasty provided relative stability for temple worship but introduced many political problems—in particular, infighting among many candidates for the kingship and for the office of high priest. In the first century B.C. what would become the Roman Empire was expanding in the east. In 63 B.C. Pompey and his Roman legions marched into Jerusalem, and the Jews and the Hasmonean family submitted to Rome. The next several decades were full of upheaval throughout the Roman domain. Julius Caesar nearly put an end to the Republic of Rome and then was assassinated in 44 B.C. A long civil war ensued, and finally in 27 B.C. Caesar Augustus emerged as the emperor of the Roman Empire. This would set the stage for the Roman rule during the ministry of the Savior in Palestine.

Herod's Temple: The Temple at the Time of Jesus

Herod the Great was the king of the Jews from 40 to 4 B.C. He was from an Idumean family who had recently converted to Judaism. Idumea, biblical Edom, was a traditional enemy of the Jews. Thus, he was viewed with resentment by many Jews on both counts—as an Idumean and as a convert. He was appointed in 40 B.C. by the Roman senate as "king of the Jews"— but it took him three years to consolidate his power. He was a shrewd politician and managed to survive many crises. He ruled Judea as a loyal vassal of Rome, and was often ruthless in dealing with any local opposition. The Romans prized peace in their empire, and while Herod's allegiance was always to Rome first, he made many attempts to placate the many factions in his domain of Judea.

First of all, he formed an alliance with the royal Hasmonean family by marrying Mariamne, a Maccabean princess. Ironically Herod was threatened by his Hasmonean wife and descendants, most of whom he eventually murdered. Second, and most

important in regards to the temple, Herod attempted to impress
both Rome and the Jews by becoming a great builder. His mon-
umental building projects are visible throughout Israel to this
day. He built imposing fortresses and luxury palaces at Masada,
Herodium, and Machaerus; a lavish city at Samaria called
Sebaste; a port city with an ingenious artificial harbor at
Caesarea; and, of course, the magnificent temple complex on the
Temple Mount in Jerusalem.

Several ancient sources, besides the New Testament, describe
in detail Herod's temple. Josephus (ca. A.D. 37–100) was an
Israelite priest and an eyewitness to the temple. He left lengthy
descriptions in his works *Jewish War* and *Antiquities of the Jews.*
In addition, the rabbinic literature, the Mishnah and Talmud,
are full of references to the temple and temple worship from this
period. In particular, a tractate in the Mishnah entitled *Middoth*
("Measurements") describes the dimensions and architectural
features of the temple, and *Tamid* ("The Daily Whole-offering"),
also in the Mishnah, gives details of the sacrifices and other rituals performed at the temple.[13]

Since 1967 excavations have been undertaken in Jerusalem
outside of the walls of the temple platform, refining our understanding of Herod's Temple Mount.[14] Because of the presence of
the Dome of the Rock and other sacred Muslim buildings on the
Temple Mount itself, there are no archaeological explorations
going on there, and thus, archaeological information is only
available for the area around the Temple Mount.

Herod began building the temple in the eighteenth year of
his reign (counting from 37 B.C.), or 19 B.C. Josephus tells us:
"Herod undertook an extraordinary work, (namely) the reconstructing of the temple of God at his own expense, enlarging its
precincts and raising it to a more imposing height. For he believed that the accomplishment of this task would be the most
notable of all the things achieved by him, as indeed it was, and
would be great enough to assure his eternal remembrance."[15]
This would entail tearing down the temple of Zerubbabel and
the building of a completely new edifice. To those who feared
that he intended to tear down the old temple and not replace it,

Herod promised not to raze the old building until everything was ready for the new one. He prepared a thousand wagons to bring stones, chose ten thousand of the most skillful workmen, and taught a contingent of priests the crafts of masonry and carpentry so that they would be able to construct those parts of the temple located within the priestly courts.

For the temple itself Herod maintained the same floor plan known to Solomon and Zerubbabel's temples, but he greatly expanded the Temple Mount complex by extending the platform to the south, and outdid even Solomon in his adornment of the temple. Though accounts of Herod's building are found in Josephus and in the Mishnah, for many years scholars have assumed that the dimensions given for Herod's temple building project were gross exaggerations. Recent archaeological excavations have for the most part vindicated Josephus's description. Herod's temple platform was one of the largest sites of its kind in the ancient world. The largest stones are forty feet long and have been estimated to weigh between forty and one hundred tons.[16]

Herod's temple was truly one of the great architectural wonders of its time. The Talmud recalled the Jerusalem and the temple from the time of Jesus thusly: "Whoever has not seen Jerusalem in her splendor has never seen a lovely city. He who has not seen the Temple in its full construction has never seen a glorious building."[17] Likewise, Josephus reports:

> The exterior of the building wanted nothing that could astound either mind or eye. For, being covered on all sides with massive plates of gold, the sun was no sooner up than it radiated so fiery a flash that persons straining to look at it were compelled to avert their eyes, as from the solar rays. To approaching strangers it appeared from a distance like a snow-clad mountain; for all that was not overlaid with gold was of purest white.[18]

Josephus tells us that the temple itself was completed in a year and a half, but work on the complex on the Temple Mount continued long after Herod died. The final touches were not completed until about A.D. 63.[19] In A.D. 70 this splendid building was destroyed by the Roman armies under Titus.

Description of Herod's Temple

The King James Version of the New Testament uses the term *temple* to translate two different Greek words: *naos,* which means "house" and refers to the temple proper; and *hieron,* which means "sanctuary" and refers to the entire temple complex. It is important to distinguish between these terms to properly visualize the New Testament narratives. For example, John 2:14 states that Jesus found the money changers in the "temple" (*hieron*); here "temple" would perhaps be better rendered as "temple precincts," from which Jesus drove out the money changers. Then he prophesied the destruction of the "temple" (*naos*), referring to the temple proper.

According to archaeological reports, Herod's Temple Mount was a trapezoid-shaped platform with the long sides running north and south. The walls around the platform measured about 1,550 feet long and about 1,000 feet wide.[20] There were at least eight gates into the Temple Mount complex.[21] Along the south wall was a long stoa running east and west. A stoa is a large covered hall whose ceiling is supported by a row of columns—in this case 162 Corinthian columns. At the eastern end was a room that is believed to be the place where the Sanhedrin met. Many of those coming to worship at the temple would enter from the two gates in the southern wall. Archaeological excavations have uncovered the remains of a bathhouse at the foot of the south stairs. Those coming to worship would cleanse and purify themselves through a ritual immersion in water before they entered the Temple Mount.

Those going to worship on the Temple Mount would then proceed north by climbing stairs passing under the stoa and entering the Court of the Gentiles. This indicated that Gentiles, or nonmembers of the covenant, were invited to come and worship the Lord but were allowed to proceed towards the temple only as far as the *Soreg,* a marble screen that surrounded the temple. Posted around this barrier were signs warning Gentiles not to pass on pain of death. Several fragments of these inscriptions were found in the excavations. One reads as follows, "No Gentile

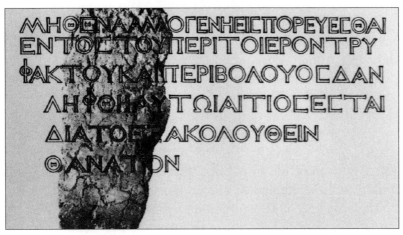

A stone barrier about four and a half feet high divided the inner temple precinct from the Court of the Gentiles. Notices written in Greek and Latin warned everyone who was not Jewish to keep out. One stone block carrying the Greek version was found in 1871. The above fragment was discovered in 1936. It had red paint in the letters to make them stand out. In the second illustration the full block inscription is overlaid on this fragment.

shall enter inward of the partition and barrier around the temple, and whoever is caught shall be responsible to himself for his subsequent death." It is most likely that the money changers carried on their business in the Court of the Gentiles and that Jesus cleansed the temple there. It was also probably here, in the Court of the Gentiles, that Mary and Joseph purchased the sacrificial offerings as part of the purification following the birth of Jesus (see Luke 2:21–24). It is likely that whenever Jesus went to teach in the temple he taught in the Court of the Gentiles.

The temple itself was situated near the middle of the Temple Mount complex, facing east and surrounded by another wall. At the northwest corner of the Temple Mount was a fortress called the Antonia, named after Mark Anthony, where, in the time of Jesus, Jewish and Roman officials were able to watch all the proceedings on the Temple Mount. Here a garrison was stationed to put down disturbances which often fomented on the Temple Mount.

The temple faced east. Israelite men and women going there would enter from the east gate, called the Beautiful Gate (see Acts 3:1–11), where they would enter a square courtyard called the Court of the Women. Josephus records, "On the side where the sun rises it had one great gateway, through which those of us who were ritually clean used to pass with our wives."[22] This courtyard was surrounded by rooms which had specific functions: rooms for the Nazarites and lepers, and storage rooms for the wood and the oil used in the temple worship. There were four large lampstands in the Court of the Women which were lit on various occasions. In addition, various chests for the collection of monetary offerings were found in this court, and this would be where the widow offered her mites (see Luke 21:1–4).

The women could congregate in this courtyard and observe through the gate the sacrifices going on at the altar and could participate in temple worship through fasting, prayer, and hymns. Proceeding to the west, Israelite men climbed fifteen curved stairs and entered into the narrow Court of the Israelites. A line in the pavement separated the Court of the Israelites, where Israelite men could observe and participate in temple worship, from the priests who officiated there. Standing in the

Court of the Israelites one could see—between the court and the temple itself, on the left hand towards the south—the large stone altar, 40 feet square and 15 feet high. To the north of the altar was the place of the slaughtering, where the sacrificial animals were killed. Behind the altar was a large bronze laver providing water for the ritual washings.

Herod's temple had two stories—the bottom story functioning in the temple ordinances, and the upper floor apparently being used for access to the lower floor for the purpose of cleaning. Workers had to be lowered into the rooms from the top for cleaning and maintenance. The building was 172 feet long and 34½ feet wide. There were three rooms on the bottom floor: the porch, the Holy Place, and the Holy of Holies. Surrounding the main floor on the north, west, and south sides were a number of smaller rooms apparently used for storage of the sacred vessels, oil, incense, and other materials used in the temple, as well as the Temple treasures—gifts dedicated to the temple.

From the descriptions given by Josephus and the Mishnah, we can reconstruct what the temple looked like with some degree of confidence. The gold-covered facade of the temple was imposing. It was square, 172 feet wide and 172 feet high. Twelve stairs ascended to the portal of the temple, which was 69 feet high and 34 feet wide. Josephus tells us this entryway "had no doors, displaying unexcluded the void expanse of heaven."[23]

Through the door one entered the porch, a room that was long and narrow, measuring only 19 feet from east to west and almost 172 feet from north to south. The porch was 26 feet wider than the rest of the building on each side, leading to the description in the Mishnah that the temple was "as a lion is narrow behind and wide in front," calling to mind one of the titles of Jerusalem, "Ariel" (Isa. 29:1), which the Mishnah interprets to mean "Lion of God."[24] At the north and the south ends were two rooms called the "Chambers of the Slaughter Knives," where the knives for the sacrifices were kept.[25]

On the west wall of the Holy Place, visible through the portal of the temple, was an elaborate gate to the Holy Place.

The portal was 34 feet high and 17 feet wide set between four pillars, two on each side. Above these doors, in the words of Josephus, "spread a golden vine with grape-clusters hanging from it, a marvel of size and artistry to all who saw with what costliness of material it had been constructed."[26] Elsewhere he describes this vine as being so large that "grape-clusters as tall as a man" hung from it.[27] The splendor of this portal was enhanced through the years as those who brought costly gifts to the temple gave them to the priests who hung them on this golden vine.

A large tapestry veil hung in front of the doors at the entrance to the Holy Place. Josephus describes this tapestry, finding cosmic symbolism in its design:

> Before these [the doors] hung a veil of equal length, of Babylonian tapestry, with embroidery of blue and fine linen, of scarlet also and purple, wrought with marvellous skill. Nor was this mixture of materials without its mystic meaning: it typified the universe. For the scarlet seemed emblematical of fire, the fine linen of the earth, the blue of the air, and the purple of the sea; the comparison in two cases being suggested by this colour, and in that of the fine linen and purple by their origin, as the one is produced by the earth and the other by the sea. On this tapestry was portrayed a panorama of the heavens.[28]

Passing through the veil and the doors, one entered the Holy Place, a room measuring 69 feet long. Actually the Holy Place and the Holy of Holies were one large room 103 feet long, 34 feet wide, and 69 feet high, completely covered with plates of gold, separated only by the veil of the temple.

In the Holy Place was the seven-branched lampstand, the shewbread table, and the incense altar where Zechariah was officiating when Gabriel appeared to him (see Luke 1:5–23). Josephus preserves a tradition as to the symbolism of these furnishings:

> The seven lamps (such being the number of the branches from the lampstand) represented the planets; the loaves on the table, twelve in number, the circle of the Zodiac and the year; while the altar of

incense, by the thirteen fragrant spices from sea and from land, both desert and inhabited, with which it was replenished, signified that all things are of God and for God.[29]

Separating the Holy Place from the Holy of Holies was a veil—the veil which was "rent in twain from the top to the bottom" at the moment when Jesus died on the cross (Matt. 27:51). Actually the veil of the temple consisted of two curtains hung about 18 inches apart. The Mishnah informs us, "The outer curtain was looped up on the south side and the inner one on the north side,"[30] providing a corridor for the high priest to walk through on the day that he entered the Holy of Holies. In this way he could enter without anyone else being able to see into the Holy of Holies.

The Holy of Holies was a cube-shaped room of 34 feet in each direction. Its walls were covered with plates of beaten gold. In Herod's temple this room was empty, since the ark of the covenant and the cherubim had been captured and probably destroyed by the Babylonians when they destroyed Solomon's temple in 587 B.C. (see 2 Kgs. 25:8–17). Rabbinic tradition identifies a stone on the floor of the Holy of Holies, rising to a height of three fingerbreadths, as the "foundation stone"[31] which, according to tradition, was the very stone with which the creation of the world began.[32] It was upon this stone that the high priest, on the Day of Atonement, would sprinkle the blood of the sacrifice and offer incense.

For the Jews, the temple of Herod was a magnificent symbol of their religion. At the three pilgrimage festivals hundreds of thousands of Jews from all over the world came to worship at the temple. From the time of the Maccabees until the destruction of Jerusalem, several different kinds of Judaism emerged, each of which had its own distinctive views about the temple.[33] Josephus records that there were three prominent sects of Judaism at the time of the Christ: Pharisees, Sadducees, and Essenes.

Prominent in the New Testament were the Pharisees and the Sadducees, both of which sects were dedicated to the law of

Moses and to the temple, where the law was carried out. The Sadducees were a small party of wealthy aristocrats mostly from priestly families. As priests they controlled the temple and enjoyed the vast revenues generated by the temple. They fervently held to the five books of Moses as constituting the law of Moses, and rejected any attempts to add to it. They were generally supportive of Roman rule, the political stability of Judea being in their best interest since it allowed them to maintain their power and influence. The Pharisees also held the five books of Moses to be the center of the Mosaic law, but they believed there was a corpus of "oral law," beginning with the Lord's speaking to Moses and continuing among the various interpreters of the law, which added what they called a "fence around the law." They generally acknowledged and respected the authority of the Sadducees over the temple, though they often vigorously debated differences in doctrine and scriptural interpretation. They were often critical of the Roman authorities.

An additional distinctive group was the Essenes. They believed that the Saducean priesthood in Israel was apostate, especially following the Maccabean revolt, which made the office of high priest a political office to be bought and sold rather than maintaining the strict hereditary succession. In their eyes, the authority was not only illegitimate but also corrupt. Led by someone they called the Teacher of Righteousness, they went into the wilderness to await God's judgment on the Gentiles as well as on the apostate Jews. They envisioned the coming of a Messiah who would destroy all of the wicked and restore them, the Essenes, as the true holy ones, or "saints," of God. A library apparently left behind by this group was found near one of their communities at Qumran. Several copies of a document in this library were found called the Temple Scroll, which contained a description and dimensions of a future temple, as well as the laws governing it. This temple was envisioned as the true and purified temple which would accompany the return of the Messiah and which would serve as the religious center for the Essenes, replacing the corrupt temple in Jerusalem.[34]

Another prominent movement was that of the Zealots. This

was a nationalistic movement whose adherents believed in armed revolt against Rome to reestablish the Jews' political independence. They found hope in the successful Maccabean revolt of 150 years earlier, in which the Jews had revolted against the Syrians and, through the intervention of God, had defeated their armies and set up an independent political state. For the Zealots, the temple was a religious symbol harking back to the glorious days of David and Solomon and to the time of the Maccabees when Judea was an independent religious state.

The temple became the focal point of the conflict between the governing Romans and the vassal Jews. On several occasions Roman officials offended the Jews by desecrating their holy place. Josephus carefully records many of these events. For example, in A.D. 6 a Roman commander named Sabinus, attempting to seize money in the treasury, met with armed resistance. Thousands of Jews who had come to Jerusalem for the festival of Pentecost rioted against the Roman legions. The Romans killed thousands of Jews, and in the riot the southern and western stoas of the temple were destroyed by fire. The Romans then sacked the temple treasury and crucified two thousand Jews.[35]

Pontius Pilate, procurator from A.D. 26 to 36, on one occasion brought the banners of the Roman legions, bearing eagles, into Jerusalem. The presence of such images was considered a violation of the commandment against images. Thousands of Jews offered to sacrifice their lives rather than submit to this desecration. Pilate gave in. On another occasion, he took funds out of the temple treasury in order to build an aqueduct which he thought would benefit the city. This act was met with riots which resulted in the deaths of many Jews.[36] During the ministry of Christ the temple was considered a volatile place. Especially on the occasions of the pilgrimage festivals when he went to teach there, vast numbers of Jews filled Jerusalem, and temple guards and Roman soldiers had to be ready for any disturbances.

Just as in the time of Antiochus IV (Epiphanes), these Roman desecrations of the temple and offenses against the law led many Jews to believe that it was their religious duty to expel the Romans. The stories of the miraculous victories against the Syrians and the rededication of the temple under the Maccabees gave these Jews hope that in a similar way the Lord would intervene on their behalf in an armed insurrection against Rome.

The Zealots gained much popular support, and beginning in A.D. 66 they led a disastrous war against Rome. Although the war lasted seven years, the conflict came to a climax in A.D. 70, when the Romans besieged and destroyed Jerusalem and the temple. The temple was burned to the ground. Most of the furnishings of the temple were destroyed, though several of the implements— the trumpets, the shewbread table, and the menorah—were seized and taken to Rome, where their images were captured in the relief on the arch in Rome built to commemorate Titus's triumph.

The destruction of the temple was catastrophic for all of Judaism and its sects. The Sadducees, in particular, lost their base of operation. Without the temple, the law of Moses, as they interpreted it, could not be fulfilled. Within a generation the Sadducees disappeared. Likewise, the Essenes and the Zealots were both destroyed by the Romans in the Jewish revolt.

The destruction of the temple was also mourned by the Pharisees. But they alone had devised a system whereby they could function without a temple. Through their "oral law," they were able to maintain the practice of Judaism without the sacrificial system of the temple, though they yearned for its restoration. Thus Pharisaism developed into Rabbinic Judaism—the form of Judaism that has survived to this day. The synagogue has provided a place for community worship and the study of the Torah. The oral tradition has been preserved in the Mishnah and Talmud, and their rabbis have been consulted for the proper interpretation of the law. In addition, their rabbis taught that prayer and "acts of lovingkindness" could substitute for the sacrifices of the temple.[37] Nevertheless, as prophesied by the biblical prophets of old, the house of Israel, including Rabbinic Judaism, awaits the rebuilding of the temple in Jerusalem.

Today, one of the most prominent features of Jerusalem is the golden Muslim shrine known as the Dome of the Rock, which is located on the spot once occupied by Solomon's and Herod's temples and which stands a little over 100 feet high. When Herod's temple stood here two thousand years ago, it rose to a height of over 150 feet, fifty feet higher than the Dome of the Rock. Following the Roman destruction of A.D. 70 the area was in ruins. These may have been cleared and leveled in the second century when Roman statues were placed on the mount by the emperor Hadrian. At the end of the seventh century the Muslim shrine was built on the current site. This view also shows the famous Western Wall, the "Wailing Wall," a place of great sacredness to modern Judaism. The massive stones of the Temple Mount retaining walls built by Herod two thousand years ago are impressive and are the only major extant remains of the glorious holy site from the time of Christ.

THREE

Temple Worship
at the Time of Christ

Sing unto the Lord, bless his name;
  shew forth his salvation from day to day.
Declare his glory among the heathen,
  his wonders among all people. . . .
Give unto the Lord the glory due unto his name:
  bring an offering, and come into his courts.
O worship the Lord in the beauty of holiness:
  fear before him, all the earth.
                    —*Psalm 96:2, 3, 8, 9*

Nephi rejoiced in the coming of Christ, which was typified by the law of Moses: "Behold, my soul delighteth in proving unto my people the truth of the coming of Christ; for, for this end hath the law of Moses been given" (2 Ne. 11:4). The temple at the time of Jesus was the focal point of worship under the Mosaic law, and all of the statutes and ordinances pointed towards the

---

◄ The Jews at the time of Jesus worshipped the Lord in the temple courtyards through song, dance, fasting, and prayer, and through discussions of the scriptures. Especially during the yearly festivals, the temple was a busy and crowded place of great activity. Jesus regularly attended the temple festivals, teaching his gospel to the large multitudes found at the temple during those times.

Savior's advent. The children of Israel came into the presence of the Lord to worship him, through blood sacrifice and a host of other offerings in similitude of the future sacrifice of Jesus Christ; to make covenants with the Lord; to repent; and to call upon the Lord in prayer. Worship at the temple was conducted under the authority of the Aaronic Priesthood, and was largely directed towards the numerous sacrifices and offerings. The making and renewing of covenants and repentance were also connected with the sacrificial system. The Levites, the priests, and the people also worshipped the Lord at the temple through group and individual prayer and the singing of hymns, many of which have been collected in the book of Psalms.

Throughout the calendar year, the Lord had instituted, under the law of Moses, a series of festivals, some of which required all Jewish males to make pilgrimage to Jerusalem and all of which entailed special rituals and ceremonies at the temple. While the forms of temple worship were being meticulously carried out at the temple, for various reasons the Jews at the time of Jesus were largely apostate. In spite of the dramatic symbolism of the Atonement present in the sacrifices performed on a daily basis at the temple, they rejected the Messiah who had come to fulfill these symbols. Nevertheless, Jesus constantly referred to the temple and its symbolism in proclaiming to his people that he was the Messiah and in explaining the nature of the mission he had come to perform.

The Temple as Sacred Space

One of the most graphic lessons taught by the temple was that in order to enter into the presence of God one must become holy. The closer one got to the Holy of Holies, the more holy or purified one had to be. All peoples were invited to come to worship the Lord God of Israel at the Temple, both those who were members of the covenant, who were considered to be Israel, and those who were not members, who were considered as Gentiles. Biblical law specifically permits acceptance of sacrifices from Gentiles (see Lev. 22:25), and the Gospel of John records that

Gentiles "came up to worship at the feast" (John 12:20). As described earlier, surrounding the temple was a marble screen called the *Soreg,* which divided the Court of the Gentiles from the courts of the women, the Israelites, and the priests and warned Gentiles not to pass on pain of death.

Many of the people going to worship at the temple would enter the mount through the so-called Huldah gates set in the southern wall. The Talmud tells us that those who entered the Temple Mount, like Moses on Mount Sinai, removed their shoes,[1] and Josephus tells us that many people dressed in a white garment.[2] In addition, all of the Israelites had to present themselves before the Lord in a state of ethical and ritual purity. There was a bathhouse positioned just outside the southern gates at which Israelite men and women symbolically purified themselves by immersing themselves in a ritual bath before ascending to the Temple Mount.

Once on the Temple Mount, Israelites passed through the Court of the Gentiles and, entering through the east gate, went into the Court of the Women. Women coming to worship could look through the gate on the west and view the sacrifices at the altar and receive the priestly benediction pronounced from stairs at the doorway of the temple. In this court the Israelites, both men and women, could pray and sing hymns. The men could enter the court of the temple itself and could stand just inside the gate to witness the sacred ordinances being performed. A line in the pavement marked the end of the Court of the Israelites and the beginning of the Court of the Priests, which surrounded the temple.

Only those holding the priesthood, priests and Levites, could enter the Court of the Priests and the temple building. And only the high priest could enter the Holy of Holies, which he did exclusively on the Day of Atonement. It must be remembered that under the law of Moses the priests represented all of Israel, and thus symbolically Israel did indeed enter into the presence of the Lord. Under the higher law, with the restored Melchizedek Priesthood, both men and women can enter the temple and present themselves before the Lord.

Through the concept of sacred space, the Lord taught in the law of Moses the same principles presented in the higher law in Doctrine and Covenants 76, where we learn that the final rewards following the probationary state are different degrees of glory: celestial, terrestrial, and telestial. These degrees of glory are various degrees of enjoying the presence of God—the telestial, the presence of the Holy Ghost only; the terrestrial, the presence of the Son; and only the celestial, the presence and the fulness of the Father, the Son, and the Holy Ghost. Attainment of these various rewards are based on the degree of holiness attained by an individual during the time of his or her probation.

Priests and Priesthood

The intention of the covenant, whether under the higher or the lower law, was stated by the Lord at Sinai: "And ye shall be unto me a kingdom of priests, and an holy nation" (Ex. 19:6). Under the lower law the priesthood was confined to the descendants of one tribe, Levi. The sacrifice of the firstborn lamb symbolically represented that Jesus Christ as the Only Begotten would offer an infinite sacrifice on behalf of all mortals. Through the Atonement, all mankind can become sons and daughters of Jesus Christ, since he ransomed all from sin and death. Symbolically, the Lord required of his covenant people the firstborn of their flocks in similitude of this infinite sacrifice. This included their firstborn sons as well. Under the law of Moses the symbolism of offering the firstborn was fulfilled when the Lord chose from the twelve tribes one of the tribes, Levi, who would represent before the Lord the firstborn (see Num. 3:12–13; 8:5–22). For the rest of Israel the typifying of the sacrifice of Christ was continued in an offering at the temple signifying the redemption or substitute sacrifice of the firstborn (see Ex. 13:13) both through the atonement of Christ and through the selection of the Levites who would serve the Lord exclusively. It is important to remember that while each family did not have access to priesthood through the patriarchal order, under the lower law the people were not deprived of the blessings of priesthood in their midst; they were dependent upon the Levites for such blessings.

In ancient Israel the Aaronic Priesthood was held exclusively by the descendants of the tribe of Levi. There were three levels of the Aaronic Priesthood: Levites, priests, and the office of high priest. The Aaronic Priesthood was given to all eligible males from the tribe of Levi. The direct descendants of Aaron were ordained as priests, and the eldest son of the eldest son all the way back to Aaron presided over the Aaronic Priesthood in the office of high priest. The priesthood was responsible for fulfilling all of the rituals and ceremonies of the Mosaic law. In short, those who held the priesthood were responsible for maintaining the holiness of the people. Those holding the Aaronic Priesthood had varying functions, depending on the offices they held.

The Levites served in various capacities surrounding the tabernacle and later the temple. They assisted the priests in many of their duties and took care of the courts and chambers of the temple, as well as the furnishings and vessels. Some were gatekeepers, porters, treasurers, choristers, and musicians.

The priests were mainly in charge of supervising and carrying out at the temple the many rituals, sacrifices, and festivals prescribed by the law of Moses. The descendants of Aaron were divided into twenty-four priestly families called "courses," each of which took a turn lasting a week officiating at the temple. They all officiated together at the important annual festivals. There is also evidence that the priests were responsible to teach the people the law (see Mal. 2:6–7; Jer. 18:18) and to regularly bless the people in the name of the Lord (see Num. 6:22–27).

The office of high priest was a hereditary one and was normally held for life. The high priest held the responsibility for the spiritual welfare of the children of Israel, and presided at many of the daily and annual ceremonies of the temple. Of particular significance was his participation on the Day of Atonement, as described in Leviticus 16. On that occasion the high priest went into the Holy of Holies and sprinkled the blood of the sacrifice on the mercy seat, symbolizing the power of the Atonement to cleanse all of repentant Israel from their sins and to render them worthy to be in the presence of the Lord.

The Levites were set apart by the laying on of hands (see Num. 8:10). The model for the consecration and setting apart of the priests was revealed by the Lord as recorded in Leviticus 8. Here it is stated that Moses took Aaron and his sons and "washed them with water" (Lev. 8:6). He then "poured of the anointing oil upon Aaron's head, and anointed him, to sanctify him" (Lev. 8:12). Moses took blood from the sacrifices and "put it upon the tip of Aaron's right ear, and upon the thumb of his right hand, and upon the great toe of his right foot" (Lev. 8:23). Finally Moses "took of the anointing oil, and of the blood which was upon the altar, and sprinkled it upon Aaron, and upon his garments, and upon his sons, and upon his sons' garments with him; and sanctified Aaron, and his garments, and his sons, and his sons' garments with him" (Lev. 8:30).

As has been discussed previously, the washing, anointing with oil, and sprinkling with blood were all symbols of holiness. The priests were washed, symbolic of the need for moral and ritual purity when serving in the presence of the Lord. They were anointed with the sacred oil, symbolic of the setting apart to the service of the Lord. They were anointed with blood, symbolic of the responsibility of officiating in the priesthood and of the power of the blood to cleanse from sin. Finally, the oil and the blood were sprinkled on their garments, symbolic of the solemn responsibility of representing all of Israel before the Lord. The English word *consecrated* is a translation of a Hebrew word meaning "to make holy."

There is no scriptural evidence for the clothing of the Levites, but Josephus records that at the time of Jesus the Levites had gained the privilege of wearing priestly linen robes.[3] The Lord revealed to Israel, as recorded in the book of Exodus, the nature of the sacred clothing which the priests and the high priest were to wear when they officiated at the temple or participated in any of the sacred ordinances of the priesthood (see Ex. 28, 39). Their clothing reminded them, as well as all other

Moses ordained Aaron as the high priest of the Aaronic Priesthood in Israel by the laying on of hands. In addition to the white robe, belt, and cap worn by all the priests, Aaron wore a multi-colored embroidered robe called the ephod and a beautifully crafted breastplate containing twelve precious stones that represented the twelve tribes. Connected to the breastplate was a pouch which contained the Urim and Thummim. On each of his shoulders, Aaron, and the high priests who succeeded him, wore an onyx stone with the names inscribed of six of the tribes. Since not all individuals in Israel enjoyed the Aaronic Priesthood, the symbols of the clothing of the high priest reminded Israel that he represented all of the tribes before the Lord. On his head the high priest wore a round cap and on his forehead a golden plate bearing the inscription, "Holiness to the Lord," representing the consecration of the priest to the Lord.

Israelites who observed them, of the sacred nature of their calling. All of the priests wore four articles of clothing: (1) white linen breeches for modesty (see Ex. 28:42); (2) a white linen coat, or robe, which, according to Jewish tradition, reached to the ankles, with sleeves to the palms of the hands; (3) a linen girdle, or belt, around the waist; and (4) a white head covering called in the King James Version a "mitre." Most scholars believe this headdress was some kind of a turban.

In addition to the four garments of the priests, the high priest, when he officiated at the temple, wore four additional garments: (5) a blue woolen robe bearing a fringe at the bottom consisting of pomegranates and bells; (6) an ephod made of wool and linen embroidered with a thread of gold and worn over the blue woolen robe (it is unclear exactly what the ephod looked like, but many believe it was a colorful, heavily embroidered apron; attached to the ephod were two onyx stones, each bearing the names of six of the tribes, which were situated on straps on the shoulders of the high priest); (7) a breastplate, worn on the chest, which bore a different stone for each of the twelve tribes and which had a pouch of some sort where the Urim and Thummim was kept (the breastplate, as well as the two onyx stones, was a graphic reminder to the high priest as well as Israel that he represented all of Israel before the Lord); and (8) a gold plate, worn upon the forehead, which hung in front of the mitre and upon which was inscribed, "HOLINESS TO THE LORD," signifying the dedication of the priests and those they represented to becoming holy and thus worthy to enter the presence of God.

On the Day of Atonement the high priest dispensed with all of the outer garments and appeared before the Lord dressed in the ordinary, pure white linen clothing of the priests.

Sacrifices and Offerings

The law of sacrifice is an eternal law. The Prophet Joseph Smith taught "that a religion that does not require the sacrifice of all things never has power sufficient to produce the faith necessary unto life and salvation."[4] From the beginning, the law of sacrifice was given to Adam and Eve in order that they might learn the necessity of sacrificing of their worldly possessions—in this case the firstlings of their flocks—and that they might exercise and develop their faith through this eternal principle. The sacrifice they were commanded to offer was specifically a blood sacrifice in "similitude of the sacrifice of the Only Begotten of the Father" (Moses 5:7).

Likewise, the law of Moses instituted a whole series of sacrifices and offerings, that the covenant people might learn to give of their worldly possessions to the kingdom of God, and to point them towards the power of the Atonement—that Christ, the creator of the world, would sacrifice his life on behalf of the world. They were able to repent and receive forgiveness only through their faith in Jesus Christ and his atonement. The Atonement was already in effect, even though the event itself had not yet taken place. The dramatic symbols of blood sacrifice were a constant reminder of the reality of that event to come.

The complex system of sacrifices and offerings are outlined in Leviticus 1–7. These sacrifices were all offered daily, at appointed times, at the temple. Various details concerning these sacrifices and offerings are found throughout the books of Exodus, Leviticus, Numbers, and Deuteronomy. For example, Numbers 28–29 gives a catalog of the additional sacrifices to be offered on the Sabbath, on the new moons, and for the various festivals. It is sufficient here to review the basics of the most important of these sacrifices and offerings in order to understand what was going on in the temple at the time of Jesus. Jewish traditions, collected in the third century A.D. in the Mishnah, offer us many additional details as to the service at the temple of Herod at the time of Jesus.

Five specific sacrifices are described in Leviticus 1–7: the burnt offering (see Lev. 1; 6:8–13); the "meat" offering, probably better translated as "meal" offering[5] (see Lev. 2; 6:14–18); the peace offering (see Lev. 3; 7:11–21); the sin offering (see Lev. 4:1 to 5:13; 6:24–30); and the trespass offering (see Lev. 5:14 to 6:7; 7:1–10).

The burnt offering was probably a continuation of the sacrifice revealed to Adam and the patriarchs. It consisted of the offering of a male of the flocks, without blemish, and symbolized the sacrifice of the Savior. An interesting ritual accompanied this sacrifice. The offerer brought the animal voluntarily to the north side of the altar, where he himself laid his hand upon the head of the beast, probably signifying that in some way the animal represented the offerer. The animal was killed by the offerer himself and then given to the priests, who sprinkled the blood upon the altar. The carcass was skinned and cut into pieces. The priests put the pieces on the altar. The priests washed the entrails and the legs with water, and then everything was burned on the altar "to be a burnt sacrifice, an offering made by fire, of a sweet savour unto the Lord" (Lev. 1:9). While the entire ceremony offers many possible symbolic interpretations of this sacrifice, one should note the prominence of the death of the animal, the water and blood, and the totality of the sacrifice. The burnt offering was made twice daily on the altar at the temple for the entire congregation of Israel—a male lamb in the morning and another in the evening.

The meal offering was an offering of thanksgiving and regularly accompanied the burnt offering. It took the form of a baked loaf made from fine flour and oil. Part of the offering was given to the Lord and burned on the altar, and part was given to the priest to eat. It was offered twice a day along with the burnt offering.

The peace offering was a communal meal consisting of any unblemished domesticated animal along with unleavened cakes. The animal was killed at the door of the temple. Certain portions were given to the Lord, to the priests, and to the offerer, who took his portion home and ate it with his family. Perhaps this meal symbolized that the Lord, the priesthood, and the people, having eaten together, were at "peace."

Two sacrifices, the sin and the trespass offerings, were connected with the laws of clean and unclean, and helped individuals to overcome ritual impurity caused by sin or the transgression of the laws of clean and unclean. Under the law of Moses, a host of human functions, some volitional and others not, rendered a person unclean—unable to enter into the precincts of the temple and to participate in religious rites performed there. In particular, sexual intercourse, seminal emissions, menstrual periods, childbirth, leprosy, and other actions or conditions were considered as defilements. Presumably these strict commandments of purity represented spiritual lessons—that the things of mortality must be overcome. Also included were "sins of ignorance," and of course willful disobedience rendered a person unworthy to participate in religious ritual. Sin of any kind involved three or four parties: the transgressor himself; the

Lord; the covenant community, or the church; and often another
party which was damaged in some way by the sin—for example,
moral transgression often involves another party, as do dishonesty, theft, and violence.

The process of repentance has always been the same. Under
the law of Moses, sacrifice was a ritual which accompanied the
repentance process and provided a concrete symbol of the
power of the Atonement to cleanse repentant people from sin
and free them from its consequences. The Psalms explain that
sacrifice without repentance is meaningless:

> For thou desirest not sacrifice;
> > else would I give it:
> > > thou delightest not in burnt offering.
> The sacrifices of God are a broken spirit:
> > a broken and a contrite heart, O God,
> > > thou wilt not despise. . . .
> Then shalt thou be pleased with the sacrifices of righteousness,
> > with burnt offering and whole burnt offering:
> > > then shall they offer bullocks upon thine altar.
> > > > (Ps. 51:16–17, 19.)

The animal sacrificed for a sin offering depended on the
rank of the person bringing the sacrifice. A high priest, or the
congregation, brought a bull, a ruler a male goat, and a common
person a female goat or a lamb. Poor people could bring pigeons
or even a small offering of flour. The offerer, like at the burnt offering, laid his hand on the head of the animal. The blood was
collected and sprinkled on the altar. Choice parts of the animal
were burned to the Lord; the rest was eaten by the priests. This
sacrifice was to remove from a person ritual impurity or any
other "sin through ignorance" (Lev. 4:2). On certain occasions
this sacrifice was offered on behalf of the congregation, but it
was largely a sacrifice offered by individuals.

The animal offered for the trespass offering was usually a ram
but sometimes a lamb. The animal was killed, blood sprinkled
on the altar, and some of the carcass burned to the Lord, the
rest being given to the priests to eat. Like the sin offering, it

symbolically cleansed a person after some infraction of the law. Transgressions of the law mentioned were the breaking of oaths and covenants, and infringing on other people's property rights, including fraud. The person guilty of such infractions could only be cleansed from such sins through repentance, restitution (which included full compensation, plus a twenty-percent penalty), and finally the transgression offering, symbolizing the completion of the repentance process.

The Daily Sacrifices and Offerings at the Temple

Jewish tradition preserved in the Mishnah contains many descriptions of the various rituals from the time of Herod's temple and much information detailing how these sacrifices were actually done at the time of Jesus.[6] The sacrificial ceremonies were systematically performed throughout the day, and the priests followed a well-organized routine. Let us review a typical day at Herod's temple.

As has been noted, the descendants of Aaron, or priests, were divided into twenty-four divisions. From the division chosen to officiate in the temple for the week, the individual priests were chosen by lot to attend to the various functions for the day. All of the priests ritually washed and purified themselves each day before participating in any of the ordinances. First, some of the priests removed the ashes from the altar in front of the temple from the day before and prepared wood for the sacrifice. Then they awaited the call from a priest assigned to watch the horizon and determine when the dawn had come. The morning sacrifice, the burnt offering, was to be offered at the first light of dawn, and then again as evening fell.

When the assigned priest announced that the eastern horizon was light "all the way to Hebron," the sacrificial ceremony began. The trumpets sounded, the gates of the temple itself were opened, and priests went into the temple to clean the ashes from the incense altar and prepare and light the seven lamps on the branches of the lampstand, or menorah. (The westernmost branch of the menorah closest to the temple was left burning day and night, but the other branches often burned out during the night.) Then the burnt offering was sacrificed. The priests gathered in one of the chambers and, with the people, read the Ten Commandments and other scriptural passages reminding them of their covenantal obligations to the Lord. At that point another priest entered the temple again to offer the incense on the golden incense altar. During the offering of the incense, symbolic of the offering of prayer (see Ps. 141:2), the people gathered both inside the temple—in the Court of the Women and the Court of the Israelites—and outside of the temple to join in prayer (see Luke 1:10).

The priests then stood on the stairs and blessed the people with the priestly blessing (see Num. 6:23–25). As representatives of the Lord, the priests officiating at the temple, after the two daily sacrifices, would stand together on the stairs and bless the people, reciting the Priestly Benediction in Numbers:

> The Lord bless thee,
> > and keep thee:
> The Lord make his face shine upon thee,
> > and be gracious unto thee:
> The Lord lift up his countenance upon thee,
> > and give thee peace (Num. 6:24–26).

Originally, at this point in the service the priests would recite the name of God, Jehovah, to the people, for the name of the Lord was to be found at the temple (see 1 Kgs. 8:29). At some point in time, in order to avoid speaking the name of the Lord too frequently, the priests said "Lord" (in Hebrew "Adonai") instead of Jehovah.

To conclude the burnt sacrifice, the limbs of the sacrifice were lifted on the outer altar to be burned, the "meal" offering (in the King James Version "meat") was made, and an offering of wine was presented on the altar. The trumpets sounded again, and the Levites sang a hymn.

In much the same way the evening sacrificial rite was conducted. In between the two daily burnt offerings, the priests were busy offering all of the rest of the individual sacrifices

The Temple of Herod

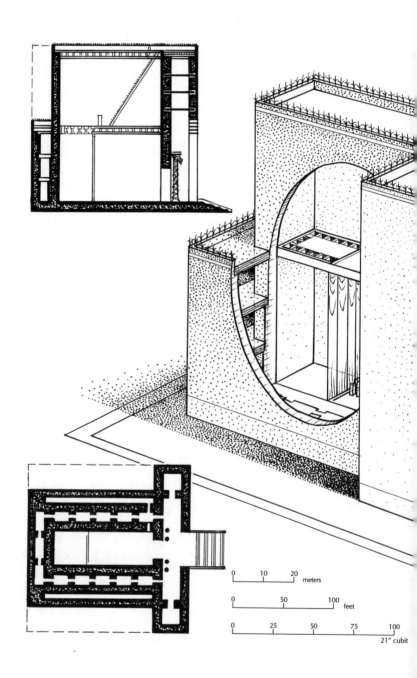

0   10   20   meters

0   50   100   feet

0   25   50   75   100

21″ cubit

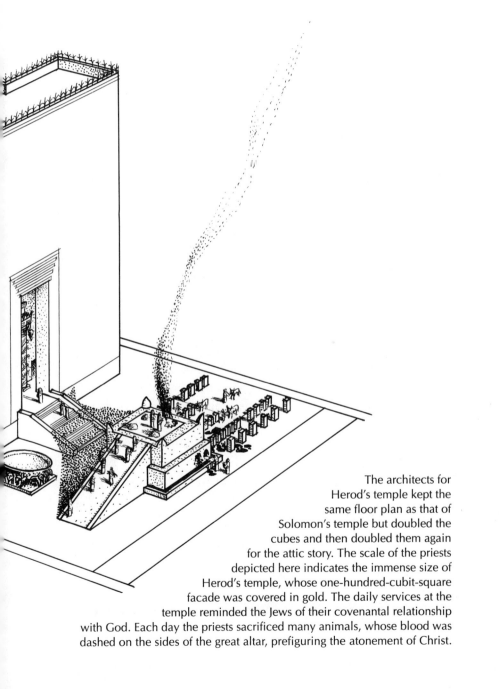

The architects for
Herod's temple kept the
same floor plan as that of
Solomon's temple but doubled the
cubes and then doubled them again
for the attic story. The scale of the priests
depicted here indicates the immense size of
Herod's temple, whose one-hundred-cubit-square
facade was covered in gold. The daily services at the
temple reminded the Jews of their covenantal relationship
with God. Each day the priests sacrificed many animals, whose blood was
dashed on the sides of the great altar, prefiguring the atonement of Christ.

which were brought that day for people's purification from the various impurities defined by the Mosaic law. These included the various thank and meal offerings; sin offerings which accompanied the purification from childbirth, the cleansing of lepers, and the fulfillment of the Nazarite vow; trespass offerings; and peace offerings.

In addition to the above five sacrifices, there was a series of other offerings of thanksgiving, financial obligations towards the redemption of the firstborn, and the maintenance of the temple which could be offered there. Around the Court of the Women was a series of chests with trumpet-shaped funnels into which these offerings could be made. It was here that the Savior witnessed the widow offering her mites.

The Sabbath was celebrated by a doubling of the daily burnt offering—four lambs instead of two—but the host of individual sacrifices in between was not permitted. In addition to the two double burnt offerings, the priests removed the old shewbread, which was then reverently eaten, and offered twelve fresh loaves along with an incense offering on the table of shewbread.

Each of the temple festivals was celebrated with variants of the five major sacrifices which added to the symbolism of the festivals. For example, the burnt offering was often doubled like the Sabbath sacrifice. At Passover all of the lambs to be eaten by the congregation were slaughtered at the temple. At Pentecost a series of "first fruit" offerings was made from the harvest of the winter's grain. The Feast of Tabernacles incorporated offerings of water and wine. And the Day of Atonement consisted of a ceremony of burnt and sin offerings, first offered by the priests and then for the congregation. At the pilgrimage festivals, each of the pilgrims coming to Jerusalem would have numerous individual offerings to be made on his or her own behalf. The temple altar was a busy place during these festivals.

Sacred Time: Feasts and Festivals

From the beginning the Lord consecrated and set apart sacred time which was to be observed by his children. The observance of sacred time was a demonstration of faith and served to establish and reinforce the relationship between God and his children. It was a time for the members of the covenant to remember their obligations to the Lord and to teach their children their sacred history. In the law of Moses the Lord revealed a whole series of sacred days which would serve in various ways to help the people remember the bounteous hand of the Lord on their behalf, to direct their hearts to him, to help them teach their children about their sacred heritage and their relationship with God, and, most important, to direct their attention to the coming of the Messiah, Jesus Christ. As part of the process of creation the Lord set apart the seventh day and set the example for its correct observance when he rested "from all his work" (Gen. 2:2). The observance of this sacred day was legislated by the Ten Commandments where the Lord commanded, "Remember the sabbath day, to keep it holy" (Ex. 20:8), and where the Lord reminded Israel that the seventh day was to commemorate the Lord's bounty in the Creation (see Ex. 20:11) and to remember the Lord's intervention in delivering Israel from bondage in Egypt (see Deut. 5:15).

The Lord reaffirmed in the Mosaic law the importance of this sacred day (see Lev. 23:3). In short, the Sabbath was a day to rest from the labors of the world and to remember the hand of the Lord in the creation of the world and in the Exodus delivering Israel from bondage and death in Egypt. As part of the Mosaic law the Lord revealed to Israel a series of feast days, or festivals—special times to remember and reflect upon God's intervention on their behalf and to help them teach their children, occasions that also served as symbols of the atonement of Christ. These days became days of covenant making and renewal.

Following the scriptural account, they are as follows: Sabbath, Passover/Feast of Unleavened Bread, Weeks/Pentecost, Day of Atonement, Tabernacles (see Lev. 23). These sacred times were celebrated with sacred ordinances: fasting, rituals, sacrifices, and specific readings from the scriptures. Each of the sacred days and festivals was celebrated in some way, especially through sacrifices, at the temple. The Lord commanded that three of these festivals were to be occasions on which all of the males in Israel were to present themselves "before the Lord," that is, make a pilgrimage to the temple in Jerusalem and present themselves at the temple, presumably in a state of ethical worthiness and ritual purity. Thus, in the New Testament, Jesus, as a law-abiding Jew, went to Jerusalem to fulfill this commandment and to celebrate the festivals.

The law of Moses contains only a brief discussion of what was to be done at these celebrations. Through the years there was undoubtedly development in the ways these festivals were celebrated. By New Testament times, as preserved in the Mishnah, Jewish practice and observation of these festivals had developed distinctive characteristics in addition to the biblical injunctions. A version of these festivals continues to be celebrated by Jews today, in spite of the fact that they do not have a temple where the prescribed sacrifices can be offered. In addition, several important religious festivals were added to the Mosaic festivals, such as the Feast of Purim and the Feast of Dedication. Following is a calendar of the major festivals:

Season/Month/Month			Festival
Spring			
	Mar.		
		1 Nisan	First Month
	Apr.		14th: Passover
			15–21: Unleavened Bread
		2 Iyyar	
	May		
Summer		3 Sivan	Weeks/Pentecost:
			50th day after Passover
	June		
		4 Tammuz	
	July		
		5 Ab	
	Aug.		
Fall		6 Elul	
	Sept.		

		7 Tishri	1st: New Year
	Oct.		10th: Day of Atonement
			15–21st: Feast of Tabernacles
		8 Marchesvan	
	Nov.		
Winter		9 Chislev	25th: Feast of Dedication
	Dec.		
		10 Tebeth	
	Jan.		
		11 Shebat	
	Feb.		
Spring		12 Adar	14–15th: Purim

These festivals can be discussed on three different levels: first, most of the festivals commemorate an important historical event; second, the festivals coincide with important agricultural and sometimes astronomical events which lend significance to their celebration; and third, each of them becomes a type of future events. For example, Passover commemorated the Exodus from Egypt when the Lord miraculously delivered the children of Israel from bondage and death; it coincided with the time of the spring planting, which focused on the need for light and fertility; and it was a type for the future deliverance offered by the Atonement.

Sabbath. One of the most important of the sacred festivals, since it occurred so frequently, was the Sabbath. The Sabbath was observed by Israel as a time to remember the Lord as the creator of the universe and as the Redeemer of Israel who delivered them from the bondage of slavery and from death. Following the example of the Lord at the Creation, the covenant people were to rest from their daily labors on the seventh day of the week. On that day they were to remember the Lord's work in the Creation and his power in delivering them from bondage in Egypt. The beginning and ending of the Sabbath, from dusk to dusk, was indicated at the temple by the sounding of trumpets. At the temple the daily sacrifices for the community were doubled, but there

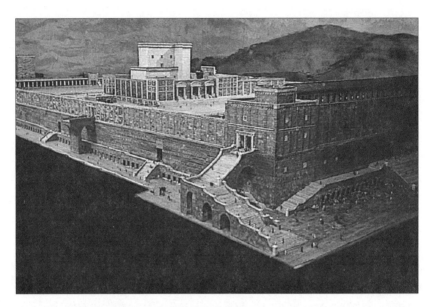

A general view from the southwest of the Temple Mount. The temple proper is seen from the back and stands in the middle of the great courtyard. Robinson's Arch, named after the Englishman who discovered it in the nineteenth century, supports the monumental stairway which led up from the main street in the valley and then turned right to the entrance of the Royal Stoa.

were no individual sacrifices offered. In addition, the shewbread was changed, the priests eating the week-old bread and replacing it with fresh.

Passover. The Passover feast originated with a sacred meal eaten by the children in Israel. It commemorated the Lord's deliverance of Israel from the angel of death which killed all of the firstborn in Egypt and which led to the deliverance of Israel from bondage in Egypt. The details of the meal were revealed to Israel as recorded in Exodus 12. On the tenth day of the first month (Nisan) an unblemished male lamb was chosen. On the fourteenth day the lamb was to be killed and the blood of the lamb was to be daubed on the doorpost of the houses where the people would eat it. The flesh of the lamb was to be roasted and eaten with unleavened bread and bitter herbs. Care was to be taken that no bones were broken in the lamb, and any of the flesh that remained was to be completely burnt as an offering to the Lord. The lamb is clearly a symbol of the Savior: the unblemished lamb whose blood was to deliver the firstborn from death. The blood on the door witnessed to the Lord and the angel of death faith and obedience exercised by those within, who would then eat the flesh of the symbol which had died to preserve them from bondage and death. That all of the flesh would be eaten and the remainder and the bones would all be burnt symbolized the totality of the sacrifice of the lamb.

The unleavened bread represented the haste with which the children of Israel would flee Egypt, since they would not even have time to allow yeast to rise. In addition, leaven was a symbol of corruption, and unleavened bread was symbolic of the purity of the sacrifice which Christ would make. The bitter herbs represented the bitter slavery which was imposed upon Israel. The Lord indicated one of the functions of this festival when he said: "And it shall come to pass, when your children shall say unto you, What mean ye by this service? that ye shall say, It is the sacrifice of the Lord's passover, who passed over the houses of the children of Israel in Egypt, when he smote the Egyptians, and delivered our houses" (Ex. 12:26–27). From the 15th to the 21st day, the people were to observe the Feast of Unleavened Bread, in which time the people were to abstain from leavened bread as well as remove all leaven from their homes, rest from their labors, remember the Lord, who provides us with what we eat, and thus be reminded of the purity expected of the covenant people.

This festival was celebrated in the spring and became enriched through time with its natural connections with the planting of the crops and the supplications to the Lord for abundance in crops and flocks. Spring begins with the vernal equinox and the astronomical phenomenon of the lengthening of the day. Thus the celebration incorporates light and life. This was the season of the death and the resurrection of Christ, who was described in the agricultural terms of this season, "Except a corn of wheat fall into the ground and die, it abideth alone: but if it die, it bringeth forth much fruit" (John 12:24).

The symbols pointing to Christ are clear: the lamb, the blood, the unleavened bread, the bitter herbs. Through time the Jews added wine to the Passover meal, and it is likely that at the time of Christ wine was also part of the Passover meal. At the Last Supper, Jesus took the unleavened bread and the wine, two of the symbols of the Passover, which he with his disciples had just celebrated in remembrance of the deliverance from Egypt, and blessed them and directed his disciples to eat them in remembrance of the new covenant and thus commemorate the historical intervention of the Atonement which delivered humankind from sin, death, and hell.

This festival was one of the greatest celebrated in Jerusalem at the time of Christ. Jews flocked into Jerusalem from all over the world. In terms of the temple, each of the lambs eaten at the Passover meal had to be sacrificed in the temple. In addition, extra sacrifices were offered at the temple during the Feast of Unleavened Bread.

Weeks/Pentecost. For seven weeks, 49 days, the children of Israel continued the harvest of the firstfruits. On the 50th day, they celebrated the Feast of Weeks, also called Pentecost, which is the Greek word for *fifty.* This was a joyous time, and people brought sacrifices of gratitude from the firstfruits to the Lord. Just as Passover commemorated the Exodus, Pentecost, in Jewish tradition, came to represent the giving of the law on Sinai, because it was believed that the law was given on the fiftieth day after Israel left Egypt.

This festival took place in the early spring as well, when in Israel the people gathered together the firstfruits of the winter grains. It was a time of thanksgiving and reminded the people of their dependence on the Lord. For the followers of the risen Christ, the symbolism of Pentecost culminated in the book of Acts when the Lord poured forth the Holy Ghost upon all (see Acts 2:1–13). It represented the giving of the law to the Gentiles and at the same time was a sort of celebration of firstfruits, with all those present receiving the Holy Ghost. As at all the festivals, special offerings were made on Pentecost at the temple.

Day of Atonement. Israel celebrated two new years. Passover was celebrated on the 14th day of the first month, but a new year called Rosh Hashanah was also celebrated on the first day of the seventh month. On the tenth day of the seventh month was the most holy of days in ancient Israel—the Day of Atonement. The Lord stated the purpose of this festival: "For on that day shall the priest make an atonement for you, to cleanse you, that ye may be clean from all your sins before the Lord" (Lev. 16:30). The Lord gave specific directions for the celebration of this solemn day. The people were to prepare themselves through fasting, prayer, and repentance. They were then to present themselves before the Lord, and the priests would offer a series of sacrifices representing the purification of the priests and all of Israel.

The high priest brought a bullock as a sin offering and a ram as a burnt offering for himself and his house, and two male goats and a ram for the congregation of Israel. He cast lots over the two goats, designating one as a sin offering to the Lord and the other as the "scapegoat," or the goat which would "escape" being slaughtered and which would be "for Azazel." The term *Azazel* either represented a name of the evil one residing in the wilderness or was a name for the wilderness itself. The priest killed the bullock, and the goat for the sin offering, and entered the Holy of Holies, representing the presence of the Lord. There he offered incense before the Lord and sprinkled the blood on the mercy seat, signifying the power of the Lord to cover over, or forgive, the sins of the high priest, his family, and all of Israel. The goat for Azazel was then brought forth, and upon its head the high priest confessed all of the sins of Israel, symbolizing for Israel that through repentance and the blood of the Atonement their sins could be removed. The high priest then offered the two rams as burnt offerings for his house and for the congregation of Israel.

This most sacred of sacrifices represented Christ, and the blood in the Holy of Holies his blood, which would allow Israel to purify themselves and become worthy to enter into his presence. In some ways the scapegoat also represented Christ, taking upon himself the sins of the people. The symbolism of this specific day was in many ways fulfilled with the literal rending of the veil of the temple, indicating that through the atonement of Christ, all men and women would be able to enter into his presence.

This festival is specifically mentioned in the Gospels, though the symbolism of the Day of Atonement pervades the life and death of the Savior. It was literally fulfilled with the death and resurrection of the Lamb of God, whose sacrifice offered for all mankind the possibility of the redemption from sin and of atonement with God through the Son.

Tabernacles. The Feast of Tabernacles was celebrated from the 14th to the 21st of the month of Chislev. This festival occurs in the fall (September or October of our solar calendar) and is primarily a joyous celebration of the harvest. It came to be associated with the forty years of wandering in the wilderness when the children of Israel lived in tents (booths) and were miraculously cared for by the Lord at various times through water from the rock, manna, and quail. The children of Israel were commanded to live in temporary booths for seven days, in commemoration of the wandering in the wilderness (see Lev. 23:42–43) and to take the boughs of "goodly trees, palm trees, thick trees, and willows," and rejoice (see Lev. 23:40). Through time the interpretation of these became citron (ethorg), myrtle, palm (lulav), and willow. It was a time of great joy and festivity.

The children of Israel were specifically commanded to read the law every seven years at the Feast of Tabernacles, symbolic of the renewal of their covenants with the Lord both as a nation and individually. The temple of Solomon was dedicated on this day as well as the altar of the rebuilt temple in the days of Zerubbabel.

The book of Zechariah identifies the Feast of Tabernacles as the festival to which all will be gathered to celebrate in the Millennium and identifies much of the symbolism associated with this festival with the first and second comings of the Messiah (see Zech. 14:16).

Prayer

The temple was a house of prayer. In his dedicatory prayer Solomon expressed this profound understanding: "And hearken thou to the supplication of thy servant, and of thy people Israel, when they shall pray toward this place: and hear thou in heaven thy dwelling place: and when thou hearest, forgive" (1 Kgs. 8:30). Prayer at the temple occurred on at least three levels. The priests offered specific prayers on behalf of the people on a daily basis and at the times of the festivals. The people joined in together with the priests throughout daily service and on special occasions. In addition, prayer is an individual matter, and those who came to worship the Lord brought their own individual petitions which they offered to the Lord at the sacred place. The temple, as the symbol of the presence of the Lord, was a powerful reminder to those who sought the Lord in prayer. Daniel, the prophet in exile, faced Jerusalem three times a day, even though the temple had been destroyed (see Dan. 6:10).

The temple was a sacred place where men and women could go into the presence of God to worship him through sacrifices and offerings. There, all could be instructed in matters of holiness and could commune with the Lord God of Israel. The repentant could be cleansed from their sins. Those who worshipped at the temple did so with thanksgiving and joy in their hearts:

> I will worship toward thy holy temple,
>> and praise thy name for thy lovingkindness and for thy truth:
> for thou hast magnified thy word
>> above all thy name.
> In the day when I cried thou answeredst me,
>> and strengthenedst me with strength in my soul.
>> (Ps. 138: 2–3.)

FOUR

Luke and the Presence of God in the Temple

How is it that ye sought me? wist ye not that I must be about my Father's business?

—Luke 2:49

Luke's Gospel account begins within the temple, at the altar of incense before the veil, as a righteous priest named Zacharias performs his duty (see Luke 1:5–25). The book ends with the disciples "continually in the temple, praising and blessing God," following their Master's ascension to heaven (see Luke 24:53). The temple figures in a surprisingly positive way throughout Luke's Gospel. In fact, sixty or more references to the temple are found in the writings of Luke (the Gospel of Luke and Acts). In the book of Luke, Jesus' first recorded words occur while he is in the temple, and his final words before his death are an address to the God of the temple. Through these passages, Luke's own understanding of the place of the temple in the ministry of Jesus

---

◄ One of the themes in Luke's Gospel is that God and His Christ could be found in the holy sanctuary by the righteous. Jesus' parents *find* him here in the temple going about his Father's work. Here Jesus sits amid the Jewish teachers discussing the things of his Father's house. The doctors of the law were "astonished at his understanding" (Luke 2:47).

and in the life of the disciples is revealed in several important ways.

Before proceeding further, however, a brief review of how the word *temple* is used in the New Testament is in order. The Greek *hieron* ("sanctuary, temple") is used once to refer to the pagan temple of Artemis (see Acts 19:27). Otherwise, it always refers to the temple at Jerusalem. The term includes the whole temple complex. Unfortunately, both this and another term, *naos*, are translated "temple" in the King James Version (KJV), which sometimes leads to confusion.

Jesus, who was not an Aaronic priest nor the high priest, technically could not enter the "temple" (*naos*)—the Holy Place and the Holy of Holies—nor could those "that sold" (Luke 19:45; or the money changers in Matt. 21:12), nor could Paul (see Acts 21:26). The original word used in each instance is *hieron*, which might be more accurately translated "temple mount" or "temple complex."

The Greek *naos* ("temple") is used in the New Testament to mean Herod's temple—that is, the sanctuary itself (the Holy Place and the Holy of Holies) and not the entire temple area (see Luke 1:21, for example). The Greek *oikos* ("house"), referring to the temple, except for Luke 11:51 and Hebrews 10:21, occurs in the New Testament only in quotations of passages in the Hebrew Bible where *bayit* ("house") is used. Therefore, most of the references to the temple should be thought of as referring to the Temple Mount or the temple complex and not to the two separate rooms of the temple proper—the Holy Place and the Holy of Holies.

The stories in which the temple plays an important role demonstrate Luke's belief that God is present in the temple and that not only are the faithful prayers of the righteous heard in the temple but also God or his messengers actually respond. Like the Psalmist, Luke believes God is present in the temple not only as a silent listener and grantor but also as an articulate speaker (see Ps. 60:6; 108:8; cf. 35:3; 50:1; 62:11; 85:8; 89:19).

The concept that the presence of God is in his holy temple is forcefully portrayed by Luke in several stories. Out of the first six episodes in Luke 1–2, three take place in the temple itself. First, an angel of the Lord appears to a righteous man as he serves before the Lord. Second, the infant Jesus is presented to the Lord in the temple following his birth and is recognized as God's salvation at the same time. Third, the young boy Jesus previews his mission concerning the temple during his visit to the holy place when he is twelve years of age.

Additionally, Luke lays stress on Jesus' actions when Jesus enters the temple and drives out the merchants in preparation for his proclamation of the good news in the temple. Another important episode in which the temple plays a significant role occurs just before Jesus' death. At this moment, Jesus speaks to his Father through the torn curtain of the temple. Finally, after his resurrection, as already mentioned, the disciples continue in the temple praising and blessing God.

According to Luke, the activities of Jesus during his ministry in Jerusalem are so intertwined with the religious celebrations of the temple that an enhanced understanding of his ministry is possible only with a knowledge of the historical background of ancient temple worship.

Zacharias at the Altar (Luke 1:5–23)

Our story begins in the "days of Herod" with a righteous priest and his wife (Luke 1:5). Both stricken with age, they are childless.

> There was in the days of Herod, the king of Judea, a certain priest named Zacharias, of the course of Abia: and his wife was of the daughters of Aaron, and her name was Elisabeth.
>
> And they were both righteous before God, walking in all the commandments and ordinances of the Lord blameless.
>
> And they had no child, because that Elisabeth was barren, and they both were now well stricken in years. (Luke 1:5–7.)

The story then shifts to the temple in Jerusalem. For Luke, the temple was not only a place of sacrifice but also a house of prayer and meditation. Zacharias at the altar of incense represents this theme. "And it came to pass, that while he executed the priest's office before God in the order of his course, according to the custom of the priest's office, his lot was to burn incense when he went into the temple of the Lord" (Luke 1:8–9).

Temple service in Jerusalem was performed by members of all priestly families who could trace their ancestry back to Aaron. These priests were assigned various duties in the daily temple activities. Twenty-four such families had returned from the exile, each tracing its descent to one of the grandsons of Aaron, one of whom was Abijah—Old Testament form (see 1 Chr. 23:6; 24:7–18) of the Greek New Testament Abia. Each of these families, or divisions of priesthood, still existed at the time of Herod. Twice a year, each division took up residence in Jerusalem for its week's duty in the temple. The family was then divided into seven groups and took responsibility for one day of the week. In all likelihood, the priests spent the night in the temple. They arose before dawn, took a ritual bath, and then dressed. In the Chamber of Hewn Stone they drew lots for their duties. On this occasion, Zacharias had the privilege of presenting the incense offering in the temple.

Since eight hundred priests were in the division, being chosen by lot to burn the incense could be a once-in-a-lifetime experience. Twice a day, morning and evening, a lamb was sacrificed and burnt at the altar before the temple. The hour of incense offering may have come just after this sacrifice in the morning and just after it in the evening. The text is unclear regarding which hour is referred to here, but the reference to "the whole multitude of the people [who] were praying without" (Luke 1:10) seems to suggest the more widely attended evening service.

At the moment when the chosen priest, in this case Zacharias, left his two assistants outside by the altar of sacrifice, he entered the Holy Place. As explained earlier in this book, this was the first room in the temple sanctuary, being a kind of anteroom to the Holy of Holies (which only the high priest could enter, and that only on one day of the year).

Here Zacharias stood before a small wooden altar covered

with gold for burning incense. The sanctity of the place, combined with the smoke of the incense and the complete solitude of the priest, made this rare moment a particularly likely one for communication with God, who dwelt in the Holy of Holies in darkness. Luke continues his story at the temple:

> And the whole multitude of the people were praying without at the time of incense.
>
> And there appeared unto him an angel of the Lord standing on the right side of the altar of incense.
>
> And when Zacharias saw him, he was troubled, and fear fell upon him.
>
> But the angel said unto him, Fear not, Zacharias: for thy prayer is heard; and thy wife Elisabeth shall bear thee a son, and thou shalt call his name John.
>
> And thou shalt have joy and gladness; and many shall rejoice at his birth.
>
> For he shall be great in the sight of the Lord, and shall drink neither wine nor strong drink; and he shall be filled with the Holy Ghost, even from his mother's womb.
>
> And many of the children of Israel shall he turn to the Lord their God.
>
> And he shall go before him in the spirit and power of Elias, to turn the hearts of the fathers to the children, and the disobedient to the wisdom of the just; to make ready a people prepared for the Lord. (Luke 1:10–17.)

Luke informs us of the activity of the people outside the Holy Place while the revelation was being given in the temple, and recounts the subsequent events following Zacharias's emergence from the holy room: "And the people waited for Zacharias, and marvelled that he tarried so long in the temple. And when he came out, he could not speak unto them: and they perceived that he had seen a vision in the temple: for he beckoned unto them, and remained speechless. And it came to pass, that, as soon as the days of his ministration were accomplished, he departed to his own house." (Luke 1:21–23.)

Stories are told in Jewish literature of similar experiences in the temple.[1] The stories are such that the people who were waiting outside had little doubt what had happened when Zacharias stayed so long inside and was unable to give them the customary blessing when he emerged from the sanctuary: "They perceived that he had seen a vision in the temple" (Luke 1:22).

The announcement, "Fear not, Zacharias: for thy prayer is heard" (Luke 1:13), introduces the message from the angel who stands "in the presence of God" (Luke 1:19). In actuality, the answer to this prayer is on two levels—namely, the general level of the people, who were waiting for the period of salvation and the manifestation of God in his temple, and the individual level of Zacharias, who desired the birth of a son. Luke attempts to make explicit what was essentially an ineffable experience as Zacharias stood there and "beckoned unto them, and remained speechless" (Luke 1:22).

The Infant Jesus at the Temple (Luke 2:22–24)

After the birth of the mortal Messiah in Bethlehem, Joseph and Mary brought him to Jerusalem to "present him to the Lord" in the temple (see Luke 2:22). According to the law of Moses, "all that openeth the matrix is mine. . . . All the firstborn of thy sons thou shalt redeem." (Ex. 34:19–20.) In remembrance of the slaying of the firstborn of the Egyptians, an event that eventually brought about redemption from physical bondage for the children of Israel, the Lord required Israel to redeem their firstborn sons from having to serve as priests. The tribe of Levi was called to serve him; therefore, each Israelite family among the other eleven tribes could "redeem" its own firstborn by offering an appropriate sacrifice at the temple (see Ex. 13:2, 12–15). This was accomplished by a payment of five shekels at the sanctuary.

Forty-one days after her delivery, Mary was bound by the Torah to offer a sin offering for her purification after the birth of a son. Apparently, the young family could not afford the one-year-old lamb and a young pigeon or turtledove for a sin offering. Therefore, they were allowed to buy two turtledoves or two young pigeons as a substitute (see Lev. 12:8). According to Luke, they sacrificed this less-costly offering (see Luke 2:24, 39).

The trip to Jerusalem was an eventful one for the young couple. As the first-century Jewish historian Josephus makes clear, the temple layout itself consisted of progressively more restricted courtyards, culminating in the Holy of Holies:

> It had four surrounding courts, each with its special statutory restrictions. The outer court was open to all, foreigners [Gentiles] included; women during their impurity [menstruation] were alone refused admission. To the second court all Jews were admitted and, when uncontaminated by any defilement, their wives; to the third male Jews, if clean and purified; to the fourth the priests robed in their priestly vestments.[2]

As for the Holy of Holies, as stated earlier only the high priest could enter on Yom Kippur—the Day of Atonement.

Let us imagine that Mary, Joseph, and Jesus entered the temple through the western gate in the southern wall and emerged into the Court of the Gentiles, where the money changers located their tables for business each day. Here the family would have found baskets or bowls, each containing two inspected birds to buy for the woman's offering after childbirth. They would have then crossed the Court of the Gentiles and come to the balustrade that warned Gentiles to go no farther.

Here at this entrance, they would have assured one of the Levites on duty that they were pure. At some point, probably at the inner wall, they would have separated, Mary and Jesus staying in the Court of the Women, and Joseph walking straight through the first eastern gate by going up a low flight of steps through the gate itself (called the Beautiful Gate because of its elaborate decorations). Near the entrance to the Court of the Women, Mary would have found a Levite and given him her birds, explaining that they were a sin offering for childbirth. She would have then entered and gone upstairs into a gallery to watch while the Levite found a priest, who then sacrificed the two birds.

The court itself comprised nearly two hundred square feet and was surrounded by porticoes. It was a place of meeting for discussing the scriptures and the events of the day. Against the walls inside the porticoes were thirteen repositories for the temple treasury, each one shaped like a chest with a shofar, or ram's-horn trumpet, set in its lid and open to receive offerings given to defray the costs of sacrifices.

Both Mary and Joseph watched for a while, at least until the sacrifice was completed. Joseph could have gone into the Court of the Israelites to watch more closely. Although sacrifice was a normal and standard part of community worship, it was not a routine activity. Most residents of Jewish Palestine probably sacrificed on only a few occasions each year. The act was surrounded by awe. The majesty of the setting, the physical actions—selecting the sacrifice, seeing the Levite pass the birds or animals to a priest, and finally the sacrifice itself—guaranteed the moment's meaning and wonder. The temple was indeed an awesome structure. According to Josephus, the outside of the structure was adorned with so much gold and polished white stone that when the sun shone upon it, it almost blinded those who looked at it.[3]

Jesus Is Found in the Temple (Luke 2:25–38)

It was in this setting at the temple that Simeon and Anna announced their witnesses of Jesus and his mission. "And, behold, there was a man in Jerusalem, whose name was Simeon; and the same man was just and devout, waiting for the consolation of Israel: and the Holy Ghost was upon him. And it was revealed unto him by the Holy Ghost, that he should not see death, before he had seen the Lord's Christ." (Luke 2:25–26.) Luke continues:

> And he came by the Spirit into the temple: and when the parents brought in the child Jesus, to do for him after the custom of the law,
> Then took he him up in his arms, and blessed God, and said,
> Lord, now lettest thou thy servant depart in peace, according to thy word:
> For mine eyes have seen thy salvation,
> Which thou hast prepared before the face of all people;

A light to lighten the Gentiles, and the glory of thy people Israel.

And Joseph and his mother marvelled at those things which were spoken of him.

And Simeon blessed them, and said unto Mary his mother, Behold, this child is set for the fall and rising again of many in Israel; and for a sign which shall be spoken against;

(Yea, a sword shall pierce through thy own soul also,) that the thoughts of many hearts may be revealed. (Luke 2:27–35.)

The text is not clear as to whether Simeon was in the temple constantly; it simply states that he had been led "by the Spirit into the temple," where he saw the "Anointed of the Lord," or, as the KJV states, "the Lord's Christ" (see Luke 2:26). The blessing of Jesus and his parents, with Mary being selected for special comments, is interesting on another level. Because the blessing is priestly in nature, Luke may be suggesting that Simeon was a priest.

As suddenly as Simeon appears, he disappears into the crowd at the temple, and another person appears—Anna, a prophetess.

And there was one Anna, a prophetess, the daughter of Phanuel, of the tribe of Aser: she was of a great age, and had lived with an husband seven years from her virginity;

And she was a widow of about fourscore and four years, which departed not from the temple, but served God with fastings and prayers night and day.

And she coming in that instant gave thanks likewise unto the Lord, and spake of him to all them that looked for redemption in Jerusalem. (Luke 2:36–38.)

Like Simeon, Anna is described as an elderly and especially devout Jew who finds the Lord's Christ in the temple.

The Young Jesus in His Father's House (Luke 2:41–49)

The next episode in the life of the young Jesus is also portrayed in the Gospel of Luke. When he was twelve years of age,

Jesus came to Jerusalem from Nazareth with his family on their pilgrimage to the temple. This event parallels the calling of young Samuel (see 1 Sam. 3:3), which, according to first-century Jewish tradition, took place at his twelfth year.[4]

Luke indicates that Joseph and Mary went up to Jerusalem yearly for the Feast of the Passover. The Torah commanded that the children of Israel were to "appear before the Lord" and not empty-handed (that is, without an offering) on three important occasions—namely, the Feast of Unleavened Bread (Passover), the Feast of Weeks, and the Feast of Tabernacles (see Ex. 23:14–17 and Deut. 16:16).

Of course, Jesus was not the only youth who attended the temple worship service. The temple choir included children, which made their hymns of praise all the more melodious.

Luke begins his narrative: "Now his parents went to Jerusalem every year at the feast of the passover. And when he was twelve years old, *they went up* to Jerusalem after the custom of the feast." (Luke 2:41, emphasis added.) This detail, "they went up," echoes the Samuel story again, as Elkanah and Hannah went up yearly to the sanctuary (see 1 Sam. 1:3, 21; 2:19). The celebration of Passover included the ritual slaying of the lamb in the temple area, a festal meal at sundown in a family circle of at least ten people, and the consumption of the entire animal. The family stayed in Jerusalem for the seven to eight days of Passover and Unleavened Bread (see Lev. 23:5–6). To make time for all the additional sacrifices, the temple service was begun at a much earlier time, especially during this spring-time feast—the most popular festival during the time of Jesus. To accommodate the large crowds, the temple gates were open from midnight on, instead of at daybreak.

Luke continues: "And when they had fulfilled the days, as they returned, the child Jesus tarried behind in Jerusalem; and Joseph and his mother knew not of it. But they, supposing him to have been in the company, went a day's journey; and they sought him among their kinsfolk and acquaintance. And when they found him not, they turned back again to Jerusalem, seeking him." (Luke 2:43–45.) Again, Luke prepares us for the fact that God and his Christ can be found in the temple. Notice the last phrase, "They turned back again to Jerusalem, *seeking him*" (Luke 2:45, emphasis added).

Luke's account continues:

> And it came to pass, that after three days they found him in the temple, sitting in the midst of the doctors, both hearing them, and asking them questions.
>
> And all that heard him were astonished at his understanding and answers.
>
> And when they saw him, they were amazed: and his mother said unto him, Son, why hast thou thus dealt with us? behold, thy father and I have sought thee sorrowing.
>
> And he said unto them, How is it that ye sought me? wist ye not that I must be about my Father's business? (Luke 2:46–49.)[5]

An alternative translation to "wist ye not that I must be about my Father's business?" may make more sense. "He said to them, Why were you searching for me? *Did you not know that I had to be in my Father's house?*"[6] A number of instances are found in biblical and extrabiblical Greek texts that support this translation.[7]

Jesus' allusion to his Father's house, following this translation, would imply that Mary and Joseph should have known *where* to find him. On the lips of a child, this concrete meaning of the expression seems better than the other more abstract sense; moreover, the Jerusalem temple is referred to indirectly as God's house in Luke 19:46. The scene also acts as the conclusion of the infancy narrative. Luke, therefore, ends his narrative as he began it, with a temple scene (see Luke 1:5–25). This is important, because the Gospel proper ends there too (see Luke 24:53), with the notice about the disciples being constantly in the temple praising God.

Moreover, the scene depicts the twelve-year-old Jesus making his way to Jerusalem—to the city that will play such an important role in his final days. He was carried there as an infant (presumably from Bethlehem) as recorded in Luke 2:22; but, in this scene, he makes his way there from Galilee.

The Ministry Begins at the Temple (Luke 4:9–13)

Of course, this is not the last time Jesus is found at the temple. When he began his ministry, Jesus approached John at the river Jordan. Following his baptism, he went into the wilderness to commune with his Father. Forty days later, Satan came to tempt him with three great trials. Unlike Matthew's account, in Luke the temptation at the temple stands last in the story.

> And the Spirit brought him to Jerusalem, and set him on a pinnacle of the temple. And the devil came unto him, and said unto him, If thou be the Son of God, cast thyself down from hence;
> For it is written, He shall give his angels charge over thee, to keep thee; and in his hands they shall bear thee up, lest at any time thou dash thy foot against a stone.
> And Jesus answering, said unto him, It is written, Thou shalt not tempt the Lord thy God.
> And when the devil had ended all the temptation, he departed from him for a season. (JST, Luke 4:9–12.)

Luke's sequence of the three temptations represents a more natural geographic movement, from the wilderness to the temple, reminding us of Israel's movements in the wilderness to Mount Sinai and eventually to the promised land. Also, the parallel to Moses is strengthened as the motifs of the forty-day period of time and the sacred mount are present.

The term *temple* as used in Luke 4:9 refers to the entire area, and the word *pinnacle* is literally a "little wing," a term used for the tip or extremity of anything, hence the edge or the summit.[8] Traditionally, the pinnacle has been identified as the tower at the southeast corner of the Temple Mount, the point described by Josephus. This pinnacle, or tower, certainly stands at a spectacular height—the drop down to the Kidron Valley from the top of Herod's portico being approximately four hundred feet.

First-century historian Josephus may have had this particular place in mind when he wrote: "For while the depth of the ravine was great, and no one who bent over to look into it from

In 1969, excavators working at the base of the southwestern wall of the Temple Mount discovered a stone bearing a broken inscription which read, "to the place of the trumpeting to [or 'for'] . . ." It is postulated that the stone once marked a place on top of the Temple Mount where the priest stood to blow the trumpet marking the beginning and the end of the Sabbath. Some scholars believe that the southwestern corner is the more logical place of the "pinnacle of the temple" where Satan tempted Jesus (see Luke 4:9–13).

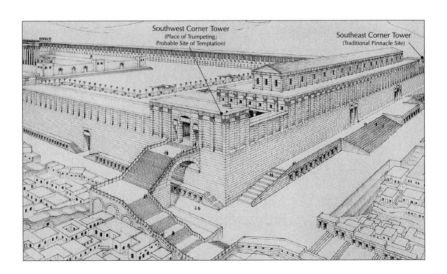

Southwest Corner Tower
(Place of Trumpeting;
Probable Site of Temptation)

Southeast Corner Tower
(Traditional Pinnacle Site)

above could bear to look down to the bottom, the height of the portico standing over it was so very great that if anyone looked down from its rooftop [pinnacle], combining the two elevations, he would become dizzy and his vision would be unable to reach the end of so measureless a depth."[9]

Some historians suggest that the southwestern corner of the Temple Mount is a more logical location of this event, since that corner has a much better angle for looking out over the lower city to the south and the upper city to the west. Recently, a carved platform stone from this site was discovered. The Hebrew inscription reads, "To the place of trumpeting."[10] Though brief and fragmentary, the inscription illustrates one of the means of communication between the priest in the temple and the people in the city. It may well have been the place were Jesus stood nearly two thousand years ago—a place where Satan wanted Jesus to tempt God and herald to the people that he was God's Son.

It is of interest to note that, according to Luke, Satan left Jesus at the temple as Jesus began his work. This may signify that the divine presence (which Jesus represents) is at the temple and that the forces of evil are about to be removed from the sacred site through his power and authority. Luke seems to indicate that one of Jesus' main purposes for going to Jerusalem was to cleanse the temple. In fact, Jesus' own statement as a twelve-year-old boy may best be explained as a preview of his mission as an adult: Jesus came as the Son of God, who took back and purified his Father's house. This view also dovetails with the ironic fact that the opposition to Jesus is also centered at the temple. These events set the stage for the death of Jesus at the hands of the chief priests and scribes, who perversely do not recognize the Son of God, who is teaching daily in the temple.

The Transfiguration (Luke 9:28–36)

Luke's record, along with Matthew, Mark, and Peter, mentions an incident upon a mountain when Jesus and three disciples went to pray sometime in October, just six months before Jesus' death (see Matt. 17:1–13; Mark 9: 2–8; and 2 Pet. 1:10–19).[11]

And it came to pass about an eight days after these sayings, he took Peter and John and James, and went up into a mountain to pray.

And as he prayed, the fashion of his countenance was altered, and his raiment was white and glistering.

And, behold, there talked with him two men, which were Moses and Elias:

Who appeared in glory, and spake of his decease which he should accomplish at Jerusalem.

But Peter and they that were with him were heavy with sleep: and when they were awake, they saw his glory, and the two men that stood with him. (Luke 9:28–32.)

Peter and Jesus spoke, but were interrupted: "While [Peter] thus spake, there came a cloud, and overshadowed them: and they feared as they entered into the cloud. And there came a voice out of the cloud, saying, This is my beloved Son: hear him." (Luke 9:34–35.)

The Transfiguration is an important episode, and it identifies Jesus as more than simply one of several messengers called "messiahs" (anointed ones) expected before the "great and dreadful day of the Lord." He is the one Messiah, after whom his predecessors are patterned. It is a clear expression that Jesus is the Son of God and, more important, that he is God's *beloved* Son, or the "chosen one" as the Greek text suggests.[12]

The nuances of the story deserve more attention. First, this story reminds us of Moses' ascent of Mount Sinai in Exodus 24. Second, parallels exist between the Mount of Transfiguration and the Mount of Olives.

Mount Sinai is, of course, the place where the Lord dwells or from which he comes (see Deut. 33:2; Judg. 5:5; Ps. 68:8, 17). Apparently, Sinai and Horeb are the same place. Moses ascends Mount Sinai, where the glory of the Lord is settled (see Ex. 24:15–18). On the sacred mountain, the Lord allows himself, or at least his "glory," to be "seen" (Ex. 24:11; 33:18–23) and reveals his "name" (Ex. 34:5–7). It is the place of making a covenant between himself and his people.

The Transfiguration story is of a similar nature—it involves a natural temple. Like Moses, the disciples are called from the cloud. Moses enters the glory of the cloud, which is like a devouring fire (see Ex. 24:16–18). Earlier in chapter 24 of Exodus, Moses has been commanded to select three worshippers (Aaron, Nadab, and Abihu), together with seventy elders, to confirm the covenant (see Ex. 24:1–8). The result is that just these people are explicitly said to have seen "the God of Israel" in his court (Ex. 24:10). The motifs of the master, three disciples, mountain, cloud, and vision here in Exodus 24 recur in the Transfiguration story.

Jesus ascends a mountain, traditionally identified as Mount Tabor. But Mount Hermon fits the context much better for two reasons: first, because it is closer to Caesarea Philippi—the vicinity of the last scene—and second, because it is higher (over nine thousand feet) than Tabor. Mark, one of the sources for Luke in the preparation of his own Gospel, states: "And after six days Jesus taketh with him Peter, and James, and John, and leadeth them up into an *high mountain apart* by themselves: and he was transfigured before them" (Mark 9:2, emphasis added).

Mount Hermon formed Israel's northern boundary. It dominates the landscape of northern Galilee and is snow covered virtually year round. Its name means "set apart" and indicates its sacred character, suitable for a peak from whose base flow the sources of the Jordan River. Note that Mark's statement, "an high mountain *apart*," may relate to the name. Mark adds, "And his raiment became shining, exceeding white as snow" (Mark 9:3). Of course, Mount Hermon had snow on its peaks nearly year round. Whichever mountain it was, the important aspect of Luke's narrative is the fact that Jesus and the three disciples ascended a mountain—a symbol of God's heavenly temple, of which the earthly temple is a representative.

The tabernacle and later the temple were symbolic of the Mountain of God at Sinai. In the Psalms, the location of the permanent Jerusalem temple is Zion. One goes up to Jerusalem (see Ps. 122:4), and at the temple gates one asks who may "ascend into the hill of the Lord" (Ps. 24:3). The staircases that connected the various temple courts and areas are representative of the stairs and gate of heaven that Jacob saw at Bethel. Many passages mention "mount Zion" (see Ps. 48:2, 11; 74:2; 78:68; 125:1; 133:3) and the "holy hill" or "mountain of his holiness" (see Ps. 2:6; 3:4; 15:1; 43:3; 48:1; 99:9). The "hill of the Lord" (Ps. 24:3) may refer not only to the entire hilltop on which the temple stood but also to the temple itself.

In 2 Peter 1, the mountain where Jesus went to pray and the Transfiguration occurred is called "the holy mount" (2 Pet. 1:18). Luke also views the mountain, not named in any of the accounts, as a place of prayer (see also Luke 6:12; 19:29; 22:39). Of course, for Luke, the temple is the place of prayer par excellence (see Luke 1:9–11; Acts 3:1).

Like a later experience at the Mount of Olives, this may have been a nighttime episode, because "Peter and they that were with him were heavy with sleep" (Luke 9:32; cf. Luke 22:39 for the other experience at night). In fact, this connection is strengthened by an earlier experience: "And it came to pass in those days, that he went out into a mountain to pray, and continued all night in prayer to God" (Luke 6:12). For Jesus, and, of course, Luke, the mountain was the site of God's presence, of a nearness to God, as was the Temple Mount in Jerusalem.

Peter, James, and John were present with Jesus on both occasions, as we learn from Mark. Jesus came to pray in both stories, and ultimately a divine messenger appeared following the prayer. As occurs often elsewhere in this Gospel, the picture of Jesus at prayer precedes an event of importance. Like what took place at the temple altar before the veil, when Zacharias offered up the incense at the hour of prayer (see Luke 1:9–11), Jesus' prayer was answered by angelic administration—in this case Elijah and Moses.[13] As was the case with Moses when he was visited by the Lord (see Ex. 34:29), Jesus' appearance was changed.

The description of the clothing is of interest because white was the color of the priestly garments and robes and of the clothing of the heavenly host who worship God in the heavenly temple (see Rev. 2:17; 6:2; 20:11).

Both Moses and Elijah were two Old Testament figures

whose appearance on earth was expected in some way by many of the Jews of the first century. Luke, unlike Mark and Matthew, tells us they also "appeared in glory" with Jesus (Luke 9:31). The Greek text indicates they communicated with him about his *exodos* (exodus), not simply about his death as the King James translators suggest by their choice of the word *decease*. The temple represents the ascent toward the presence of God. In the Jerusalem temple and on Sinai, one literally and figuratively ascended to higher elevation to come into the presence of the Lord. Here Luke may be suggesting not just simply Jesus' death, "which he should accomplish at Jerusalem," but also Jesus' entire journey to the Father, ending in the ascension to the right hand of glory.

Another parallel to the Mount of Olives experience is the fact that an angel appears following Jesus' prayer. Moses and Elijah, however, do not appear to Jesus as the consoling angel does in Luke 22:43 to sustain him in his moment of suffering. Nor should they be understood as merely informing him about the details of his "exodus." Several other details tie these events together.

Moses and Elijah came to the mount to communicate with Jesus. Moses "came to the mountain of God, even to Horeb" (Ex. 3:1); later, he brought all the children of Israel to the same mountain, "for they were departed from Rephidim, and were come to the desert of Sinai, and had pitched in the wilderness; and there Israel camped before the mount" (Ex. 19:2). When Jezebel sought the life of Elijah, he went to Horeb (Sinai): "And he arose, and did eat and drink, and went in the strength of that meat forty days and forty nights unto Horeb the mount of God" (1 Kgs. 19:8).

Moses' work was continued and finished by Joshua. Elijah's work was finished by Elisha (a name related to the name Joshua). The new "exodus" of Jesus (whose Hebrew name was Joshua) would also deliver the people from bondage—but in this case it would bring to fulfillment the work of both Moses and Elijah, just as a Joshua had done earlier in both cases. The substitute sacrifice of Jesus was, in fact, the basis of all vicarious efforts performed in the temple.

Peter's statement, "Let us make three tabernacles; one for thee, and one for Moses, and one for Elias" (Luke 9:33), uses the same Greek word (*skene*) as the Septuagint (Greek Old Testament) for the ancient tabernacle of Moses. This event directly ties the Transfiguration experience with the temple. Peter's discussion with Jesus also demonstrates that he not only saw the two men but also recognized them.

The appearance of the cloud is another Old Testament temple allusion. It is the physical representation of the glory and presence of God, whether at the holy mount, the tabernacle, or the temple in Jerusalem (see Ex. 16:10; 19:9; 24:15–18; 40:34; 2 Sam. 22:12; 1 Kgs. 8:10–11; Ezek. 10:3–4; Ps. 18:11). The cloud points the way on the march out of Egypt (see Ex. 13:21ff). It accompanies the people throughout their journeyings (see Num. 14:14). At each special revelation, it rests on the tabernacle (see Ex. 33:9ff). Above all, at the making of the covenant, the cloud, with lightning on the top of the mountain, both conceals and reveals the presence of the Lord (see, for example, Ex. 19:16; 24:15ff; Deut. 5:19–22).

A renewal is promised for a future day: "And the Lord will create upon every dwelling place of mount Zion, and upon her assemblies, a cloud and smoke by day, and the shining of a flaming fire by night: for upon all the glory shall be a defence" (Isa. 4:5). This is reemphasized in Revelation 21: "And I heard a great voice out of heaven saying, Behold, the tabernacle of God is with men, and he will dwell with them, and they shall be his people, and God himself shall be with them, and be their God" (Rev. 21:3). This alludes to a passage in Psalms: "For in the time of trouble he shall hide me in his pavilion: in the secret of his tabernacle shall he hide me; he shall set me up upon a rock" (Ps. 27:5).

On another level, the appearance of the cloud while they talk about Jesus' exodus relates to John's vision of when Christ will come again: "And I looked, and behold a white cloud, and upon the cloud one sat like unto the Son of man, having on his head a golden crown, and in his hand a sharp sickle. And another angel came out of the temple, crying with a loud voice to him that sat on the cloud, Thrust in thy sickle, and reap: for the time is come for thee to reap; for the harvest of the earth is ripe. And he that sat on the cloud thrust in his sickle on the earth; and the earth was reaped." (Rev. 14:14–16.)

All of these suggest that, for Luke, the Mount of Transfiguration was a sacred experience for Jesus and the disciples and of such importance that it prefigured the Mount of Olives experience and in another way was tied to the Mountain of God—Mount Sinai.

Like Moses before, Jesus and the three Apostles ascend the holy mountain of God. There, atop the sacred mount, they are brought into the presence of the Lord through sacred prayer. The command of the Father to the disciples to "hear" the Son may also refer to Jesus' standing—the full embodiment of the Father's will. Jesus noted at the beginning of his ministry that the temple was "my Father's house" (John 2:16); but now, at the end of his mission, he will enter the temple and call it "my house" (Luke 19:46).

Jesus' Lament over Jerusalem and the Temple (Luke 13:34–35)

Jesus' statement, "How often would I have gathered thy children together, as a hen doth gather her brood under her wings, and ye would not!" (Luke 13:34) may suggest more frequent visits to Jerusalem, and so presumably also to the temple, than the Gospels mention. The concluding statement, "Behold, your house is left unto you desolate: and verily I say unto you, Ye shall not see me, until the time come when ye shall say, Blessed is he that cometh in the name of the Lord" (Luke 13:35) is altogether a troubling prophecy.

Prayer in the Temple (Luke 18:9–15)

Jesus' view of the temple in Jerusalem was very much different from that of many of the Jews of his day. He was not concerned with correct measurements of the temple courts and never complained about the ritual impurity of the priests as did the Qumran community near the Dead Sea.

For Jesus, the Jerusalem temple was primarily meant to be a house of praise. In fact, those who attended the temple offered up praise to God through the singing of the hymns found in the book of Psalms and through prayer. The temple was the place where one should acknowledge the power of the Lord. Through the prostration (some thirteen times during a temple visit) of the people, the Israelites showed their humility. Nevertheless, sincere and humble prayer was the major manifestation of this act of pure sacrifice. In the parable on prayer (see Luke 18:9–15) Jesus has a Pharisee and a tax collector go up to the temple. The tax collector "went down to his house justified," not because he had offered a sacrifice but because of his prayer and sincere repentance.

> Two men went up into the temple to pray; the one a Pharisee, and the other a publican [tax collector].
>
> The Pharisee stood and prayed thus with himself, God, I thank thee, that I am not as other men are, extortioners, unjust, adulterers, or even as this publican.
>
> I fast twice in the week, I give tithes of all that I possess.
>
> And the publican, standing afar off, would not lift up so much as his eyes unto heaven, but smote upon his breast, saying, God be merciful to me a sinner. (Luke 18:10–13.)

The prayer is reminiscent of Psalm 51: "The sacrifices of God are a broken spirit: a broken and a contrite heart, O God, thou wilt not despise" (Ps. 51:17). Jesus then concluded the parable, "I tell you, this man went down to his house justified rather than the other: for every one that exalteth himself shall be abased; and he that humbleth himself shall be exalted" (Luke 18:14). Jesus declared elsewhere that God does not desire sacrifice but mercy (see Matt. 9:13; 12:7), that is, a merciful heart of repentance: "I say unto you, that likewise joy shall be in heaven over one sinner that repenteth, more than over ninety and nine just persons, which need no repentance" (Luke 15:7). The temple should not merely gather and serve Israel, but unite all nations in prayer (see Mark 11:17). It is for this reason that Jesus will come to Jerusalem one last time to cleanse the temple by driving the merchants and money changers out of the Court of the Gentiles.

The Royal Entry into the Temple (Luke 19:28–48)

Jesus' last pilgrimage to the temple occurred just before his death. His long journey was over, and Luke's account joins the other three Gospels in telling the story of Jesus' entry into Jerusalem and the temple. "And when he had thus spoken," Luke writes, "he went before, ascending up to Jerusalem" (Luke 19:28). Luke has already prepared us for this story with various Jerusalem references that have marked the travel account that has preceded it (see Luke 9:51, 53; 10:30; 13:4, 22, 33, 34; 17:11; 18:31; 19:11).

Jesus arrives at the environs of the holy city and prepares to make his way into it, entering it as one hailed as king (and going directly to the temple in it, as we eventually learn).

> And they brought him [the colt] to Jesus: and they cast their garments upon the colt, and they set Jesus thereon.
> And as he went, they spread their clothes in the way.
> And when he was come nigh, even now at the descent of the mount of Olives, the whole multitude of the disciples began to rejoice and praise God with a loud voice for all the mighty works that they had seen;
> Saying, Blessed be the King that cometh in the name of the Lord: peace in heaven, and glory in the highest. (Luke 19:35–38.)

The allusion to Psalm 118 is obvious: "Blessed be he that cometh in the name of the Lord: we have blessed you out of the house of the Lord. God is the Lord, which hath shewed us light: bind the sacrifice with cords, even unto the horns of the altar. Thou art my God, and I will praise thee: thou art my God, I will exalt thee. O give thanks unto the Lord; for he is good: for his mercy endureth for ever." (Ps. 118:26–29.) Luke omits the Grecized Aramaism *hosanna* of Mark 11:9, because of his usual custom of eliminating Semitic words or phrases that his intended readers (non-Jews) would scarcely understand. Psalm 118 forms part of the Hallel Psalms (used on the feasts of Passover or Tabernacles) to greet pilgrims coming to Jerusalem. But, in this instance recorded in Luke, the crowd substitutes the word *King* for the word *he.*

The enthusiastic and shouting crowd continues its journey with Jesus, but as he draws near to Jerusalem, he weeps over it (see Luke 19:41). With dramatic contrast, Luke depicts Jesus weeping over the city, the temple, and the inhabitants, who are totally unaware of their own fate (see Luke 19:41–44).

Upon entering the city, Jesus proceeds directly into the temple—this time as God's Son, sent by his Father to the temple (the Court of the Gentiles, not the sanctuary proper) to sacrifice himself for mankind—and in a prophetic act purges it of those who by their mercantile traffic are profaning its character as a house of prayer. This cleansing of the temple has been of incredible interest to New Testament students and scholars. Luke's story begins:

> And he went into the temple, and began to cast out them that sold therein, and them that bought;
> Saying unto them, It is written, My house is the house of prayer: but ye have made it a den of thieves.
> And he taught daily in the temple. But the chief priests and the scribes and the chief of the people sought to destroy him,
> And could not find what they might do: for all the people were very attentive to hear him. (Luke 19:45–48.)

Great quantities of money, whether from the annual half-shekel tax or from the various tithes and offerings, poured into the temple's treasury, making it one of the wealthiest institutions in the ancient world.

Several studies demonstrate that many Jews at the time of Jesus expected God to someday cleanse the temple and take up residence there, bringing in the time of salvation.[14] It appears that the fulfillment of this expectation is at the core of Luke's narrative. The baby Jesus is recognized in the temple as God's salvation. It is in the temple that the boy Jesus proclaims he must be about his Father's work. As an adult, Jesus enters the temple and drives out the merchants.

While it may be difficult to completely understand Jesus' actions at the time of the cleansing, it is possible to suggest one interpretation. Josephus tells us of the temple's great wealth and the political power of the ruling priests, especially the high priest.[15] He also relates the fact that in the decades preceding the temple's destruction, the ruling priests committed acts of theft, violence, and bribery.[16] Several texts dating from A.D. 70 assert that it was because of Israel's sin that the Herodian temple was destroyed. The lack of equity mentioned in some texts may refer to the unfair and oppressive taxation by the temple priesthood. Lamenting the fate of Jerusalem, one text from the period states: "You, priest, take the keys of the sanctuary, and cast them to the highest heaven, and give them to the Lord and say, 'Guard your house yourself, because, behold, we have been found to be false stewards.' "[17]

It is significant that the priests are characterized as "false stewards," a characterization that coheres with some of Jesus' parables (see Matt. 24:45–51 and parallels; Mark 12:1–9 and parallels; Luke 16:1–8). Other Jewish literature from the period speaks in similar terms. The so-called Targum Johnathan to the Prophets contains criticisms of the first-century priesthood.[18]

Similar criticisms, only fuller and more explicit, appear in the later rabbinic writings following the destruction of the temple. Reflecting on an earlier time when the temple still stood, one text relates the story of Rabbi Simeon ben Gamaliel (ca. A.D. 10–80) when he vigorously protested because the price of a pair of doves had been raised to one gold denar, a price some twenty-five times the proper charge. It should be remembered that the dove was the poor man's sacrifice (see Lev. 5:7; 12:8). Such a charge would obviously have been resented.[19] Apparently, the high priestly families profited in ways that the rabbis considered at best questionable and at other times clearly oppressive.[20]

It is likely that the profiteering and extortion that resulted in the accumulation of so much gold took years and perhaps had something to do with the refurbishing of the temple that continued throughout most of the first century. If these sources give a correct interpretation of events, then it certainly follows that Jesus was unhappy with what he discovered in the temple. Apparently, Jesus also viewed the temple establishment, particularly the ruling priests, as an oppressor of the poor. He regarded the Corban tradition as potentially contrary to the commandment that enjoins support and honor for one's parents, as will be discussed later in this book. Economic oppression, evidently in the name of religion, is clearly one of the problems Jesus confronted in the courageous and incredible act recorded in Luke 19.

Jesus' protest, however, was not directed against the sacrifices, but against the trafficking in sacrificial animals. His complaint seems to have been limited to the activity of buying and selling. Yet, there was nothing inappropriate about buying and selling, which included, of course, the changing of money. Jesus' complaint may have been prompted by overcharging. Whatever motivated him on this occasion, one thing does seem clear: By this significant act of cleansing the temple, Jesus as "the King that cometh in the name of the Lord" takes possession of and transforms his "Father's house" (see Luke 2:49) into "my house" (Luke 19:46). Another irony of this cleansing story is the fact that reestablishing God's dominion at the Temple Mount is completed only through the death of Jesus, which is forced by the temple authorities' insistence that Jesus is not the Son of God (see Luke 23:66–71).

During this particular cleansing, Jesus declared that it had been written that the temple was the "house of prayer" (see Matt. 21:13; Mark 11:17; and Luke 19:46). The allusion is probably to the prophet Isaiah's writing: "Even them will I bring to my holy mountain, and make them joyful in my house of prayer . . . ; for mine house shall be called an house of prayer for all people" (Isa. 56:7).

Jesus wanted the Jerusalem temple to become a place of prayer for all nations; he predicted that if the Jewish nation did not significantly alter its policies, the temple would instead become a place of trampling under the feet of the nations.

Teaching Daily in the Temple (Luke 20–21)

Jesus left the temple for the evening but returned to the temple on "one of those days" to teach again in the temple. Unlike the other Gospel accounts, Luke emphasizes that Jesus was "*daily* in the temple" proclaiming the "good news" (Luke 19:47, emphasis added; 20:1 and 21:37). In fact, according to Luke, Jesus' ministry in Jerusalem is confined to teaching in the temple. Having assumed possession of the temple, Jesus now teaches and preaches in the temple and is eventually confronted by Jerusalem authorities, who want to know where he gets the authority to do so.

Instead of immediately answering them or challenging their authority, he poses a counterquestion: "The baptism of John, was it from heaven, or of men?" (Luke 20:4.) Sensing the implication of the dilemma and realizing the possible reaction of the people who are present if they answer, they refuse to respond directly to the question. Obviously, if they accepted John's commission from God—John having declared Jesus to be greater than himself—such an acceptance would imply that they believed Jesus had been called of God to proclaim the "good news."

This reaffirms what was implied in the episode of the cleansing of the temple and will be reinforced later in the temple, where Jesus will be indirectly presented as the Beloved Son of God (see Luke 20:13), the cornerstone (see Luke 20:17), teacher (see Luke 20:39), and David's son and Lord (see Luke 20:41–44).

It surely was striking for those present to hear him give a parable about "a certain man" who planted a vineyard (see Luke 20:9–16). In telling the parable, Jesus predicts that, following the killing of the son, the owner of the vineyard will come and destroy those murderous tenant farmers. Shortly before this scene, as we have already mentioned, Jesus talked about the destruction of Jerusalem, which suggests that the same event is in mind here. The shared image of a stone, associated with destruction, also supports this connection (see Luke 19:44; 20:18). The chief priests who oppose him understand the parable—it applies to them (see Luke 20:19).

The people, when they hear of the coming destruction, pray that it will not happen. They are affected, nevertheless, by what their leaders do, and the conquest of Jerusalem will mean death and suffering for all its inhabitants.

Jesus continues his discourse in the temple: "And he beheld them, and said, What is this then that is written, The stone which the builders rejected, the same is become the head of the corner? Whosoever shall fall upon that stone shall be broken; but on whomsoever it shall fall, it will grind him to powder." (Luke 20:17–18.) This, of course, is a quotation from Psalm 118:22. This quotation is inserted in a question, "What is this then that is written?" No answer is given either by Jesus or by those present. To be sure, the context suggests some connection between the builders who reject the stone and the tenant farmers who murder the son.

Of course, Jesus has already predicted that he will be "rejected" by the elders, scribes, and chief priests (see Luke 9:22). The same verb is used in both places. Jesus' statement proclaims a reversal of status from dishonor to high honor, which means that the rejection of the stone by the builders will produce the exact opposite of their intention. This ironic reversal is the hidden purpose of God being realized through Jesus' rejection, suffering, and death.

The use of such an architectural symbol was all the more real for those who sat or stood to listen to Jesus in the temple. The stones used to build the Temple Mount walls were gigantic. On the western wall (the "Wailing Wall" in Jewish tradition) the largest stone is about 40 feet long; an even larger one in the south wall weighs over 100 tons. This particular foundation stone can still be seen in Jerusalem today. One can imagine the chief architect requesting a special stone. At the quarry, the workers spend an enormous amount of time and energy preparing a huge foundation stone for the Temple Mount. After all the work, the stone is found to have a hairline fracture—in spite of the lost labor and great cost, the stone is rejected.

Jesus' use of such a metaphor in the temple is all the more interesting in light of his own understanding of his mission as the suffering servant. It also provides a striking connection to the parable of the vineyard—a parable that revealed the destiny of Jerusalem and the Temple Mount itself. Luke now continues his story of Jesus' teaching ministry in the temple.

A Widow in the Temple (Luke 21:1–4)

In this setting, Jesus made his comment about the widow who put her offering into the temple treasury. Of course, the text says nothing about her being elderly, crippled, or childless. Our usual "mental picture" of her is only a figment of our imagination. She could just as easily have been a young woman with several fatherless children.

> And he looked up, and saw the rich men casting their gifts into the treasury.
> And he saw also a certain poor widow casting in thither two mites.
> And he said, Of a truth I say unto you, that this poor widow hath cast in more than they all:
> For all these have of their abundance cast in unto the offerings of God: but she of her penury hath cast in all the living that she had. (Luke 21:1–4.)

The Court of the Women, as described earlier, was a very spacious court surrounded by porticoes. Against the walls inside the porticoes were thirteen boxes, shaped like shofar trumpets, into which temple donations could be placed to help cover costs at the sacred site. This is the likely place called in the KJV "the treasury," where the widow deposited two mites.

Each of the receptacles was identified with a particular title: New Shekel Dues, Old Shekel Dues, Bird-offerings, Young Birds for the Whole-offering, Wood, Frankincense, Gold. Six of them were identified with the title Freewill-offerings.[21]

Why does Luke record this saying in the temple? Often the story is used to demonstrate that it is not the amount but the spirit in which one gives that really matters. While this may be a good modern application, there may be another interpretation. The context of the story must be examined for us to understand

Jesus sat in the temple and spoke of the things of the kingdom. While speaking, he made note of a poor widow who had just made a donation to the temple treasury.

the implications of this story as it relates to the temple in Jerusalem and those whose sacred duty it was to administer therein. The mention of widows in the preceding story (see Luke 20:45–47) acts as a link to this story about a widow.

The story is also related to the "Corban" dilemma in Mark 7:10–13, where Jesus states categorically that human needs take precedence over misguided religious vows when they conflict. The Hebrew word *corban* means "gift" or "offering" and is used in the Old Testament to refer to the freewill offering "unto the Lord," that is, to the holy sanctuary (see Lev. 1–2). In rabbinic literature, *corban* also related to an oath that turns whatever it is applied to into an offering no longer suitable for its normal purpose. In controversy with the scribes and Pharisees, Jesus accuses them of declaring such oaths binding even when they conflicted with a person's legal duties toward parents, thus placing their tradition higher than the commandments of the Mosaic law.

In the immediate context, moreover, Jesus condemns the scribes who devour the estates of widows. Then he comments: This widow has put in everything that she had, her whole livelihood. In a sense, her religious thinking has accomplished exactly the very thing the scribes were accused of doing. In the preceding story, Jesus was displeased with what the scribes were doing to widows' estates; here he is no more pleased with what he sees. He heaps no praise on the woman but rather laments the tragedy of the day. She had been taught and encouraged by the chief priests and scribes to donate as she does.

Jesus condemns the very value system that motivated her action. In short, Jesus' comment contains words of lament, not praise. This story is part of the large condemnation of what the temple authorities have done with the temple: "Ye have made it a den of thieves" (Luke 19:46). Jesus is reversing their actions and teachings by taking control of the temple and teaching the news of his kingdom to the people.

The Fate of the Jerusalem Temple (Luke 21:5–7)

Clearly, Jesus takes possession of the temple. His teachings in the temple are an attempt to establish holiness upon the sacred mount. To accomplish this he must physically and spiritually cleanse the temple. This cleansing is accomplished by casting the merchants out and by teaching the good news to circumvent the false teachings of the Jewish leaders about temple service and worship.

As prophesied repeatedly, if Israel does not respond, tragic consequences await its people. This outcome is foreshadowed in Jesus' lament over the city as he arrives (see Luke 19:41–44). As Jesus continues his teaching in the temple, he utters a long discourse that deals with the fate of Jerusalem and its temple. In the midst of Jesus' public teaching in the temple, he hears some of the people speaking "of the temple, how it was adorned with goodly stones and gifts" (Luke 21:5). Obviously, his comments that follow are not just a warning but are a prophetic pronouncement—an ominous prediction: "The days will come, in the which there shall not be left one stone upon another, that shall not be thrown down" (Luke 21:6). His words are unmistakably clear. They saw fulfillment in the burning and destruction of the temple in late August/early September A.D. 70, just a mere seven years after the temple was finally completed in A.D. 63.

Josephus, who witnessed the destruction of the temple, contradicts himself in another place as to who was responsible for the fire, but on one occasion wrote: "The flames, however, owed their origin and cause to God's own people."[22] The end of the temple is a sad story, with as many as six thousand people perishing in the flames of the temple porticoes when a "false prophet" told them that God had commanded them to go to the temple to receive the signs of their salvation. Jerusalem's walls were breached, the temple defiled, and the people driven into exile while thousands of their dead remained behind without proper burial. These unimaginable events, however, were in the future, as Jesus continues to proclaim the kingdom in the temple.

Jesus Before the Sanhedrin (Luke 22:66–71)

Luke's record depicts the last few hours of Jesus life in graphic specificity. Jesus' passion—his suffering, betrayal, trial, scourging, and execution—are all portrayed with shocking detail. These horrible events stand in stark contrast to the first Easter morning. Yet, these incidents are in reality the culmination of Jesus' mission to the least, last, and lost.

All the Gospel writers agree that Jesus was arrested and questioned before the rulers of the Jews—the supreme Jewish legislative, religious, and judicial body, the Sanhedrin. While we cannot be certain about the location of this trial, it may be reasonable to suppose that it occurred at the temple. The largest structure on the Temple Mount was a grand hall extending across the southern end of the platform, from east to west, sometimes identified as the Royal Stoa or Herod's Basilica. Archaeological and literary evidence suggests that it was built in the style of a basilica; the stoa was divided into a central nave and side aisles by four rows of forty columns each. Josephus said that "the thickness of each column was such that it would take three men with outstretched arms touching one another to envelop it."[23]

The Royal Stoa, or Herod's Basilica, was the largest structure on the Temple Mount. The covered area protected individuals from the sun's heat in the summer and the winter's chilly winds. This grand hall extended across the southern end of Herod's great platform and was, as depicted here, the probable place where the Sanhedrin convened from A.D. 30 to A.D. 70, the year the temple was destroyed. Here is seen the eastern end of the structure. An apse, built adjacent to the eastern wall of the Hall of Columns, was the area where two rows of semi-circular benches were placed to accommodate the seventy-one elders that sat in judgment. Each of the 162 Corinthian monolithic pillars was 50 feet high.

One row consisted of pilasters built into the southern wall. A second row, forty monoliths topped by Corinthian capitals, created an aisle adjacent to the nave. A third row divided the nave from an aisle on the other side. The fourth, northernmost row formed an open colonnade, not a wall as on the southern side. Through this open row of columns one could proceed into the temple court. Josephus stated:

> The middle aisle was one and a half times as wide and twice as high, and thus it greatly towered over those on either side. The ceilings (of the porticoes) were ornamented with deeply cut wood-carvings representing all sorts of different figures. The ceiling of the middle aisle was raised to a greater height, and the front wall was cut at either end into architraves with columns built into it, and all of it was polished, so that these structures seemed incredible to those who had not seen them, and were beheld with amazement by those who set eyes on them.[24]

Josephus emphasized the beauty of this place when he wrote that it was "more noteworthy than any under the sun."[25] The Sanhedrin, according to reliable sources, met at the eastern end of the nave.

Luke reported: "And as soon as it was day, the elders of the people and the chief priests and the scribes came together, and led him into their council" (Luke 22:66). A large stairway provided an impressive entrance to the stoa. It may have been through this entrance that Jesus entered the temple one last time. Once inside, the council questioned him further:

> Art thou the Christ? tell us. And he said unto them, If I tell you, ye will not believe:
> And if I also ask you, ye will not answer me, nor let me go.
> Hereafter shall the Son of man sit on the right hand of the power of God.
> Then said they all, Art thou then the Son of God? And he said unto them, Ye say that I am.
> And they said, What need we any further witness? for we ourselves have heard of his own mouth.
> And the whole multitude of them arose, and led him unto Pilate. (Luke 22:67 to 23:1.)

From the Sanhedrin meeting, Jesus was taken to Pilate to be questioned, judged, and condemned at the Antonia Fortress overlooking the Temple Mount. In the next scene Jesus is mocked, beaten, stripped of all clothing in an ultimate act of humiliation. Finally, he is executed by the horribly cruel method of Roman crucifixion—a most extreme form of punishment reserved for slaves, dangerous and violent criminals, and political enemies of Rome. With faithful disciples watching, Jesus dies an agonizing death on the cross, yet one last reference to the temple during Jesus' mortal life is recorded by Luke.

The Temple Veil Rent (Luke 23:44–49)

The Gospels agree that the "veil of the temple was rent in twain from the top to the bottom" just before or just after Jesus' death (see Matt. 27:51; Mark 15:38; and Luke 23:45). Three differing interpretations of the tearing of the temple curtains have been proposed: (1) it was a sign of the destruction of the temple; (2) it was a sign of the rejection of the temple and temple worship; and (3) it was a sign that through Jesus' death the way to God was now open to all true believers beyond the Mosaic ordinances. However, a careful reading of the text suggests another interpretation that fits with Luke's general theme.

Both Matthew and Mark place the tearing of the curtain *after* the death of Christ, but Luke indicates that it immediately *preceded* Jesus' death:

> And it was about the sixth hour, and there was a darkness over all the earth until the ninth hour.
>
> And the sun was darkened, and the veil of the temple was rent in the midst.
>
> And when Jesus had cried with a loud voice, he said, Father, into thy hands I commend my spirit: and having said thus, he gave up the ghost.
>
> Now when the centurion saw what was done, he glorified God, saying, Certainly this was a righteous man.
>
> And all the people that came together to that sight, beholding the things which were done, smote their breasts, and returned.
>
> And all his acquaintance, and the women that followed him from Galilee, stood afar off, beholding these things. (Luke 23: 44–49.)

If we link the tearing of the temple curtain with Jesus' final cry from the cross rather than allow it to stand alone or to be linked with the eclipse of the sun, then we may understand why Luke fashions the text this way. In his account, after the tearing of the curtain Jesus addresses God: "Father, into thy hands I commend my spirit" (Luke 23:46). We might conclude that this image presents Jesus as communing at the last moment before his death with the Father, who is present in the temple.

Two items in Luke's writings seem to indicate this possible interpretation. They are the parallelism of the deaths of Jesus and Stephen and the Lucan understanding of the ninth hour.

Luke parallels Jesus' death and Stephen's death with several elements. Both Jesus and Stephen ask for forgiveness for their murderers. Both commit their spirits before they die. Both utter an articulate cry right before dying. Both are buried by good, righteous, and devout men. The final and most important parallel has to do with Stephen's seeing the heavens open and his vision of God. A striking parallelism between Luke 23 and Acts 7 is described as we read of an opening into the place of God's presence (the heavens) in Acts and the opening of the place of God's presence (the temple) in the book of Luke.

Luke's understanding of the ninth hour also supports the preceding interpretation of Luke 23:45–46. Luke, as Acts 3:1 shows, had a very definite understanding of the ninth hour as "the hour of prayer" in the temple. Later in the book of Acts, Luke records: "There was a certain man in Caesarea called Cornelius, a centurion of the band called the Italian band, a devout man, and one that feared God with all his house, which gave much alms to the people, and prayed to God alway. He saw in a vision evidently about the *ninth hour* of the day an angel of God coming in to him." (Acts 10:1–3, emphasis added.) Again, Luke connects the ninth hour with prayer.

For Luke, then, Jesus' last words represent a prayer to the God of the temple. Notice that two other elements often associated with temple prayer are present in Luke's account—for example, the centurion's statement that he praised God (see Luke 23:47). This is appropriate for the prayerful context that Luke has established for Jesus' final moments before his death.

Further, Luke may have presented the crowd's reaction to Jesus' death in a manner befitting the specific context of temple prayer—namely, that they "smote their breasts" (Luke 23:48). The only two places in which Luke writes about people performing this action are in this passage and in Luke 18:13. As described earlier, Luke 18:10–14 is a parable about a Pharisee and a tax collector who went up to the temple to pray. It is said that the publican, "standing afar off, would not lift up so much as his eyes unto heaven, but smote upon his breast, saying, God be merciful to me a sinner" (Luke 18:13).

On the Day of Atonement, the high priest entered the Holy of Holies through the temple veil, wearing only the simple white robes of a priest and carrying a large golden spoon filled with coals and incense to be offered before the Lord. The elaborate curtain protected the entrance to the Holy of Holies. Exodus 26 records the commandment: "And the vail shall divide unto you between the holy place and the most holy" (v. 33) and describes it as being made of "blue, and purple, and scarlet, and fine twined linen of cunning work" (v. 31). In Herod's temple there appears to have been two veils separated by a space. According to Luke, this curtain was torn before Jesus' death on the cross.

This interpretation presupposes both Luke's acceptance of the idea of God's presence in the temple and presents the temple as the center of Jesus' activity—both of which are attested in Luke's writings, as already indicated.

The Commission of Disciples and the Temple (Luke 24:50–53)

Luke concludes his Gospel story with a carefully described incident in which Jesus gives his disciples a high priestly blessing while he ascends: "And he led them out as far as to Bethany, and he lifted up his hands, and blessed them" (Luke 24:50).

Having finally recognized and worshipped him, the disciples return to Jerusalem, where they spend the ensuing days in the temple praising God: "And they worshipped him, and returned to Jerusalem with great joy: and were continually in the temple, praising and blessing God. Amen." (Luke 24:52–53.) Thus, the

Gospel of Luke ends where it began—at the temple of Jerusalem (see Luke 1:5).

For Luke, this is also the fulfillment of the Mount of Transfiguration discussion (see Luke 9:31; cf. 9:51). It is also the event to which Jesus himself referred in his answer to the Sanhedrin: "Hereafter shall the Son of man sit on the right hand of the power of God" (Luke 22:69). But Luke has something more in mind than simply demonstrating the fulfillment of prophetic insight.

The scene is full of temple imagery. The raising of one's hands while pronouncing a blessing indicates a possible high priestly blessing. This reminds us of Aaron in the book of Leviticus:

> And Aaron lifted up his hand toward the people, and blessed them, and came down from offering of the sin offering, and the burnt offering, and peace offerings.
>
> And Moses and Aaron went into the tabernacle of the congregation, and came out, and blessed the people: and the glory of the Lord appeared unto all the people. (Lev. 9:22–23.)

The blessing refers to one mentioned in Numbers 6, as already noted earlier: "Speak unto Aaron and unto his sons, saying, On this wise ye shall bless the children of Israel, saying unto them, The Lord bless thee, and keep thee: the Lord make his face shine upon thee, and be gracious unto thee: the Lord lift up his countenance upon thee, and give thee peace. And they shall put my name upon the children of Israel; and I will bless them." (Num. 6:23–27.) Another ironic point in Luke's narrative appears here—Jesus does for the disciples what Zacharias could not do when he left the temple after his vision (see Luke 1:22). It seems reasonable to assume that Christ was now the true High Priest who enters the heavenly Holy of Holies.

It is striking that the temple in Luke is not replaced by the Church, as the disciples still return to the earthly counterpart of the heavenly temple to worship Jesus and God. The temple itself appears as something positive and is bound with the Church. This continues in the second part of Luke's work—the Acts of the Apostles.

FIVE

The Early Church
and the Temple in Acts

*And they, continuing daily with one accord in the
temple, and breaking bread from house to house, did eat
their meat with gladness and singleness of heart,*

*Praising God, and having favour with all the people.
And the Lord added to the church daily such as should be
saved.*

—*Acts 2:46–47*

Luke begins the second part of his writing effort with a brief
historical summary of his previous work, the Gospel of Luke.
"The former treatise have I made, O Theophilus, of all that Jesus
began both to do and teach, until the day in which he was taken
up, after that he through the Holy Ghost had given commandments unto the apostles whom he had chosen" (Acts 1:1–2).
Luke adds a fascinating comment: "To whom also he shewed

◄ On the day of Pentecost, after Jesus' resurrection, his disciples were suddenly
filled with the Holy Spirit, and their proclamations in the temple were heard not
as a Galilean dialect of Aramaic (their native language) but as all the languages
spoken by the pilgrims visiting the city for this special celebration (see Acts 2).
The disciples' presence in the temple following Jesus' departure demonstrates
the temple's continued importance among the early Christian Saints.

himself alive after his passion by many infallible proofs, being
seen of them forty days, and speaking of the things pertaining to
the kingdom of God" (Acts 1:3). Known as the forty-day ministry, this episode has sparked extraordinary interest among
Latter-day Saints.[1]

Because the scriptural record does not inform us of the exact
nature of Jesus' instruction during this forty-day period, we
cannot with certitude know what happened. We can make certain assumptions about the purpose of this forty-day period,
however. In all likelihood, sacred instruction regarding the fulness of the gospel was discussed. The writings of Paul, Peter,
James, Jude, and John suggest they had access to doctrinal
knowledge beyond what Jesus taught during his mortal ministry.
Such hints suggest that Jesus taught the disciples about salvation
for the dead and the sacred ordinances of temple worship.

As one can imagine, because the record is silent, numerous
stories and legends circulated within the Christian community
purporting to reveal the "secret teachings" of Jesus during the
forty-day ministry. Some striking parallels are evident between
our current understanding of the gospel and some of the material
found in these writings. Nevertheless, much of the material is far
afield from what we would be comfortable with as being an accu-
rate description of this episode. Much care and caution are
needed in analyzing this literature. Because our present task is to
discuss temple worship and symbolism *in the New Testament,* we
have avoided most pseudepigraphical sources of this kind, uti-
lizing for the most part contemporary historical writings and
documents to add context to our discussion.

The Upper Room—a Temple (Acts 1)

The "upper room" (Greek *hyperoon*), where the early Saints
gathered after the ascension of the Lord and where the Pentecost
event occurred, already had an established significance for the
disciples.[2] Luke recorded: "And when they were come in, they
went up into an upper room. . . . These all continued with one
accord in prayer and supplication." (Acts 1:13–14.)

Luke seems to represent this center as the prototype for the early Church's meeting places of worship. The Greek word *hyperoon* in the New Testament appears only in Acts and always in contexts that denote a place of worship. According to Acts, Tabitha, a member of the community of widows in Joppa, was laid in such an upper room after she died (see Acts 9:37, 39). Acts 20 describes an early meeting for Sunday worship in an upper room at Troas in Asia Minor (see Acts 20:7–8). This report, given in the first person, specifically observes that "there were many lights" in the room (Acts 20:8). Moreover, inside the "house of Peter" in Capernaum, which was transformed into an early house church by the second half of the first century, numerous fragments of oil lamps have been found.[3]

Upper rooms had already acquired some religious significance in the Old Testament (see, for example, 2 Kgs. 4:10–11 and Dan. 6:10, which all use Greek *hyperoon* in the Septuagint). There may be some connection between the upper room mentioned in Acts 1 and the one discussed later in Acts 12. The owner is Mary, the mother of John called Mark (see Acts 12:12). From the first-person report in Acts 21:15–18 we learn that Luke visited the Holy City at least once (A.D. 57). The use of the article before "upper room" in Acts 1:13 implies that Luke himself knew the location of this room.

According to this understanding of Luke, the "upper room" of Acts 1:13 and the location of the Last Supper are identical. If the identification is correct, then the traditional meeting place for the Saints following the Resurrection would also be the traditional location of the Last Supper. Traditionally, this upper room was located on a southwest hill—Mount Zion.[4]

That the "upper room" had special significance to the early Church beyond a simple meetinghouse may be assumed. Apparently the Prophet Joseph Smith believed that the disciples had a place dedicated to the performance of ordinances at the time of Pentecost. He stated, "At one time God obtained a house where Peter was[hed] and ano[inte]d &c on the day of pentecost."[5]

The Pentecost (Acts 2)

The story continues on the Day of Pentecost (fifty days following Passover). The Holy Spirit descends on the leaders of the Church, and they immediately preach the good news about Jesus of Nazareth to a stunned audience. Luke's narrative is filled with allusions to the Hebrew Bible, especially the experience at Mount Sinai. Although Luke does not tell us where the followers of the risen Christ were assembled when the Spirit came, the subsequent scene seems to be in the temple court.

As with the Sinai experience, the Spirit's coming on the Day of Pentecost was attended by "a sound from heaven as of a rushing mighty wind," filling the house where they were gathered, and was marked by the appearance of "tongues like as of fire." Then the followers "were all filled with the Holy Ghost, and began to speak with other tongues." (Acts 2:2–4.) Pentecost was not only an agricultural festival but also a celebration of the giving of the Torah on Sinai fifty days following the exodus from Egyptian bondage.

At Sinai, the symbolic representation of God's heavenly temple, the Israelites met and received the law from him on tables made of stone. To prepare the people to receive his commandments and covenant, God commanded Moses to go to the people and "sanctify them to day and to morrow, and let them wash their clothes, and be ready against the third day: for the third day the Lord will come down in the sight of all the people upon mount Sinai" (Ex. 19:10–11). Here they became the people of God—"a kingdom of priests, and an holy nation" (Ex. 19:6). In the midst of lightnings, thunders, and voices, the children of Israel covenanted to be the Lord's people (see Ex. 19:18–20).

Luke's allusion to the creation of the nation of Israel may be symbolic of what God has done through the new passover (the atonement of Christ) and the reception of the new law written on the fleshy tables of the disciples' hearts and the creation of a new Israel (the Church) on this most joyous celebration.

As a result of their preaching in the temple court and the moving of the Holy Spirit among the Jews who had come to

Jerusalem to celebrate this important festival, about three thousand were baptized (see Acts 2:41). These new believers in Christ Jesus

> continued stedfastly in the apostles' doctrine and fellowship, and in breaking of bread, and in prayers.
>
> And fear came upon every soul: and many wonders and signs were done by the apostles.
>
> And all that believed were together, and had all things common;
>
> And sold their possessions and goods, and parted them to all men, as every man had need.
>
> *And they, continuing daily with one accord in the temple,* and breaking bread from house to house, did eat their meat with gladness and singleness of heart,
>
> Praising God, and having favour with all the people. And the Lord added to the church daily such as should be saved. (Acts 2:42–47, emphasis added.)

For the followers of Jesus of Nazareth, the temple still continued to represent a house of God. Unlike the Qumran Essenes (those who collected the Dead Sea Scrolls library), who abandoned Jerusalem and the temple in Jerusalem, the early Christian Saints remained in Jerusalem to be near the temple and to participate in its services and benefits.[6] Indeed, the early Saints in Jerusalem felt themselves to be so perfectly expressing the true Jewish faith that they kept up their daily attendance at the temple, especially at the hour of prayer.

Peter, John, and Others at the Temple (Acts 3–5)

Luke's record continues as Peter and John go to the "temple at the hour of prayer, being the ninth hour" (Acts 3:1). Here Peter heals the man born lame who sat at the Beautiful Gate asking alms of those who entered the temple to pray and worship.

> Now Peter and John went up together into the temple at the hour of prayer, being the ninth hour.

And a certain man lame from his mother's womb was carried, whom they laid daily at the gate of the temple which is called Beautiful, to ask alms of them that entered into the temple;

Who seeing Peter and John about to go into the temple asked an alms.

And Peter, fastening his eyes upon him with John, said, Look on us.

And he gave heed unto them, expecting to receive something of them.

Then Peter said, Silver and gold have I none; but such as I have give I thee: In the name of Jesus Christ of Nazareth rise up and walk.

And he took him by the right hand, and lifted him up: and immediately his feet and ankle bones received strength.

And he leaping up stood, and walked, and entered with them into the temple, walking, and leaping, and praising God.

And all the people saw him walking and praising God:

And they knew that it was he which sat for alms at the Beautiful gate of the temple: and they were filled with wonder and amazement at that which had happened unto him. (Acts 3:1–10.)

The scene is full of praise, song, and worship. Music, including both Levitical choirs and musicians, filled the temple courts at the time of prayer. Praise and prayer mingled with trumpets, lutes, lyres, harps, and a cymbal as the choir sang at the Levite choir stand.

Peter then took occasion to preach in the temple (see Acts 3:11–26). Soon thereafter, the priests, the captain of the temple, and the Sadducees "laid hands on them" (Acts 4:3). The Jewish leaders commanded them not to preach in Jesus' name anymore. Luke records that they continued preaching, teaching, and baptizing anyway (see Acts 5:12–16), but again he makes specific reference to the temple: "And by the hands of the apostles were many signs and wonders wrought among the people; (and they were all with one accord *in Solomon's porch*)" (Acts 5:12, emphasis added). Again, the high priest and those that were with him laid their hands on the Apostles and put them into prison; but an "angel of the Lord by night opened the prison doors, and brought them forth" (Acts 5:17–19).

The angel instructed the Apostles to *"go, stand and speak in the temple* to the people all the words of this life" (Acts 5:20, emphasis added). The disciples did exactly what had been commanded by the messenger, and "early in the morning" they entered the temple and began to preach the gospel to those who would listen (Acts 5:21). "Now when the high priest and the captain of the temple and the chief priests heard these things [about the empty prison], they doubted of them whereunto this would grow. Then came one and told them, saying, *Behold, the men whom ye put in prison are standing in the temple,* and teaching the people." (Acts 5:24–25, emphasis added.)

Again, the Apostles were arrested and brought to the high priest "without violence: for they feared the people, lest they should have been stoned" (Acts 5:26). This time, in private counsel, the Apostles were rebuked and beaten by the Jewish leaders and departed "from the presence of the council, rejoicing that they were counted worthy to suffer shame for his name" (Acts 5:41). The episode concluded with Luke's reflection: "*And daily in the temple,* and in every house, they ceased not to teach and preach Jesus Christ" (Acts 5:42, emphasis added).

As in Jesus' own ministry, the temple in Jerusalem had become a center of missionary activity for the new Church.

Stephen and the Temple (Acts 6–7)

Chronologically, Stephen's discourse before the Sanhedrin is the next reference to the temple in the New Testament. In it, Stephen recounts the temple history in Israel, beginning with the tabernacle. Those who argue for a rejection of the temple and temple worship rely primarily on three key references in the book of Acts.[7] Two of these references are found here (see Acts 6:13–14 and Acts 7:48–50).

First, Luke stresses that the charges regarding Stephen's teachings about the temple (Stephen was accused of teaching that Jesus would destroy it) are presented by *false* witnesses (see Acts 6:13). We may assume that Luke intentionally placed this insight here so that Stephen's subsequent speech will be read so as not to confirm such false rumors that Jesus would destroy the temple, which obviously were widespread in Jerusalem. In fact, his speech may be an effort to expose the erroneous attitude behind the charges. For Luke, Stephen's enemies view "the law" as equivalent to "the customs which Moses delivered us" (Acts 6:13–14) without reference to its divine origin (cf. 6:11). Likewise, they identify God with "this holy place" (Acts 6:11, 13) and with "this place" in particular (Acts 6:14). In both cases, God's authorship progressively disappears from consideration. This is the mentality that Stephen seems to be exposing and criticizing.

Second, Luke presents these charges as distortions—not of Jesus' historical teaching but of Stephen's teachings about him. In his Gospel, Luke already has taken great pains to avoid connecting such teaching against the temple with Jesus (such as the clarifying statement found in Mark or Matthew that could be read in another way). Sensitive to the rumors, Luke carefully divorces such rumors of Jesus' opposition to the temple from Jesus' own ministry in the book of Acts also.

Third, clearly the rumor in Acts presents Jesus only as the future destroyer of the temple. Stephen and Jesus are not accused of wishing to supplant the temple but rather the customs handed down by Moses (see Acts 6:14).

Finally, Acts 6:14 lacks any reference to the temple as the work of human hands. To be sure, this motif does appear in Acts 7:48–50, at the close of Stephen's discourse. But there it appears as part of his wider critique of things that tend to unduly restrict divine revelation and the worship of God to Jerusalem.

Stephen's speech (see Acts 7:2–53) is a most interesting historical overview of the people of Israel. At the very first, Stephen widens the meaning of Exodus 3:1, 12 to make the entire promised land, not just Mount Horeb, the "place" the Lord designates for Israel to worship him once he has effected their future deliverance from Egyptian bondage. Similarly, Stephen later broadens the notion of an acceptable "place" of revelation from Mount Sinai (see Acts 7:30, 38) to include the tabernacle, which traveled with the children of Israel into Canaan (see Acts 7:44–45).

Stephen's teachings represent no radical departure from the

Old Testament. Solomon's own prayer at the dedication of his temple recognizes God's transcendence:

> But will God indeed dwell on the earth? behold, the heaven and heaven of heavens cannot contain thee; how much less this house that I have builded?
>
> Yet have thou respect unto the prayer of thy servant, and to his supplication, O Lord my God, to hearken unto the cry and to the prayer, which thy servant prayeth before thee to day:
>
> That thine eyes may be open toward this house night and day, even toward the place of which thou hast said, My name shall be there: that thou mayest hearken unto the prayer which thy servant shall make toward this place.
>
> And hearken thou to the supplication of thy servant, and of thy people Israel, when they shall pray toward this place: and hear thou in heaven thy dwelling place: and when thou hearest, forgive. (1 Kgs. 8:27–30.)

Without rejecting temple worship as a sign of true devotion, Stephen nevertheless emphasizes that without the right attitude about worship, a building built by man is meaningless. "Howbeit the most High dwelleth not in temples made with hands; as saith the prophet, Heaven is my throne, and earth is my footstool: what house will ye build me? saith the Lord: or what is the place of my rest? Hath not my hand made all these things?" (Acts 7:48–50.)

Luke understands Stephen's criticism to apply to the temple only in the measure that this institution is used to ground an erroneous understanding of what Moses, David, and Solomon had done. The focus of the debate is found in verses 46–47. Referring to David, Stephen says he "found favour before God, and desired to find a tabernacle for the God of Jacob. But Solomon built him an house." (Acts 7:46–47.) One biblical scholar has suggested an alternative translation that helps place the proper emphasis in the discourse: "Instead of translating 7:47 in an adversarial sense [But Solomon built him an house], this verse might be better read parenthetically 'though [it was] Solomon [who] built him [= God] a house [= Temple].' "[8]

Viewed in this way, verse 47 qualifies and completes the two previous verses, 45 and 46, in the spirit of Solomon's own prayer found in 1 Kings 8, as quoted above. In this case, Solomon can be seen as continuing the service of Moses and David. Stephen already has presented the prophets (including Moses among them) as those who revealed the coming of the "Just One" (see Acts 7:37; cf. 7:52). Likewise, he upholds the law as "living words" given to Israel in the desert through angelic instruction (see Acts 7:38; cf. 7:53) and depicts the origin of the tabernacle in similar terms (see Acts 7:44). Thus, the law appears as divine revelation that includes the original command from God to build the tabernacle and so gives legitimate roots to the establishment of the temple in Jerusalem by Solomon, provided the temple is worthy of his continued presence.

Persecution intensified with the martyrdom of Stephen and James, and the Church was scattered. Yet disciples remained in

The Acropolis of Athens was built during the golden age of Greece. It consisted of a complex of different temples to the different deities worshipped by the ancient Greeks. The largest and most splendid of the temples was the Parthenon (see top of photograph of Acropolis model); it was the temple to Athena, the patron goddess of Athens. This temple contained an image of the goddess which represented to the people her continuing protection of them.

Jerusalem for many years. Several important conferences occurred there that had significant impact on Church growth and organization.

Paul Before Pagan Temples (Acts 17)

The speech by Paul in Athens is ostensibly for a Gentile audience, set in the shadows of pagan temples. The Athenian Acropolis, an architectural showpiece unparalleled in Greece outside the sanctuaries of Delphi or Olympia, had been devoted to the service of the pagan gods, especially the city goddess Athena, for several centuries before Paul arrived to proclaim the "good news" about Jesus Christ.

By the eighth century B.C., the Greeks had begun to build temples to their gods. The typical Archaic *temenos* was an enclosed

The temple of Nike found on the Acropolis of Athens housed a statue of the goddess of victory. This temple (which can also be seen in the model), along with the other structures of the Acropolis, provides background to the story, recorded by Luke, of Paul's address about "temples made with hands" (Acts 17:24).

area containing a rectangular building facing a high, raised, rectangular altar. The Greek temple, *naos,* was considered the dwelling place of the divinity; and the main chamber of the temple was used to display the cult statue of the god. In Athens, the Parthenon was dedicated in 438 B.C. with a forty-foot-high cult statue of gold and ivory of the patron goddess. The Propylaea, the monumental entrance to the Acropolis; the Erechtheum; and the temple of Athea Nike (Victory) were all added to the site.

The city's religious attitudes, expressed in temples, shrines, and altars, were proverbial in both Greek and Roman thought. Paul's reference to the Athenians' piety (see Acts 17:22) and an altar to an "unknown god" (Acts 17:23) are seen in this light. Of course, the name of Athens was synonymous with philosophical pursuit of truth. As a university town in Paul's time, Athens continued to attract philosophical and philhellenic intellectuals. Even Paul demonstrates his knowledge of Greek literature when he quotes the Stoic poet Aratus (Acts 17:28). This is the historical background necessary to understand Paul's statement about "temples made with hands" in Acts 17:24–25, the third and final reference used by those who argue for Luke's supposed rejection of the temple.

The crux of Paul's discourse is its stress on God's independence from human efforts. Paul asserts that God does not receive human service as though he needed it: "God that made the world and all things therein, seeing that he is Lord of heaven and earth, dwelleth not in temples made with hands; neither is worshipped with men's hands, as though he needed any thing, seeing he giveth to all life, and breath, and all things" (Acts 17:24–25).

This certainly does not mean that any human service for God is irrelevant, but that while he demands such service, he does not rely on it. This reflects Luke's own understanding of Stephen's intent, with the exception that Stephen's audience (the Jews) should have known better than to view the temple as they did.

For Luke, the temple is an appropriate place for Israel to

pray and for the proclamation of the good news, as shown by the numerous stories preserved by him in both the Gospel of Luke and the book of Acts. Ultimately, the attitude with which worshippers use the temple makes all the difference. Though the temple at Jerusalem may serve God's purpose, it is not indispensable to him.

It is of interest to note that Luke, as well as the other New Testament writers, is very precise about distinguishing the altar of the true and living God from the altars of the pagan gods. The Greek *thysiasterion* always refers to the altars in the temple at Jerusalem, including the altar of burnt offering (see Matt. 5:23f; 23.10ff, 35, Luke 11.51, 1 Cor. 9.13, 10.18, Heb. 7.13, Rev. 11:1), the altar of incense (see Luke 1:11), and, more important, the altar that John saw in the heavenly temple (see Rev. 6:9; 8:3, 5; 9:13; 14:18; 16:7). For altars of alien gods, in the New Testament the Greek *bomos* is always used.[9] The precise vocabulary in the Greek New Testament argues that pagan and divinely sanctioned places of worship were clearly distinguished from each other.

Another point to remember in relationship to Paul's statement here is that on the Acropolis near where Paul delivered this discourse stood a temple dedicated to the Greek goddess of victory, Nike. This small amphiprostyle Ionic temple rises gracefully on the edge of the rock, where the ancient Athenians worshipped the goddess of victory, expressing their hopes for triumph over their enemies. In this marble temple dedicated to Athena Nike stood a wooden image of her. The original wings on the statue had been removed by the people to prevent her departure from the temple and from Athens.[10] One scholar has compiled a convincing list of similar attempts during the classical period to prevent the gods from leaving their temples, in some instances by chaining them to their shrines.[11]

Along with these specific examples of people's attempts to keep a god within a temple by such means, there is also the fact that most pagan temples had at least one cult statue representing a god within the temple itself. For example, at Athens the citizens had placed a gold and ivory forty-foot-tall statue of Athena

The gold and ivory statue of Athena Parthenos found in the most holy place within the Parthenon not only was an artistic wonder, but represented the presence of the goddess in the temple. In this replica she wears her *aegis,* a small goatskin cloak fringed with snakes, and a high-crested helmet. On her right hand is a small winged figure of Nike. To the right of the pedestal is a figure of a man to indicate the enormity of the statue, which was some forty feet tall.

within the Parthenon. These statues represented the god's presence in the house. It may also be in this context that Paul tries to prove the futility of the people's belief that they could entrap God, either by placing a statue or by chaining that statue, in a house "made with hands."

Paul, Jerusalem, and the Temple (Acts 21)

The last mention of the temple at Jerusalem in the book of Acts occurs during Paul's final journey to Jerusalem, sometime around May, A.D. 57. He arrives in Jerusalem for the celebration of Pentecost and to deliver financial contributions to the suffering Saints in Jerusalem. Church leaders, obviously concerned about Jewish attitudes towards the Apostle to the Gentiles, ask Paul to demonstrate his obedience to customs by participating in the purification rituals required of those who have returned from Gentile countries. They also ask him to help defray the sacrificial expenses of four fellow members who are about to discharge a vow: "Do therefore this that we say to thee: We have four men which have a vow on them; them take, and purify thyself with them, and be at charges with them, that they may shave their heads: and all may know that those things, whereof they were informed concerning thee, are nothing; but that thou thyself also walkest orderly, and keepest the law" (Acts 21:23–24).

The four men were presumably members of the Jerusalem Church who had taken a temporary Nazarite vow (see Num. 6:2–21). Helping someone to defray the expenses of discharging a vow at the temple was regarded in first-century Judaism as an act of charity, which Paul gladly accepts. Here again Luke preserves for us an important historical passage. The New Testament is clear in showing that Paul did not participate nor condone activity in pagan ritual or temple attendance. Yet Paul appears in the Jerusalem temple on several occasions, participating in religious celebrations and worship, evidently distinguishing his belief about the appropriateness of worship in God's house from his disapproval of those institutions dedicated to false gods.

Luke continues his report: "Then Paul took the men, and the next day purifying himself with them entered into the temple, to signify the accomplishment of the days of purification" (Acts 21:26). During one of the days of purification, certain Jews from Asia recognize Paul and accuse him of bringing Gentiles into the temple—a breach of the Mosaic law.

As already stated, stone fragments of inscriptions from the Temple Mount have been recovered that warned Gentiles not to enter the inner courts of the temple on pain of death. These were attached to the balustrade which separated the Court of the Gentiles from the area surrounding the sanctuary. The temple authorities were entitled to put even Roman citizens to death for this offense. Nothing was calculated to infuriate Jews of Jewish Palestine and of the dispersion alike more than a suspected disparagement of the Jerusalem temple.

> The Jews which were of Asia, when they saw him [Paul] in the
> temple, stirred up all the people, and laid hands on him,

Crying out, Men of Israel, help: This is the man, that teacheth all men every where against the people, and the law, and this place: *and further brought Greeks also into the temple,* and hath polluted this holy place.

(For they had seen before with him in the city Trophimus an Ephesian, whom they supposed that Paul had brought into the temple.)

And all the city was moved, and the people ran together: and they took Paul, and drew him out of the temple: and forthwith the doors were shut.

And as they went about to kill him, tidings came unto the chief captain of the band [Roman soldiers], that all Jerusalem was in an uproar. (Acts 21:27–31, emphasis added.)

While it is impossible to know which gates are intended by Luke in the above passage, both sets of doors (the entrance gate to the Court of the Women and the entrance gate to the Court of the Israelites) were massive, requiring twenty men to push them shut. In any case, the closing of the gates leading from the inner courts to the outer courts may be of symbolic significance for Luke. The Jewish Saints, including Paul, believed that Jesus of Nazareth fulfilled Hebrew scripture. They do not appear to have committed any crime against the people or customs of their fathers while in Jerusalem. Yet they are now forced from their home—their Father's house. The temple doors are shut against them and their message. For Luke, the temple may now cease to fill the role hitherto allotted to it—a place of prayer and a place where God's presence is found.

The expulsion of God's messenger (and his message) from the house formerly called by his name may have sealed its fate: it was now ripe for the destruction which overtook it not many years later (A.D. 70), as prophesied by Jesus.

Throughout Luke's narrative, both in the Gospel of Luke and the Acts of the Apostles, there is a tension between the fact that the reader already knows that Jesus prophesied of the temple's ultimate doom (see Luke 21:6) and the fact that the early Saints continued to attend and participate in the temple for several decades following their Master's resurrection. Yet here the story

In A.D. 60 Paul visited Jerusalem for the last time. Wrongly charged with bringing Gentiles into the inner precincts of the temple, he was set upon by an angry mob. Roman troops from the nearby Antonia Fortress rescued him, and allowed him to speak, as he stood on the steps leading from the temple to the military fortress, to the crowd gathered in the Court of the Gentiles.

is finally played out symbolically as the temple doors (the Beautiful Gate perhaps) are closed against Paul, and therefore against the "good news."

Luke continues his dramatic account of the riot in the temple as the Roman soldiers take control of the situation:

Then the chief captain came near, and took him [Paul], and commanded him to be bound with two chains; and demanded who he was, and what he had done.

And some cried one thing, some another, among the multitude: and when he could not know the certainty for the tumult, he commanded him to be carried into the castle.

And when he came upon the stairs, so it was, that he was borne of the soldiers for the violence of the people.

For the multitude of the people followed after, crying, Away with him. (Acts 21:33–36.)

Paul stands on the stairs and makes a passionate speech to the mob. He reviews his own conversion, but also gives us a little historical insight about an earlier trip to Jerusalem and the temple.

Paul's Vision in the Temple (Acts 22:17–21)

During his fervent plea to the massive crowd from the steps leading to the Antonia Fortress, Paul reviews his first visit to Jerusalem following his dramatic conversion on the road to Damascus: "And it came to pass, that, when I was come again to Jerusalem, even while I prayed in the temple, I was in a trance; and saw [Jesus] saying unto me, Make haste, and get thee quickly out of Jerusalem: for they will not receive thy testimony concerning me" (Acts 22:17–18).

Paul's vision in the temple parallels that of Isaiah's temple vision (see Isa. 6:1–13). Both Isaiah and Paul were warned that the people of Jerusalem would pay no attention to their message, but Isaiah was told nevertheless to persist in his witness to them, whereas Paul was told to leave the city.

Responding to the Lord, Paul says that he is just the man to bear such a testimony, since the people know how wholeheartedly he persecuted the Church. They must realize, Paul believes, that the reasons for his change of mind must be overwhelmingly persuasive (see Acts 22:19–20). Yet the Lord commands him in the temple vision: "Depart: for I will send thee far hence unto the Gentiles" (Acts 22:21). Obviously, this story fits nicely into Luke's own theme that the temple is a house of prayer and a place where one finds the presence of the Lord.

The Final View of the Temple Area (Acts 22:22 to 23:31)

After Paul relates his story, the people respond to his message as Jesus predicted years earlier: "And then [they] lifted up their voices, and said, Away with such a fellow from the earth: for it is not fit that he should live. And as they cried out, and cast off their clothes, and threw dust into the air, the chief captain commanded him to be brought into the castle." (Acts 22: 22–24.)

The castle was, of course, the fortress called Antonia. This was possibly the same location of Jesus' own trial before Pilate (see John 18:28 to 19:16). The building was located next to the temple, which gave it a commanding view of the whole Temple Mount. Broad courtyards provided accommodation for troops, and a Roman cohort was stationed there permanently. Particularly at festivals the soldiers kept watch on the people in the temple area to repress any insurrectionary movement. Stairs led down at the point where the fortress impinged on the temple area porticoes, so that the soldiers could descend rapidly. The tribune and his soldiers and centurions ran down these steps to apprehend Paul, and from the steps Paul addressed the people.

On the following day, Paul is brought "down" from the Antonia Fortress to the Temple Mount to meet with the Sanhedrin (Acts 22:30). Again Paul takes the opportunity to plead his case before the Jewish leaders: "And Paul, earnestly beholding the council, said, Men and brethren, I have lived in all good conscience before God until this day" (Acts 23:1). The meeting does not go well, and through some thoughtful reflection Paul decides to divide his persecutors by declaring his belief in the resurrection. Immediately there arises a verbal battle between the Pharisees and Sadducees present. Luke continues: "And when there arose a great dissension, the chief captain, fearing lest Paul should have been pulled in pieces of them, commanded the soldier to go down, and to take him by force from among them, and to bring him into the castle" (Acts 23:10).

During the night the "Lord stood by him" and said: "Be of

good cheer, Paul: for as thou hast testified of me in Jerusalem, so must thou bear witness also at Rome" (Acts 23:11). He is soon whisked away from Jerusalem during the middle of the night when the Romans discover a plot to kill him (see Acts 23: 12–31).

Jerusalem and the temple are left behind as Paul makes his way to Rome in the closing chapters of the book of Acts. Luke knows, in light of later events, about the temple's historical demise when the Roman armies surrounded Jerusalem and destroyed the temple during their siege of the city. But during the time of its existence Luke places the temple in proper context. It is a place of prayer and a place where God can communicate with his faithful children. Neither Stephen's nor Paul's statements that "the most High dwelleth not in temples made with hands" (Acts 7:48; 17:24; cf. Isa. 66:1–2) imply a rejection of the temple, but rather they are an argument against the notion that God can be confined to a structure. The book of Acts relates the experiences of the early Church and its relationship to continued temple service and worship. It also demonstrates the essential difference between the divinely appointed structure built by the Israelites and those pagan buildings constructed by man.

Yet, at some point, God's presence does leave the temple, the mount, and the city, just as Jesus prophesied years earlier. Without the Lord's divine protection, the building is left to the people in revolt against the Roman Empire. Like the Babylonians before, Rome attacks and destroys God's abandoned house because the majority of people refuse to repent and obey the Lord who commanded them to build it originally.

In the closing chapters of Acts, Paul makes one last journey to Jerusalem. While there, he relates a vision he received in the temple years earlier. In that vision, Jesus told Paul that his mission would be to the Gentiles, far away from the Holy Land. (See Acts 22:17–21.) While his missionary efforts to this point have taken him as far as Greece, now Paul begins a journey that leads him to testify of Christ Jesus before Roman governors and that takes him to the city of Rome, where he may have preached before Caesar himself, thus fulfilling the revelation he received in the temple at Jerusalem.

SIX

Jesus and the Temple
in the Gospel of John

In the beginning was the Word,
and the Word was with God,
and the Word was God. . . .

And the Word was made flesh,
and dwelt among us, . . .
full of grace and truth.

—*John 1:1, 14*

All of the Gospel writers realize that the coming of the Messiah was an event quite unlike any other. And in the Book of Mormon, an angel told King Benjamin that God himself would come to earth: "For behold, the time cometh, and is not far distant, that with power, the Lord Omnipotent who reigneth, who

---

◄ The temple symbolized both the justice of God, in that the law of Moses dictated specific punishments for disobedience, and the mercy of the Lord, symbolized especially by the ordinance of blood sacrifice which taught the power of the Atonement to cleanse the people from impurity and sin. On one occasion the Pharisees brought to Jesus in the courtyard of the temple a woman who had been taken in adultery. Their motive was to test Jesus. After drawing on the ground with his finger, the Lord gave an unexpected judgment for such a serious offense of the law, "He that is without sin among you, let him first cast a stone at her" (John 8:7).

141

was, and is from all eternity to all eternity, shall come down from heaven among the children of men, and shall dwell in a tabernacle of clay, and shall go forth amongst men" (Mosiah 3:5). Amulek further explained, "For according to the great plan of the Eternal God there must be an atonement made. . . . It shall not be a human sacrifice; but it must be an infinite and eternal sacrifice. . . . And that great and last sacrifice will be the Son of God, yea, infinite and eternal." (Alma 34:9, 10, 14.) Jesus Christ, though he was God in the premortal life, came to earth as a mortal, the Son of God, infinite and eternal, the only one who could atone for the sins of the world and overcome death and hell. The four Gospels, each in its own way, attempt to explain, through the events they record and the teachings they preserve, who Jesus was and the wonderful mission he had come to perform.

Jesus often describes who he is with symbolic titles, or metaphors, which have the power to convey great spiritual truths to those who are prepared. For example, John preserves powerful symbols in the teachings of the Savior and others, not found in the other Gospels, in which Christ is identified as "the Word" (John 1:1, 14), "the Lamb of God" (John 2:29, 36), the source of "living water" (John 4:10, 14; 7:38), the "bread of life" (John 6:48), "the light of the world" (John 8:12; 9:5), "the good shepherd" (John 10:14), a "Comforter" (see John 14:16), and "the true vine" (John 15:1). These symbols and metaphors teach about Christ on many different levels. On the superficial level they identify Jesus with objects or ideas that are well known in everyday life. Everyone, especially those who lived in Palestine at the time of Jesus, knows the importance of sacrificial lambs, water, bread, light, shepherds, comforters, and vines. Comparing Jesus, as the Creator, "the Word," to these objects effectively explained the significance of the Savior to give and sustain the life we know.

Throughout the history of Israel, as contained in the Old Testament, these objects had acquired further significance. Sacrificial lambs, at Passover, represented both deliverance from the angel of death as well as redemption from Egypt (see Ex.

13:14–15). In the wilderness the Lord had miraculously provided water and bread (see Ex. 15:23–27; 16:4–8), and Israel followed the Lord, who manifested himself as a pillar of fire from which they received light (see Ex. 13:21). Because of the Lord's intervention on their behalf and his constant care, Israel referred to the Lord as their shepherd (see Ps. 23). The Lord referred to his people as a "vine" which he delivered out of Egypt (see Ps. 80:8) and planted in the promised land (see Ex. 15:17; cf. Isa. 5; Jer. 2:21). Thus, on a deeper level, through allusions to historical events, these symbols represent the convenantal relationship with the Lord and his intervention on behalf of his people to deliver, provide for, and protect them.

Jesus used these symbols grounded in everyday objects and sacred history to teach a yet more profound level of spiritual truth. The life the Savior offers us is eternal life, the kind of life he enjoys. The bread and water which he provides as nourishment to sustain our temporal lives are types of the spiritual sustenance which leads us to the everlasting life to be had through his atonement. The Light of Christ, which illuminates our daily lives, is the "light of life" (John 8:12). The symbols of the shepherd and the vine define the relationship shared by the Savior and his disciples. Christ, who shepherds us through mortality, is the Shepherd who gives his life that his sheep might be resurrected from the dead. As the vine he is the giver and sustainer of the life of the branches.

It is not surprising that many of these symbolic titles are connected in one way or another with the temple, as it is in the temple that we learn more fully the meaning of Christ and our relationship to him. Throughout his mortal ministry Jesus is portrayed as a fulfillment of the symbols connected with the temple and the temple festivals.[1] In his sermons Jesus uses familiar metaphors derived from temple symbolism and from the temple festivals to explain who he is and the nature of his sacred mission. Many of these symbols and metaphors were misunderstood by those who heard them. Even the disciples did not completely understand some of the Savior's teachings until after the Resurrection. Metaphors may be the only way to describe the coming of the Savior, since there was no one before or after him like unto him. In addition, these metaphors have the power to reveal sacred spiritual truth to those who are prepared, "Who hath ears to hear, let him hear" (Matt. 13:9), and at the same time to conceal that truth from those who are not prepared, "because they seeing see not; and hearing they hear not, neither do they understand" (Matt. 13:13). An examination of some of these titles in light of their temple context can add much to our understanding of the Savior and his mission.

John's Testimony (John 1)

John, in the prologue to his Gospel, identifies Jesus Christ as the "Word" by whom "all things were made." He "was with God, and . . . was God. . . . In him was life; and the life was the light of men." He "was the true Light, which lighteth every man that cometh into the world. . . . But as many as received him, to them gave he power to become the sons of God, even to them that believe on his name." Finally, John bears his own personal testimony: "We beheld his glory, the glory as of the only begotten of the Father." (John 1:1–14.) The Word, creation, life, light, and glory are all important aspects of the temple and its teachings.

Further, John tells us, "And the Word was made flesh, and dwelt among us" (John 1:14). The Greek verb in the phrase "dwelt among us" is *skenein,* and it literally means "he tabernacled (or pitched his tent) among us." On the surface the metaphor, of course, refers to the incarnation, that Jesus as God took upon himself a mortal tabernacle. In addition, the image of Jesus "pitching his tent among us" refers to the symbolism of the presence of God associated with the tabernacle, and echoes the giving of the Mosaic law at Sinai when the Lord commanded Israel to build the tabernacle, "that I may dwell among them" (Ex. 25:8).[2] With this deceptively simple metaphor John teaches us more than the fact that Jesus took upon himself a body, but also that the coming of the Savior in the flesh fulfilled the symbolism of the tabernacle and the temple—both of which represented the condescending presence of the Lord in the midst of his covenant people.

John the Baptist introduced Jesus to his disciples as "the Lamb of God, which taketh away the sin of the world" (John 1:29), an obvious allusion to the ordinance of sacrifice which was performed daily in the temple to teach and remind the people of the power of the Atonement. The burnt offering of a firstborn, unblemished male lamb was offered twice a day for the community, and as many times as necessary for individuals, to remind the people of the coming sacrifice of the Redeemer of Israel. The blood of the lamb was a graphic reminder of the price which was to be paid by the Savior to make redemption possible, and was the symbol and promise that the Israelites could indeed be purified of their many sins. This allusion in John foreshadows both the death of the Savior and his resurrection. As taught by the Passover symbols, the death of the lamb and the placement of his blood on the doorpost of the faithful had the power to deliver those who believed from the angel of death.

Temple Festivals in John

John structures the chronology of his book by noting the occurrence of the temple festivals, especially Passover, throughout the ministry of Christ. The following chart identifies where in the Gospel of John these chronological notes appear.

2:13   "And the Jews' passover was at hand, and Jesus went up to Jerusalem"

5:1   "After this there was a feast of the Jews; and Jesus went up to Jerusalem"

6:4   "And the passover, a feast of the Jews, was nigh"

7:2   "Now the Jews' feast of tabernacles was at hand"

10:22   "And it was at Jerusalem the feast of the dedication, and it was winter"

12:1   "Then Jesus six days before the passover came to Bethany"

12:12 "On the next day much people that were come to the
       feast, when they heard that Jesus was coming to
       Jerusalem . . ."

John's Gospel records that the ministry of Jesus covered two
years, as measured by three Passovers: at the beginning, the
middle, and the end. Regarding the beginning of Jesus' ministry,
John notes, "And the Jews' passover was at hand, and Jesus went
up to Jerusalem" (John 2:13). Passover is again mentioned in
John 6:4, and it is the festival which Jesus celebrated in the final
week of his life and ministry (see John 12:12). In the Gospel of
John, the Savior is crucified precisely at the moment when the
Passover lambs were being killed for all of Israel, highlighting
the testimony of John that Jesus was the "Lamb of God." The
feast mentioned in John 5:1 is not identified. An early Christian
tradition identifies it with Pentecost.[3] The feasts of Tabernacles
(see John 7:2) and of the Dedication (see John 10:22) are also
mentioned. On each occasion Jesus delivers a sermon which alludes to symbols known from these temple festivals. In each
case Jesus shows how he fulfills the symbols given in the Mosaic
law and how he replaces the festivals with new commandments.
In each case his teaching is met with misunderstanding and
often with violent opposition. At the same time those disciples
close to him slowly learn more about who he really is and the
magnitude of his calling in mortality.

As an obedient Jew, Jesus would have gone to Jerusalem
three times a year: at Passover, Pentecost, and Tabernacles (see
Ex. 23:14–17; Deut. 16:16). John's Gospel includes many events
not recorded in the other Gospels. While most of the events
recorded in the synoptic Gospels of Matthew, Mark, and Luke
occur in Galilee, most of the events in John occur in Jerusalem
and in the context of the celebration of one of the temple festivals. Thus John has deliberately chosen those events from the
life of the Savior that are connected with the temple in
Jerusalem.

The Cleansing of the Temple (John 2:13–25)

John records that Jesus began his ministry when he went up to Jerusalem to celebrate Passover and there cleansed the temple. The other three Gospels record another cleansing of the temple at the end of his ministry. There is a powerful symbolism in the authority manifested by the Savior in cleansing the temple. Jeremiah, in Old Testament times, similarly went to the temple of Solomon and declared that it had been defiled by the hypocrisy that existed there—that murderers, thieves, adulterers, and idolaters had made the temple "a den of robbers" (Jer. 7:1–16).

The money changers were probably located in the Court of the Gentiles, where they sold animals for sacrifice and changed the money into the currency and denominations needed for temple offerings. Jesus was apparently upset with the commercialization that had taken place at the temple and with those who were making unjust profits from temple concessions. In the incident recorded by John, Jesus says to the money changers, "Take these things hence; make not my Father's house an house of merchandise" (John 2:16). Here Jesus is possibly alluding to Zechariah's prophecy of a millennial temple which would not be corrupted by such concessions: "In that day there shall be no more the Canaanite [or the merchant] in the house of the Lord of hosts" (Zech. 14:21). John records that the disciples understood Jesus' anger in the context of a messianic psalm: "For the zeal of thine house hath eaten me up" (Ps. 69:9; cf. John 2:17). In this episode Jesus implicitly compares himself to the prophet Jeremiah, who also objected to hypocrisy in temple worship (see Jer. 7). More important, he tells us by what authority he cleansed the temple, as the Son of God, when he declares, "Make not my Father's house an house of merchandise" (John 2:16).

The Jews respond to this dramatic action by asking Jesus to give them a sign proving his claim to divine authority. Jesus answers them in veiled language: "Destroy this temple, and in three days I will raise it up" (John 2:19), referring to his death and resurrection. Many misunderstand. In fact, at Jesus' trial before the Sanhedrin a witness is brought forward to testify that Jesus foretold the destruction of the temple (see Matt. 26:61; Mark 14:58). Jesus, by making the play on the word *temple,* referring to his Father's house and to his body, taught that he would come and fulfill the symbolism in the temple. He would be the Lamb of God sacrificed for the sins of the world, and in this way they would destroy his body, the "temple." He would then be resurrected from the dead. Apparently the significance of this scene was only fully appreciated after the Resurrection when "his disciples remembered that he had said this unto them; and they believed the scripture, and the word which Jesus had said" (John 2:22). Ironically, on a literal level the destruction of the "temple," Herod's temple, would also occur, as Jesus prophesied in Matthew 24. And in the future the Lord has promised he will restore and rebuild the temple (see Ezek. 40–44).

Again the Jews ask for a sign clarifying who Jesus is that he would have the authority to cleanse the temple. John recorded that on this Passover "many believed in his name, when they saw the miracles which he did" (John 2:23). But Jesus was cautious and he "did not commit himself unto them, because he knew all men, and needed not that any should testify of man: for he knew what was in man" (John 2:24–25).

Thus, the festival of Passover became the bookends of Christ's ministry. As a law-abiding Jew, Jesus participated in Passover at the inception of his ministry, cleansed the temple, taught the people at the temple, and performed miracles. At the end of his ministry Jesus would once again come to Jerusalem to celebrate Passover. On that occasion he would institute at the Last Supper the sacrament, in which he would fulfill many of the symbols of Passover. In the Gospel of John, Jesus himself becomes the sacrificial lamb of Passover, being offered while the slaughter of the sheep takes place.

Where Ought Men to Worship, Jerusalem or Gerizim? (*John 4*)

We next hear about the temple in the Gospel of John when Jesus meets with the Samaritan woman at the well of Jacob. Jesus and his disciples, after celebrating Passover in Jerusalem, passed through Samaria, on their way back to Galilee, and stopped at the well to rest. Jesus remained at the well, while his disciples went into a nearby city to get provisions.

The Samaritans and the Jews had been enemies for centuries. The Old Testament records that when Solomon's son Rehoboam became king in 922 B.C., the northern ten tribes, led by the Joseph tribes of Ephraim and Manasseh, revolted and set up their own kingdom with Jeroboam as king. This Northern Kingdom eventually was called Samaria, after its capital city, and Jeroboam established sacred shrines at Dan and Bethel and erected idols there. In addition, he founded new religious festivals to replace the need to go and worship at Jerusalem (See 1 Kgs. 12.) The Southern Kingdom, led by the tribe of Judah, considered those of the Northern Kingdom to be apostates, yet by their actions they show that they were both far from obedience to the law. In 721 B.C., after repeated warnings by prophets in the north, Samaria was conquered by the Assyrians, who destroyed many of their cities and sent many of their people, taken into exile, to various cities in the Assyrian empire (see 2 Kgs. 17). The Assyrians then imported groups of people from various places in the Assyrian empire who settled in Samaria and began to intermarry with the remnant of the northern tribes which remained. These foreign peoples brought with them their own gods and idolatrous religious practices. Before long the people inhabiting Samaria were of mixed blood and were confirmed polytheists, worshipping the various imported foreign gods as well as the God of Israel. On account of this intermarriage and mixing of religious practices, the Samaritans were considered by the Jews as non-Israelites with apostate religious beliefs and practices.

When the Jews returned from exile in Babylon in 539 B.C., the Samaritans offered to help them build their temple, but the Jews rejected their help, which further exacerbated the hostilities (see Ezra 4). Josephus records that after Alexander the Great conquered the Near East in 332 B.C., the Samaritans were allowed to build a temple on Mount Gerizim, the site of the ancient covenant renewal ceremony performed by Joshua and the tribes of Israel after the conquest of Canaan (see Josh. 8:33; 24).[4] The Samaritans at the time of Christ had their own scriptures, the Samaritan Pentateuch, which proclaimed the proper place for the temple to be on Mount Gerizim, rather than in Jerusalem as indicated in the Jewish scriptures.[5] Hostile relations continued through the centuries, finally exploding in 128 B.C. when John Hyrcanus, the Hasmonean king of the Jews, destroyed the Gerizim temple. At the time of Jesus the Samaritans and the Jews hated and avoided each other. Although the Samaritan temple on Gerizim had been destroyed for over a century, the Samaritans' loyalty to it remained.

The meeting of Jesus and the Samaritan woman at the well is emotionally charged because of these issues. First, the woman wants to know why Jesus, a Jew, is conversing with a Samaritan: "How is it that thou, being a Jew, askest drink of me, which am a woman of Samaria? for the Jews have no dealings with the Samaritans" (John 4:9). To this Jesus responds, "If thou knewest the gift of God, and who it is that saith to thee, Give me to drink; thou wouldest have asked of him, and he would have given thee living water" (John 4:10), water which, he says further on, will be in those who partake of it "a well of water springing up into everlasting life" (John 4:14).

Then she brings up the doctrinal question at the heart of the hatred between the Jews and the Samaritans—where is the proper place to worship? Should the temple be on Mount Gerizim as the Samaritans believe or in Jerusalem as the Jews believe? Jesus answers, "The hour cometh, when ye shall neither in this mountain, nor yet at Jerusalem, worship the Father." Jesus clearly tells her "salvation is of the Jews." (John 4:21–22.) Although for many years the Jews had been in a state of apostasy by not living up to their covenants with the Lord, it was they who had the priesthood authority and the scriptures, and it would be through them that salvation, in the person of Jesus Christ, would come. Jesus then goes on to explain that "the hour cometh, and now is, when the true worshippers shall worship the Father in spirit and in truth: for the Father seeketh such to worship him" (John 4:23). In other words, there would come a time when the worship of the Lord would transcend either of the physical locations of the temples, as subsequent events showed.

The woman then says, "I know that Messias cometh, which is called Christ. when he is come, he will tell us all things. To this the Lord responds with one of the clearest statements of his messiahship: "I that speak unto thee am he." (John 4:25–26.) In the ensuing two days Jesus teaches those Samaritans who have been raised in the false traditions of their fathers, who have not worshipped the God of Israel at Jerusalem, but who have the faith and the humility to accept him who has the power to give unto them "water springing up into everlasting life." The scriptures record that many Samaritans believed on Christ on account of the woman's testimony, but many more because they heard the Savior himself (see John 4:39–42). The Apostle Philip continued the mission to the Samaritans after the Resurrection and had great success (see Acts 8).

Jesus and the Sabbath (John 5)

Jesus left Galilee and returned to Jerusalem to celebrate another religious feast: "After this there was a feast of the Jews; and Jesus went up to Jerusalem" (John 5:1). As noted earlier, this feast is never identified in the Gospel of John, though an early Christian tradition identified it as Pentecost.[6] At the end of his sermon Jesus mentions Moses, "For had ye believed Moses, ye would have believed me: for he wrote of me" (John 5:46). Since Pentecost is the festival which was associated with the giving of the law to Moses on Sinai, it is possible that Jesus alludes to Moses in the context of the celebration of Pentecost.

Actually, the narrative concerns a healing on the Sabbath. There is a man who waits at the pool of Bethesda for the miraculous healing power of God. He has not been able to walk for thirty-eight years. Jesus comes to him on the Sabbath and says, "Rise, take up thy bed, and walk" (John 5:8). The critics of Jesus confront the man and ask him why he is carrying his bed on the Sabbath. He replies, "He that made me whole, the same said unto me, Take up thy bed, and walk" (John 5:11). In addition the multitude persecutes Jesus because he has healed on the Sabbath. Jesus responds to these charges, "My Father worketh hitherto, and I work" (John 5:17). The Jews understood the import of this statement and "sought the more to kill him, because he not only had broken the sabbath, but said also that God was his Father, making himself equal with God" (John 5:18).

Thus Jesus took advantage of the Sabbath day to teach the Jews who he was. Not only could the Son of God heal on the Sabbath, but Jesus went on to explain that the Father had "committed all judgment unto the Son" (John 5:22) and that through the resurrection of the Son all men would be resurrected (see John 5:25–29).

The Feast of Passover and the Bread of Life (John 6)

Chapter 6 of John is the account of the feeding of the five thousand and the following bread of life sermon in which Jesus attempts to explain to the Jews who he is with symbols taken from Passover, for "the passover, a feast of the Jews, was nigh" (John 6:4). The Jews were familiar with the significance of bread on many different levels: the bread of life, the manna connected with the Exodus, and the shewbread in the temple. Jesus identifies himself with the bread and teaches his people about the sacrament. In John, it is only here, in the context of Passover, that Jesus teaches about the sacrament. In the synoptic Gospels, Jesus' teachings on the sacrament are preserved in the accounts of the Last Supper—a Passover meal.

The story of the feeding of the five thousand contains references to the temple and the Exodus which was being celebrated at Passover. The twelve baskets of bread remaining from the feeding of the five thousand are reminiscent of the twelve loaves of shewbread put before the presence of the Lord in the temple. Some have also suggested that Jesus' crossing the Sea of Galilee after the feeding is reminiscent of the crossing of the Red Sea.

After crossing the Sea of Galilee, Jesus teaches the sermon of the bread of life. First, Jesus notes that those who have come to him have come "not because ye saw the miracles, but because ye did eat of the loaves, and were filled" (John 6:26). The importance of bread on the physical level is obvious—it has been the staff of life throughout the history of mankind. Jesus urges them to "labour not for the meat which perisheth, but for that meat which endureth unto everlasting life" (John 6:27) and identifies himself as that meat: "Believe on him whom he hath sent" (John 6:29). The people ask for a sign, "that we may see, and believe thee" (John 6:30), and cite as a past example the Lord's gift of manna in the wilderness, which they call "bread from heaven" (John 6:31). While manna was perceived to be the bread from heaven because it was divinely given, Jesus tells them that the Father will give them the "true bread from heaven" (John 6:32), which is "he which cometh down from heaven, and giveth life unto the world" (John 6:33).

The people then ask that Jesus give them the bread of life, and he responds, "I am the bread of life: he that cometh to me shall never hunger; and he that believeth on me shall never thirst" (John 6:35). At this the people murmur—just as in the wilderness. Jesus reminds them that he is not Moses, nor is he manna, for "your fathers did eat manna in the wilderness, and are dead" (John 6:49). Jesus teaches, "I am the living bread which came down from heaven: if any man eat of this bread, he shall live for ever: and the bread that I will give is my flesh, which I will give for the life of the world" (John 6:51). Then Jesus proceeds to teach them about the sacrament: "Verily, verily, I say unto you, Except ye eat the flesh of the Son of man, and drink his blood, ye have no life in you" (John 6:53). This of course is a dramatic statement, particularly to a people who were commanded by the Mosaic law not to eat blood in any form.

At Passover the covenant people partook of the flesh of the lamb, which had died in order to provide them deliverance from the angel of death. In addition, they partook of other symbolic foods to remind them of important elements of their sacred history: unleavened bread, bitter herbs, and probably, at the time of Jesus, wine. But most were unable to accept this same symbolic gesture in relationship to Jesus Christ. They were unable to accept him as the Son of God, asking themselves, "Is not this Jesus, the son of Joseph, whose father and mother we know? how is it then that he saith, I came down from heaven?" (John 6:42.) The Gospel of John records, "From that time many of his disciples went back, and walked no more with him" (John 6:66).

The Feast of Tabernacles: The Light of the World and the Source of Living Water (John 7–8)

Following Passover, Jesus returned to Jerusalem: "Now the Jews' feast of tabernacles was at hand" (John 7:2). The Feast of Tabernacles was a joyous occasion held at the same time as the fall harvest. It began on the fifteenth day of the seventh month and lasted seven days. It was primarily a feast of thanksgiving for the bounty of the harvest and the Lord's hand which had made it all possible. In addition it was associated with the wandering in the wilderness, commemorating the forty years the children of Israel spent in the wilderness living in tents or booths. Israel was specifically commanded to read the law on this occasion and recommit themselves to its observance (see Deut. 31:10–11). The temple of Solomon was dedicated on this occasion (see 1 Kgs. 8:2), which added further sanctity to the day.

At the time of Jesus, the Feast of Tabernacles was celebrated, as outlined in the Bible, by the people's living in booths for seven days. On each of the seven days, the people, carrying in their hands the feast's symbols—the citron fruit and the branches of the myrtle, palm, and willow trees—would make a procession to the temple, where they would walk around the altar singing the so-called Hallel Psalms (Ps. 113–18). As they proceeded around the altar, they recited Psalm 118:25: "Save now, I beseech thee, O Lord [Heb. *hosanna*]: O Lord, I beseech thee, send now prosperity."

In addition, the Feast of Tabernacles at the time of Jesus had also incorporated a water libation ritual. In the Mishnah the ceremony is known as the "rejoicing of the place of water-drawing," a title apparently derived from Isaiah 12:3: "Therefore with joy shall ye draw water out of the wells of salvation." The rabbis taught that this ceremony was to ensure rain and the continued fertility of the people's crops.

During the seven days of the festival the priests would descend to the pool of Siloam and draw water. They would then lead a joyous procession to the altar of burnt offerings at the temple, where they would offer the water to the Lord by pouring it into a bowl on the altar. The people in the procession sang the Hallel Psalms and played flutes. The Mishnah says, "He that never has seen the rejoicing of the place of water-drawing has never in his life seen joy."[7]

The Mishnah also records a ritual involving four gigantic lampstands found in the Court of the Women: "There were golden candlesticks there with four [or five] golden bowls on the top of them. . . . They made wicks from the worn out drawers and girdles of the priests and with them they set the candlesticks alight, and there was not a courtyard in Jerusalem that did not reflect the light of the place of drawing."[8] In the context of Tabernacles, the light reminded Israel of the presence of the Lord in the wilderness in the pillar of fire which gave them light (see Ex. 13:21).

In the spring Jesus had delivered his sermon about the bread of life during the Passover season. By the fall Jesus was reluctant to go to Jerusalem "because the Jews sought to kill him" (John 7:1). Jesus sent his disciples to Jerusalem, but he stayed behind because, as he said, "my time is not yet come" (John 7:6). Later, Jesus went up to the feast secretly (see John 7:10). "Now about the midst of the feast Jesus went up into the temple, and taught" (John 7:14). His sermon was about the fact that Moses had given the law and yet the covenant people did not obey it—a

Jesus' presence in the temple not only allowed the righteous to hear him, but also demonstrated his power as his enemies continued to be foiled in their attempts to trap him or capture him while he stood in this sacred spot: "And no man laid hands on him; for his hour was not yet come" (John 8:20).

timely topic, since Tabernacles was the festival which was used for covenant renewal: "Did not Moses give you the law, and yet none of you keepeth the law? Why go ye about to kill me?" (John 7:19.) Not only did the people reject Jesus but they sought to kill him. The many signs which Jesus had performed had indicated who he was: "Then cried Jesus in the temple as he taught, saying, Ye both know me, and ye know whence I am: and I am not come of myself, but he that sent me is true, whom ye know not. But I know him: for I am from him, and he hath sent me." (John 7:28–29.)

John records:

> In the last day, that great day of the feast, Jesus stood and cried, saying:
> If any man thirst, let him come unto me, and drink.
> He that believeth on me, as the scripture hath said,
> out of his belly shall flow rivers of living water.
>
> (John 7:37–38.)

This is a difficult passage to interpret, since it is not clear what scriptural passage is being quoted here. Several passages are similar.[9] Many scholars believe the closest parallel to be Psalm 78:15–16[10], which speaks about Moses providing the children of Israel with water in the wilderness:

> He clave the rocks in the wilderness,
> and gave them drink as out of the great depths.
> He brought streams also out of the rock,
> and caused waters to run down like rivers.

We immediately think of Jesus speaking to the Samaritan woman and promising her that he could give her living water. John goes on to parenthetically explain that Jesus was talking about the giving of the Spirit (see John 7:39). In John the symbolism of the giving of the Spirit, which was to occur after the death of the Savior, is noted in John 19:34, where it is stated that when the soldier pierced Jesus' body, blood and water came out—literally from his belly. This same theme is noted in Revelation 22, where in the celestial city a "river of water of life" (Rev. 22:1) proceeds from the throne of the Lamb and waters the tree of life, and all are invited to "come. And let him that is athirst come. And whosoever will, let him take the water of life freely." (Rev. 22:17.)

Building on the series of symbols of the feast, Jesus clearly identifies himself as the fulfillment of the festival of Tabernacles. He begins by comparing himself with Moses—"one like unto Moses"—who led the children of Israel in the wilderness. The water of life—so prominent throughout the seven days of Tabernacles—is none other than Jesus himself. There is great irony in the people's drawing water and singing messianic psalms and yet not being able to recognize and accept the living water offered by the Messiah in their midst.

In the middle of the Tabernacles narrative we find the story of the woman taken in adultery. While Jesus is teaching in the temple, the scribes and Pharisees bring to him a woman whom they say "was taken in adultery, in the very act" (John 8:4). They announce to the Savior, "Now Moses in the law commanded us, that such should be stoned: but what sayest thou?" (John 8:5.) We are not told whether the woman has already been judged by the Sanhedrin, or whether they have brought her to Jesus first. We are told that they are tempting Jesus, "that they might have to accuse him" (John 8:6). Perhaps she has already been judged by the Sanhedrin and deemed worthy of the death penalty, and they are attempting to trap Jesus. If he says she should not be stoned, they can accuse him of denying the law of Moses, and if he says she should be killed, they can accuse him of speaking against Rome—as the Sanhedrin had been denied the power of capital punishment by the Romans during this period. In any case their motives are not pure—they are concerned neither with the law nor with the spiritual welfare of the woman.

At first Jesus does not respond but begins to write with his finger in the dust. We do not know what he was writing and apparently John did not think it was important to the story. Finally Jesus looks up and says, "He that is without sin among you, let him first cast a stone at her" (John 8:7). With this statement Jesus unveils the hypocrisy of those standing before him. Those who wish to accuse, condemn, and punish must examine their own hearts before they judge. One by one those who have brought the woman leave. At last Jesus is left alone with the woman. He speaks to her: "Woman, where are those thine accusers? hath no man condemned thee? She said, No man, Lord. And Jesus said unto her, Neither do I condemn thee: go, and sin no more." (John 8:10–11.) The God of heaven and earth demonstrates his power to forgive sin. Many years before, near the very site where Jesus stood, Solomon had prayed to the Savior and said, "Then hear thou in heaven thy dwelling place, and forgive, and do, and give to every man according to his ways, whose heart thou knowest" (1 Kgs. 8:39). The Lord, in the flesh, demonstrated his ability to discern the hearts of men and women—those who had impure motives he dismissed, and the repentant one he forgave. The temple has forever reminded those who worship there of both justice and mercy. Through the Atonement, which it represents, all can be freed from the bondage of sin.

The next day Jesus once again explained who he was in symbolic language: "I am the light of the world: he that followeth me shall not walk in darkness, but shall have the light of life" (John 8:12). Within the context of Tabernacles, it is clear: All of the light symbolism connected with the Exodus and the coming of the Messiah in the book of Zechariah, as commemorated in the ritual of the burning lamps in the temple, was to point to the light of the world. Ironically, in John the "light shineth in darkness; and the darkness comprehended it not" (John 1:5).

Jesus concludes this sermon with an unmistakable statement as to his identity: "Before Abraham was, I am. Then took they up stones to cast at him. but Jesus hid himself, and went out of the temple, going through the midst of them, and so passed by." (John 8:58–59.)

Prophecies of the last days in Zechariah 9–14 connect the Feast of Tabernacles with the triumphal entry of the Savior, judgment and the Second Coming, and the gathering of all the nations during the Millennium to worship the Lord God of Israel.[11] Zechariah 9:9 describes the coming of the Messiah as the King entering Jerusalem on a donkey. This prophecy was fulfilled in Jerusalem with the triumphal entry, which occurred at the time of Passover, but was celebrated with the symbols of the Feast of Tabernacles, the waving of the palm fronds (see John 12:12–19). This passage further prophesies the life-giving waters that would accompany the Messiah: the coming of the latter rains (see Zech. 10:1), for which the people petitioned the Lord at Tabernacles; the "fountain opened to the house of David" to cleanse Israel (Zech. 13:1); and the "living waters" to go out from Jerusalem (Zech. 14:8). The "day of the Lord" is a day of judgment, and the Messiah will "stand in that day upon the mount of Olives" (Zech. 14:1, 4). The coming of the Lord will usher in a period characterized by the flooding of the earth with light and truth: "And it shall come to pass in that day, that the light shall not be clear, nor dark: but it shall be one day which shall be known to the Lord, not day, nor night: but it shall come to pass, that at evening time it shall be light" (Zech. 14:6–7). Furthermore, "it shall be in that day, that living waters shall go out from Jerusalem" (Zech. 14:8), "and the Lord shall be king over all the earth" (Zech. 14:9).

Just as Israel every year gathered their crops in the fall, so would the Lord's harvest be gathered in the Millennium and be commemorated by the Feast of Tabernacles: "And it shall come to pass, that every one that is left of all the nations which came against Jerusalem shall even go up from year to year to worship the King, the Lord of hosts, and to keep the feast of tabernacles" (Zech. 14:16). Zechariah adds that upon those who do not come up to worship the King, there "shall be no rain" (Zech. 14:17). The association of rain with the harvest may seem strange to someone not familiar with agriculture in the Holy Land. Virtually all of the rain which Israel would receive would fall in the months between Tabernacles and Passover. Thus, the harvest time was the proper and critical time for Israel to petition the Lord for water.

For all those who come to worship the Lord "shall there be upon the bells of the horses, HOLINESS UNTO THE LORD" (Zech. 14:20). In other words, the entire society would become sacred, perhaps reminiscent of the time spoken of in Revelation when there would be no temple (see Rev. 21:22) since the entire society would become sacred and enjoy the presence of the Lord.

All of these elements—gathering, light, water, the kingship of the Lord, holiness, and the temple—coalesce in the celebration of the Feast of Tabernacles, which looked back to the wandering in the wilderness and the dedication of Solomon's temple and looked forward to the Second Coming and the Millennium. Jesus used all of these symbols to teach the people that he had come as the fulfillment of this festival.

The Feast of the Dedication (John 10)

We next find Jesus back in Jerusalem: "And it was at Jerusalem the feast of the dedication, and it was winter. And Jesus walked in the temple in Solomon's porch." (John 10: 22–23.)

The Feast of the Dedication is not one of the festivals pre-scribed in the Mosaic law. The origins of the Feast of the Dedi-cation are found in the apocryphal books which recount the Jewish revolt led by the Maccabees against the Syrian armies who had desecrated the temple and which tell of the cleansing and rededication of the temple (see 1 Maccabees 4:36–59; 2 Macca-bees 1:8; 10:1–5).[12] The Jews called this festival *Hanukkah*, meaning "dedication," the same Hebrew word (in various nominal and verbal forms) which appears in the dedication and consecra-tion of the altar of the tabernacle (see Num. 7:10–11), Solomon's temple (see 1 Kgs. 8:63; 2 Chr. 7:5), and the second temple in the days of Zerubbabel (see Ezra 6.16). The festival reminds one of dedication, consecration, and making holy for the Lord.

The book of 2 Maccabees tells us that the Jews celebrated the first Hanukkah "for eight days with rejoicing, in the manner of the festival of booths, remembering how not long before, during the festival of booths, they had been wandering in the moun-tains and caves like wild animals. Therefore, carrying ivy-wreathed wands and beautiful branches and also fronds of palm, they offered hymns of thanksgiving to him who had given suc-cess to the purifying of his own holy place." (New Revised Standard Version Bible [NRSV], 2 Macc. 10:6–7.) Eight days is reminiscent of Solomon's dedication of the temple (see 1 Kgs. 8:65), as well as of the rededication of the cleansed temple under Hezekiah (see 2 Chr. 29:17). The book of 1 Maccabees describes the rededication of the temple commemorated at the Feast of the Dedication:

> They rose and offered sacrifice, as the law directs, on the new altar of burnt offering that they had built.
>
> At the very season and on the very day that the Gentiles had profaned it, it [the temple] was dedicated with songs and harps and lutes and cymbals.
>
> All the people fell on their faces and worshiped and blessed Heaven, who had prospered them.
>
> So they celebrated the dedication of the altar for eight days, and joyfully offered burnt offerings; they offered a sacrifice of well-being and a thanksgiving offering.

They decorated the front of the temple with golden crowns and small shields; they restored the gates and the chambers for the priests, and fitted them with doors.

There was very great joy among the people, and the disgrace brought by the Gentiles was removed. (NRSV, 1 Macc. 4:53–58.)

John's narrative includes many details that highlight the association of Jesus' sermon with the festival at hand, and like each of the other narratives about the temple festivals, Jesus' sermon points us towards how he fulfilled the symbolism associated with the festival.

In the sermon that Jesus gave just before the Feast of the Dedication, he proclaimed himself "the good shepherd" (John 10:14) who would give his life for his sheep. Scholars have suggested that since the yearly scripture reading in the synagogue at the time of the Feast of the Dedication included Ezekiel 34, an Old Testament passage about sheep and shepherds, Jesus is building upon this passage, which would have been fresh in the minds of people in his audience.[13]

John records that it was "winter" during the Feast of the Dedication, reminding us the weather in Jerusalem in December was cold. Further, he notes that Jesus was walking "in the temple in Solomon's porch." (John 10:22–23.) Of course, as we have noted, "in the temple" (Greek *en to hiero*) means in the temple complex rather than in the temple itself. The stoa, or rows of columns, south of the temple were closed and would provide some protection from the cold winter winds. The oldest part of the porch which surrounded the temple was at the time of Jesus believed by many to date back to the time of Solomon, thus the appellation "Solomon's porch."[14]

Just as in each of the other festival narratives the question posed to Jesus is, who is he? here the Jews ask him, "How long dost thou make us to doubt? If thou be the Christ, tell us plainly." (John 10:24.) Jesus answers: "I told you, and ye believed not: the works that I do in my Father's name, they bear witness of me" (John 10:25). He then continues the theme of the good shepherd: "But ye believe not, because ye are not of my sheep, as I said unto you. My sheep hear my voice, and I know them, and they follow me." (John 10:26–27.) He concludes with the direct statement, "I and my Father are one" (John 10:30), a statement which the Jews understand to be blasphemy and they take up stones to stone him.

The Savior then explains his relationship to the Father: "Say ye of him, whom the Father hath sanctified, and sent into the world, Thou blasphemest; because I said, I am the Son of God?" (John 10:36.) This statement is a direct allusion to the Feast of the Dedication. The Greek word used here for "hath sanctified" is *hagiazein,* which literally means "to make holy" and is the same term used in the Greek Old Testament in the description of Moses dedicating the tabernacle (see Num. 7:1), and in the description of Solomon consecrating the courtyard front of the temple where the daily burnt offerings were to be offered. It is also a word used in the rededication of the temple by Hezekiah (see 2 Chr. 29:17).

Most important, this word is found in the story of the Maccabean rededication of the temple: "They also rebuilt the sanctuary and the interior of the temple, and consecrated [*hegiasan*] the courts" (NRSV, 1 Macc. 4:48). In the context of the Feast of the Dedication, Jesus taught the people of his divinity. He attempted to show them that the sanctification of the temple the people celebrated in the Feast of the Dedication actually pointed towards him—that he was the one sanctified by the Father. He admonished: "If I do not the works of my Father, believe me not. But if I do, though ye believe not me, believe the works: that ye may know, and believe, that the Father is in me, and I in him." (John 10:37–38.) The people attempted again to kill him, but he escaped.

"In My Father's House Are Many Mansions" (John 13–17)

At the end of Jesus' ministry, Jesus went up once again to celebrate Passover in Jerusalem: "Now before the feast of the passover, when Jesus knew that his hour was come that he should depart out of this world unto the Father . . ." (John

13:1). The chronology of the Last Supper differs in John from the synoptic Gospels. In Matthew, Mark, and Luke the Last Supper is the Passover feast held along with the rest of Israel. In John it is a meal held the day before the Passover, which would have Jesus being crucified on the cross at the hour the Passover lambs were being killed at the temple. There have been many ingenious solutions proposed to this discrepancy, but none have achieved consensus. While the emphasis on Jesus' fulfilling the symbols of Passover is the same in all four Gospels, the Gospel of John highlights the association of Jesus with the Passover lamb.

The atonement of Christ fulfilled many of the symbols of the Passover feast. Passover celebrated the miraculous intervention of the Lord to deliver his children from bondage and death in Egypt; the Atonement was the intervention of the Lord in cosmic history delivering his children from the bondage of sin and death. The firstborn male lamb, unblemished, whose blood was shed to deliver Israel from the angel of death at Passover, was now to be the Lord himself, who would shed his blood at Passover. The Last Supper took place in the context of Passover, and the bread and wine, which became the simple symbols of the "new covenant," were important symbols of the Passover feast.

The Gospel of John preserves Jesus' final sermon to his Apostles on the occasion of the Last Supper, though oddly enough, John leaves to the other three Gospels the description of the meal itself and the institution of the sacrament. This sermon is full of important allusions to temple symbolism.

After the meal Jesus taught his Apostles humility when he girded himself with a towel and washed their feet. Ordinances of washing were well known to Jews under the law of Moses. The bronze basins on the grounds of the temple were used by the priests to cleanse and purify themselves to officiate before the Lord on behalf of the people. In addition, Israelite men and women were required to cleanse themselves by immersing themselves in a ritual bath as part of the purification system to render themselves worthy to enter the Temple Mount (see also JST, John 13:10). Jesus was teaching them that his washing their feet was symbolic of the power of the sacrifice of the Savior to cleanse them "every whit" (John 13:10). The symbolism of the washing of the feet has been restored in the latter days in the washings associated with the endowment. Jesus' act foreshadowed the humility he would show in carrying out the Atonement.

After Judas left, the Savior returned to his message of humility, teaching his Apostles the necessity of love: "By this shall all men know that ye are my disciples, if ye have love one to another" (John 13:35). Jesus then announced to his disciples: "In my Father's house [Greek *en te oikia tou patros mou*] are many mansions: if it were not so, I would have told you. I go to prepare a place for you." (John 14:2.) Jesus, echoing the language of his cleansing of the temple at the beginning of his ministry in John—"make not my Father's house [Greek *ton oikon tou patros mou*] an house of merchandise" (John 2:16)—invited his Apostles into the presence of his Father, into the heavenly temple, the house of his Father. Just as the earthly temple was a model which taught the covenant people the process of entering into the presence of God, Jesus specifically taught his disciples how they too could enter into the "Father's house." In the law of Moses the blood of the lamb symbolized the power of the Atonement to bring Israel back into the presence of God. Jesus taught them that it was only through him that they could enter into the presence of their Father in heaven: "And if I go and prepare a place for you, I will come again, and receive you unto myself; that where I am, there ye may be also. . . . I am the way, the truth, and the life: no man cometh unto the Father, but by me." (John 14:3, 6.)

Jesus then taught his Apostles the process by which they could regain the presence of God: The first step was to believe "that I am in the Father, and the Father in me" (John 14:11). Next was to do the works of the Son (see John 14:13), to pray to the Father in the name of the Son (see John 14:14), to love the Savior and keep his commandments (see John 14:16). Then the Lord promised to send his followers two Comforters—the First Comforter, the Holy Ghost, to "teach you all things, and bring all things to your remembrance, whatsoever I have said unto you" (John 14:26); and the Second Comforter, the Savior himself. "I will not leave you comfortless: I will come to you" (John 14:18). "He that hath my commandments, and keepeth them, he it is that loveth me: and he that loveth me shall be loved of my Father, and I will love him, and will manifest myself to him. . . . If a man love me, he will keep my words: and my Father will love him, and we will come unto him, and make our abode with him." (John 14:21, 23.)

Joseph Smith clarified these matters:

> After a person has faith in Christ, repents of his sins, and is baptized for the remission of his sins and receives the Holy Ghost, (by the laying on of hands), which is the first Comforter, then let him continue to humble himself before God, hungering and thirsting after righteousness, and living by every word of God, and the Lord will soon say unto him, Son, thou shalt be exalted. When the Lord has thoroughly proved him, and finds that the man is determined to serve Him at all hazards, then the man will find his calling and his election made sure, then it will be his privilege to receive the other Comforter, which the Lord hath promised the Saints, as is recorded in the testimony of St. John, in the 14th chapter, from the 12th to the 27th verses. . . .
>
> Now what is this other Comforter? It is no more nor less than the Lord Jesus Christ Himself; and this is the sum and substance of the whole matter; that when any man obtains this last Comforter, he will have the personage of Jesus Christ to attend him, or appear unto him from time to time, and even He will manifest the Father unto him, and they will take up their abode with him.[15]

Jesus continued explaining the relationship between the Father, the Son, and disciples of Christ, using the metaphor of a vine: "I am the true vine [Greek *ampelos alethine*], and my Father is the husbandman. . . . I am the vine, ye are the branches: He that abideth in me, and I in him, the same bringeth forth much fruit: for without me ye can do nothing." (John 15:1, 5.) The vine refers to the grapevine, one of the staples of life in the Mediterranean world and a prominent symbol in the scriptures. The vine produced grapes which could be eaten fresh or dried into raisins. The juice was made into wine and vinegar, and even the leaves were eaten. In addition, the non-bearing branches were cut off, dried, and used for fuel.

In the Old Testament the Lord refers to his chosen people as a vine which he brought out of Egypt and planted in the promised land (see Ps. 80:8–10; Jer. 2:21; cf. Ex. 15:17), or as a vineyard (see Isa. 5:1–7). A similar metaphor, from the Old Testament period, comparing the world to a vineyard is found in Zenos's allegory of the olive tree (see Jacob 5). In the New Testament, a vineyard is used as a metaphor for the world in the parable of the wicked husbandmen (see Mark 12:1–12; Luke 20:1–18) and for the world—or perhaps more specifically the Church—in the parable of the laborers (see Matt. 20:1–10). In the Book of Mormon, Nephi refers to the gathering of Israel in terms of this "true vine": "Yea, at that day, will they not receive the strength and nourishment from the true vine? Yea, will they not come unto the true fold of God?" (1 Nephi 15:15.) This allusion, written nearly six hundred years before Christ, suggests that already in Israelite culture the "true vine" was an image used to describe the Savior. Likewise, the image of the "true fold" prefigures the metaphor of the Good Shepherd known in John (see John 10:1–18).

Jews at the time of Jesus were constantly reminded of this imagery by the beautiful golden vine with gold grape clusters the size of a man, prominently displayed within the doorway of the temple. Such imagery in the ancient world represented the bounteous harvests which the Lord had promised to the faithful. From the beginning, temples have been associated with the covenantal promises of fertility—promises of children as well as multiplication in flocks and the crops. Such a symbol on Herod's temple was a reminder of these promises made with the Lord as recorded in Deuteronomy 27–28, fulfilled when the spies brought back huge grape clusters (see Num. 13:23). Those who had received blessings from the Lord brought expensive thanksgiving offerings which were hung on this golden vine.

Jesus builds upon this familiar imagery. As the Messiah he is the representative of Israel, represented in the Old Testament by a vine or vineyard. His point of emphasis is that he is the source of life to his disciples, the branches, that makes possible their good works and further converts, which is the fruit. Many subtle lessons are inherent in this metaphor. True life is not to be had simply by being a descendant of Israel, the vineyard. Nor can it be found through the temple and its elaborate ceremonies under the law of Moses without the Messiah. Just as Jesus was the source of "living water," the "true bread from heaven," and the "light of the world," so he is the "true vine"—the only source of spiritual support and nutrition. Just as he is the "Good Shepherd" who gives his life for the world, so he is the source of life from the Father.

He who does not receive his life from the vine cannot bear fruit, and he is "cast forth as a branch," becomes withered, is gathered, and is burned (John 15:6). Jesus concluded: "Herein is my Father glorified, that ye bear much fruit; so shall ye be my disciples. . . . These things have I spoken unto you, that my joy might remain in you, and that your joy might be full. This is my commandment, That ye love one another, as I have loved you." (John 15:8, 11, 12.)

Jesus ended his sermon in the upper room with an eloquent prayer in which he mentioned many of the important concepts of temple worship, both ancient and modern. The temples in the Old Testament were places of glory—the light and truth which indicates the presence of God. Men and women in Israel went to the tabernacle and the successive temples in order to observe this glory and partake of it that they too might become more holy. By experiencing the presence of the Lord, little by little, they could come to understand what he was like and how better to become like him. In his prayer to the Father, Jesus asked, "And now, O Father, glorify thou me with thine own self with the glory which I had with thee before the world was" (John 17:5). He concluded: ". . . that they all may be one; as thou, Father, art in me, and I in thee, that they also may be one in us: that the world may believe that thou hast sent me. And the glory which thou gavest me I have given them; that they may be one, even as we are one." (John 17:21–22.)

It is only through Christ that one can enter into the mansions in the Father's house, and enjoy eternal life there. The golden vine at the temple, with its dazzling reflected sunlight, pointed towards the "true vine," the only source of light, life, and glory. On that night at Passover season in Jerusalem, the disciples learned of the fulfillment of all of the temple symbolism. To enter into the heavenly house of the Father one must first enjoy oneness with him, possible only through his Son. And that was only possible through the love of God and his Son.

In the following three days the love of God would be made manifest to the whole world as the Father would give his Only Begotten Son, and his Son would give his life, on the cross, in the shadow of the temple, for the sins of the world. In Gethsemane the "light of the world" would be overshadowed by darkness for a time, but then he would rise and overcome the darkness. On the third day in the tomb, the "light and life" would overcome death. Through the Atonement, the Father would glorify his Son and the Son would offer this glory to the Father and to all who would come unto him and receive it in his name. Forty days later, in the shadow of the temple, on the Day of Pentecost, the celebration of the harvest of the firstfruits, the Lord would send the Comforter.

SEVEN

Matthew and the Destruction of the Temple

Verily I say unto you, There shall not be left here one stone upon another, that shall not be thrown down.
—*Matthew 24:2*

The Gospel of Matthew presents Jesus Christ as the Messiah, the fulfillment of the Old Testament prophecies. All of the symbolism of the temple pointed towards him. Those who accepted him received the blessings of the new covenant. Because the covenant people as a whole rejected him, however, Jesus prophesied great tribulations and the destruction of the temple.

◀ In the last week of his mortal ministry, Jesus taught a sermon in which he lamented to Israel, "O Jerusalem, Jerusalem, thou that killest the prophets, and stonest them which are sent unto thee, how often would I have gathered thy children together, even as a hen gathereth her chickens under her wings, and ye would not!" (Matt. 23:37.) He then went to the Mount of Olives to the east of Jerusalem and taught his amazed disciples that the splendid temple of Herod, the culmination of the pride of Judaism, would be totally destroyed, and "there shall not be left here one stone upon another, that shall not be thrown down" (Matt. 24:2).

Jesus as the Fulfillment of the Old Testament

A central theme in the Gospel of Matthew is that Jesus was the fulfillment of the promises and covenants contained in the Old Testament. Matthew begins his account with the genealogy of Jesus, pointing out that he was a descendant of Abraham, the son of David, and the rightful heir to the Davidic throne (see Matt. 1:1–17). He constantly cites Old Testament passages in his Gospel which were fulfilled by Jesus Christ. For example, he notes that Jesus was born of a virgin (see Matt. 1:22–23) as a fulfillment of a prophecy by Isaiah (see Isa. 7:14), that Jesus was born in Bethlehem (see Matt. 2:5–6) as a realization of a passage in Micah (see Micah 5:1–3), and that the Savior would come out of Egypt (see Matt. 2:15) as alluded to in Hosea (see Hosea 11:1).

Central to the Gospel of Matthew is the idea that Jesus had come to establish a new covenant with Israel. The Sermon on the Mount is portrayed, after the type of Moses' receiving the law on Sinai, as a new giving of the law—the higher law. Jesus states in his sermon, "Think not that I am come to destroy the law, or the prophets: I am not come to destroy, but to fulfil" (Matt. 5:17), and he presents the commandments of the higher law, which involve avoiding anger, lust, dishonesty, and retribution—and he does so with authority: "Ye have heard that it was said by them of old time . . . but I say unto you . . ." (Matt. 5:21–22; see also verses 27–28, 31–32, 33–34, 38–39, 43–44). Finally, at the Last Supper, Jesus initiates the sacrament by quoting a phrase, "new covenant," from Jeremiah 31:31: "For this is my blood of the new testament [Greek *covenant*]" (Matt. 26:28).

The Blessings and Curses of the Covenant
(Deut. 27–28; Matt. 5, 23)

The book of Deuteronomy clearly spells out for the children of Israel the blessings and curses connected with the covenant. The Lord commanded Moses, as recorded in Deuteronomy

27–28, to hold a covenant renewal ceremony when the children of Israel finally conquered the promised land, a commandment which was fulfilled by Moses' successor, Joshua (see Josh. 8, 24). This ceremony was held at Shechem, a city in the inheritance of Joseph, which stood between two mountains. In this ceremony the people recommitted themselves to observe the Mosaic covenant, marching through the valley between the two mountains while elders of six of the tribes stood on Mount Gerizim and shouted out, "Blessed . . . , Blessed . . . , Blessed . . . ," as they enumerated the blessings promised to those who obeyed the covenant. On the other mountain, elders of the six remaining tribes shouted out, "Cursed . . . , Cursed . . . , Cursed . . . ," as they enumerated the curses promised to those who did not live up to their covenants. The blessings consisted of prosperity, protection, and deliverance, that "the Lord shall establish thee an holy people unto himself" (Deut. 28:9). The cursings were the reverse: plague and pestilence, destruction, and ultimately that "the Lord shall scatter thee among all people, from the one end of the earth even unto the other" (Deut. 28:64).

In Matthew, Jesus' Sermon on the Mount begins, "Blessed . . . , Blessed . . . , Blessed . . ."; these are the Beatitudes, descriptions of the kingdom of heaven and of the characteristics of those who become holy to the Lord (see Matt. 5:1–12). The Israelites would be immediately reminded of the blessings listed by Moses in previous covenant ceremonies and recorded in the law (see Deut. 28). Jesus' last public sermon recorded in Matthew begins, "Woe . . . , Woe . . . , Woe . . . ," reminiscent of the curses accompanying the Mosaic covenant, and in this sermon Jesus enumerates the hypocrisy of those who claimed to be the covenant people and yet did not understand nor obey the law (see Matt. 23). The ministry of Christ, as recorded in Matthew, is framed by references to the blessings and cursings of the covenant known from the book of Deuteronomy, references that are suggested by the blessings promised by the Beatitudes and the woes pronounced on the scribes and Pharisees.

One of the most dramatic events to occur as part of these curses is the destruction of the second temple in Jerusalem as the first had been destroyed years before. Through iniquity among the covenant people and their rejection of Jesus as the Messiah, the covenant was broken and the consequences were realized. The final chapters in Matthew include the Savior's prophecies of the events preceding the temple's destruction.

The Triumphal Entry and the Cleansing of the Temple (Matt. 21:1–16)

At the end of Matthew, when Jesus entered Jerusalem to celebrate the final Passover of his life, he was acclaimed by the people as the Messiah. As he entered the city riding a donkey, he fulfilled the prophecy made in Zechariah that "thy King cometh unto thee, meek, and sitting upon an ass" (Matt. 21:5; cf. Zech. 9:9). The people responded with gestures reserved for kings: waving branches and throwing their garments before him, and singing from the messianic Psalm 118, "Hosanna to the Son of David: Blessed is he that cometh in the name of the Lord; Hosanna in the highest" (Matt. 21:9; cf. Ps. 118:26–29).

Jesus next went to the temple, which was crowded by the tens of thousands of pilgrims who had come to Jerusalem to celebrate Passover. There he made a whip and drove out those "that sold and bought in the temple, and overthrew the tables of the money-changers, and the seats of them that sold doves" (Matt. 21:12). He explained his action by quoting scripture: "It is written, My house shall be called the house of prayer; but ye have made it a den of thieves" (Matt. 21:13). The reference to the temple as "the house of prayer" is probably an allusion to Isaiah 56:7, and the phrase "a den of thieves" is a quote from a dramatic sermon delivered by the prophet Jeremiah, who more than six hundred years earlier had come to the temple and had warned the people of their hypocrisy.

Jeremiah saw the temple of Solomon functioning in its splendor, complete with the system of sacrifices and offerings prescribed by the law of Moses. At the same time he saw that the people who came there to worship were morally corrupt: murderers, liars, adulterers, and idolaters (see Jer. 7). He warned them not to trust in the temple to save them and prophesied their imminent destruction if they did not repent. Looking to the past he reminded them of the temple at Shiloh, where the tabernacle was kept in the time of Eli and Samuel. Because of the wickedness of the people, the Lord had allowed Shiloh to be utterly destroyed and the ark of the covenant captured. On this occasion Jeremiah delivered the word of the Lord, "Is this house, which is called by my name, *become a den of robbers in your eyes?* Behold, even I have seen it, saith the Lord." (Jer. 7:11, emphasis added.)

Jesus' quotation of Jeremiah adds much significance to the cleansing. Inherent in Jesus' action was a statement against the hypocrisy of those who claimed to be members of the covenant and fastidiously attended to their ritual obligations at the temple, and yet who did not live according to the ethical standards of the law. The people at the Temple Mount that heard Jesus were familiar with the words of Jeremiah and with the fact that Jeremiah's prophecy of the destruction of the temple had been fulfilled within the prophet's lifetime. Thus Jesus' reference to Jeremiah was an ominous foreshadowing of the destruction of the temple. Just as it had not saved the covenant people in 587 B.C., because of their wickedness, so it would not deliver them from the Romans in A.D. 70.

Following the cleansing of the temple Jesus delivered his final public sermon, warning the people of the "woes" to befall them (see Matt. 23). In each case, the "woes" were pronounced on those who were hypocrites, such as those who made long prayers yet devoured the houses of widows (see Matt. 23:14), those who paid tithing on their minuscule crops of herbs and yet ignored judgment, mercy, and faith (see Matt. 23:23), and those who rigorously attended to the laws of ritual purity and ignored their inner vessels by practicing extortion and excess (see Matt. 23:25–26).

At the end of his sermon Jesus recited a lament over Jerusalem:

> O Jerusalem, Jerusalem, thou that killest the prophets, and stonest them which are sent unto thee, how often would I have

gathered thy children together, even as a hen gathereth her
chickens under her wings, and ye would not!

Behold, your house is left unto you desolate.

For I say unto you, Ye shall not see me henceforth, till ye shall
say, Blessed is he that cometh in the name of the Lord. (Matt.
23:37–39.)

Jesus repeated the psalm which had been sung with such joy
at his triumphal entry into Jerusalem, "Blessed is he that cometh
in the name of the Lord." Because his people had rejected him,
he sadly promised them they would not see him again until his
second coming.

"There Shall Not Be Left Here One Stone upon Another" (Matt. 24)

Following this public sermon the Savior took his disciples
and spoke to them privately. Their first question was what
would happen to the buildings of the temple, to which the Lord
responded, "There shall not be left here one stone upon another,
that shall not be thrown down" (Matt. 24:2).

Jesus and his disciples ascended the Mount of Olives and
viewed the splendid city of Jerusalem and the Temple Mount.
There his disciples questioned him as to the timetable of the
events of destruction he had earlier prophesied. The text in
Matthew 24 was revised by the Prophet Joseph Smith as part of
his inspired translation of the Bible. This particular chapter,
Matthew 24, was of such significance that it is included in the
Pearl of Great Price. The timetable of events is much more clear
in Joseph Smith—Matthew, and we will follow the order of this
version.

The disciples asked the Savior two questions, which he answered in order: "[1] Tell us when shall these things be which
thou hast said concerning the destruction of the temple, and the
Jews; and [2] what is the sign of thy coming, and of the end of
the world, or the destruction of the wicked, which is the end of
the world?" (JS-M 1:4.) Jesus' answer to the first question, which

concerns the destruction of the temple, appears in verses 5–20 of Joseph Smith—Matthew, and his answer to the second question, about the end of the world, appears in verses 21–55. Matthew 24 thus contains prophecies of the conditions which will attend the destruction of the temple in A.D. 70 as well as those preceding the Second Coming.

We are concerned here only with those prophecies about events leading up to the destruction of Jerusalem and the temple, and we will follow the text of Matthew 24 as found in the Pearl of Great Price (i.e., in JS-M). In summary, Jesus prophesied the coming of false Christs (v. 6), that the Apostles would be persecuted and killed (v. 7), that betrayal and hatred would spread (v. 8), that false prophets would deceive many (v. 9), that iniquity would abound (v. 10), the appearance of the abomination of desolation (v. 12), that the Saints would flee to safety (v. 13), and that great tribulations would come upon the Jews in Jerusalem (v. 18).

These prophecies were all fulfilled. The historian Josephus records in his *Antiquities* and *Jewish War* accounts of several false Messiahs and false prophets who came among the Jews and deceived many after the death of Jesus.[1] He also vividly describes the hatred and iniquity among the people living in the Holy Land and the great tribulations that came upon the Jews and Jerusalem.

The followers of Christ were persecuted from the beginning, and many sought their lives. The book of Acts records the deaths of the first martyrs: Stephen (see Acts 7) and James, the brother of the Lord (see Acts 12:2). Before the destruction of the temple in A.D. 70, many of the Apostles had been killed.

From the time of the death of Christ, tensions between the Jews and Rome increased. The Zealots believed in armed insurrection, that just as in the time of the Maccabees, the Lord would intervene in their behalf if they revolted against Rome. This attitude spread throughout the populace, and in A.D. 66 war broke out between the Jews and the Romans. Although the war lasted seven years, for all practical purposes the conflict came to a climax in A.D. 70 when the Romans besieged

Jerusalem and the temple. It was in this period that the prophecies of Jesus were fulfilled: "For then, in those days, shall be great tribulation on the Jews, and upon the inhabitants of Jerusalem, such as was not before sent upon Israel, of God, since the beginning of their kingdom until this time; no, nor ever shall be sent again upon Israel" (JS-M 1:18).

Jesus, in Matthew 24, told his disciples that one of the signs of the destruction of the temple was the "abomination of desolation, spoken of by Daniel the prophet" (Matt. 24:15; JS-M 1:12). Daniel describes the "abomination that maketh desolate" in connection with the pollution of the temple and the cessation of the daily sacrifice (Dan. 11:31). A fulfillment of this prophecy occurred in the desecration and destruction of the temple by the Roman legions in A.D. 70.

The Arch of Titus in Rome was erected to commemorate the Roman victory over Judea in A.D. 70. This close-up relief shows laurel-crowned Roman soldiers parading into Rome with the golden menorah and other plundered treasures. The soldiers also brought the silver trumpets and table of shewbread from the Jerusalem temple.

Eusebius recorded that the members of the Church in Jerusalem were warned by revelation of the impending destruction of Jerusalem. Those who heeded the word of the Lord, and the warning in Matthew 24:16, fled to safety in a town in Peraea called Pella.[2]

The siege lasted for months. Famine became so severe that mothers actually resorted to eating their own children. The Jewish rebels had built up such a strong defense against the superior Roman armies that the Romans resolved to make of Jerusalem and its Jewish defenders a lesson for any in the Roman Empire who might have similar thoughts of rebellion. Those Jews who tried to escape had been crucified before the walls as a lesson to those inside, and the temple provided one of the final defenses.

Josephus was an eyewitness to the siege and destruction, and his description is chilling. He records that Titus, the Roman general, had ordered the preservation of the temple, but on that day in the heat of battle the temple was destroyed:

> One of the soldiers, awaiting no orders and with no horror of so dread a deed, but moved by some supernatural impulse, snatched a brand from the burning timber and, hoisted up by one of his comrades, flung the fiery missile through a low golden door, which gave access on the north side to the chambers surrounding the sanctuary. As the flame shot up, a cry, as poignant as the tragedy, arose from the Jews, who flocked to the rescue, lost to all thought of self-preservation, all husbanding of strength, now that the object of all their past vigilance was vanishing. . . .
>
> While the temple blazed, the victors plundered everything that fell in their way and slaughtered wholesale all who were caught. No pity was shown for age, no reverence for rank; children and greybeards, laity and priests, alike were massacred; every class was pursued and encompassed in the grasp of war, whether suppliants for mercy or offering resistance. The roar of the flames streaming far and wide mingled with the groans of the falling victims; and, owing to the height of the hill and the mass of the burning pile, one would have thought that the whole city was ablaze. And then the din—nothing more deafening or appalling

could be conceived than that. There were the war-cries of the Roman legions sweeping onward in mass, the howls of the rebels encircled by fire and sword, the rush of the people who, cut off above, fled panic-stricken only to fall into the arms of the foe, and their shrieks as they met their fate. . . . You would indeed have thought that the temple-hill was boiling over from its base, being everywhere one mass of flame, but yet that the stream of blood was more copious than the flames and the slain more numerous than the slayers.[3]

Because the children of Israel had once again broken their covenants, the prophecy made in Deuteronomy was again fulfilled, just as in 587 B.C. when Jerusalem was destroyed by the Babylonians: "The Lord shall bring a nation against thee from far, from the end of the earth, as swift as the eagle flieth; a nation whose tongue thou shalt not understand; a nation of fierce countenance, which shall not regard the person of the old, nor shew favour to the young. . . . And he shall besiege thee in all thy gates, until thy high and fenced walls come down, wherein thou trustedst, throughout all thy land." (Deut. 28:49–50, 52.) Jesus' prediction about the temple was fulfilled: "There shall not be left here one stone upon another, that shall not be thrown down" (Matt. 24:2). Of the captives taken from Jerusalem, some were killed, others enslaved, and some sent to fight to the death in the gladiatorial arenas of the Roman Empire. But the Jews were not destroyed. As the Lord had promised his covenant people: "The Lord shall scatter thee among all people, from the one end of the earth even unto the other" (Deut. 28:64). There they await the prophesied gathering.

Titus and his Roman legions encamped around the city of Jerusalem in the
spring of A.D. 70 and erected a siege wall to cut off outside supplies as well as
any possible escape. The siege began at the Feast of Passover, trapping many
Jewish pilgrims from around the world in the city. Josephus reported that there
was well over a million people at the time. The Jews held the Romans at bay
through the spring and into the summer, although the city was ravaged by
famine and disease. In spite of the critical lack of food, the daily sacrifices continued at the temple with the fervent hope that the Lord would intervene. Those
Jews who attempted to escape were immediately crucified in full view of the
city walls. Still the city refused to surrender to the superior Roman forces. The
Romans attacked the walls with battering rams and one by one broke through
Jewish defenses and scaled the walls of the Temple Mount. On the 9th of Ab
(sometime in August), the same day of the year that Solomon's temple was destroyed by the Babylonians in 587 B.C., the temple was set ablaze. The Passover
of A.D. 70 was the last Passover celebrated with the sacrificial lamb, which,
according to the law of Moses, had to be killed at the temple.

EIGHT

The Temple Made Without Hands in Hebrews

*For Christ is not entered into the holy places made
with hands, which are the figures of the true; but into
heaven itself, now to appear in the presence of God for us.*
—Hebrews 9:24

The book of Hebrews may have been originally addressed to
Jewish priests converted to the Church (see Acts 6:7), among
whom some may even have been Essenes (the group who are
identified with the Dead Sea Scrolls). If we cannot be certain
about the specific groups, we may reasonably assume the ad-
dressees were at least Jewish Christians, who were thus familiar
with ancient Old Testament temple worship.

The Saints' Promises in Hebrews

Paul cautions the Hebrew Saints: "Be not slothful, but followers of them who through faith and patience inherit the

◄ The early disciples often met in the temple to pray and preach. Later, Paul
wrote his famous letter to the Hebrew Saints (some of whom may have been
temple priests) in which he explained the earthly tabernacle's role as a pattern
of the heavenly temple.

promises" (Heb. 6:12). These promises relate to what Paul believes was the very purpose of the Mosaic law and temple—a pattern of heavenly things,[1] first, by entering into the rest of the Lord (see Heb. 4:3, 10); second, by being made a high priest forever (see Heb. 7:17); and third, by entering into the holiest (Heb. 10:19). This hope is summarized by Paul in Hebrews 6:

> That by two immutable things [God's promise and God's oath], in which it was impossible for God to lie, we might have a strong consolation, who have fled for refuge to lay hold upon the hope set before us:
> Which hope we have as an anchor of the soul, both sure and stedfast, and which *entereth into that within the veil;*
> Whither the forerunner is for us entered, even Jesus, made an high priest for ever after the order of Melchisedec (Heb. 6:18–20, emphasis added).

Paul understood that the veil of the temple in Jerusalem guarded its innermost sanctuary, the Holy of Holies. This place was entered only once a year and only by the high priest (see Heb. 9:1–5). This priestly function of opening an approach to God for the people yearly is now served by Jesus for all time. Melchizedek is, therefore, a prototype of Christ, the eternal High Priest. (See Heb. 7:23–25.)

The promise is nothing more nor less than entering into the eternal Holy of Holies (the presence of God) through the veil. The one who entered first, our "forerunner," is Jesus—the eternal High Priest. Paul now takes time to show that the earthly tabernacle (temple) is but a shadow—a prototype—of the heavenly temple. The earthly temple, and its furnishings, has its counterparts in heaven. The rich symbolism of the ancient temple is understood in light of the coming of Jesus.

The Heavenly Temple (Heb. 8–9)

Hebrews 8–9 discusses the old covenant (*testament* in the King James Version), the ancient tabernacle, and true worship. To this point (Heb. 8) the epistle has addressed several subjects, and Paul states: "Now of the things which we have spoken this is the sum" (Heb. 8:1). The Greek *kephalaion* can be translated "main point" and, like the King James Version (KJV) word *sum,* indicates we have arrived at the core of the epistle.[2] "We have such an high priest," Paul continues, "who is set on the right hand of the throne of the Majesty in the heavens; a minister of *the sanctuary,* and of *the true tabernacle,* which the Lord pitched, and not man" (Heb. 8:1–2, emphasis added).

Here the author introduces us to the "true tabernacle" not made with hands (see Heb. 9:11).[3] This "true tabernacle" is the heavenly tabernacle, or temple, in which Christ functions as the High Priest, and it is contrasted with the earthly Mosaic tabernacle and the mortal priests who serve there. The mortal priests "serve unto the example and *shadow of heavenly things,* as Moses was admonished of God when he was about to make the tabernacle: for, See, saith he, that *thou make all things according to the pattern* shewed to thee in the mount" (Heb. 8:5, emphasis added).

The Mosaic tabernacle is only a "shadow" or a "pattern" of the heavenly temple (true tabernacle, or temple). In contrast to the earthly tabernacle set up by Moses (see Ex. 25:8–9), the heavenly one was set up by God, or, as the author of Hebrews states, it is the one "which the Lord pitched, and not man" (Heb. 8:2). Obviously, the earthly temple can be destroyed, but the heavenly temple lasts forever. God only visits the earthly counterpart. The Saints come into the earthly temple for a short period, whereas they will dwell in the eternal temple forever; and, finally, the heavenly sanctuary is the home of men and beasts, while the ancient temple had only representations of the cherubim and lions—the walls and veils of the temple.

The idea of a heavenly temple and a heavenly throne was quite common to Jewish thought of the period and was based on several passages found in the Hebrew Bible.

The first reference to the heavenly temple in the Old Testament is in Exodus 15: "Thou shalt bring them in, and plant them in the mountain of thine inheritance, in the place, O Lord, which thou hast made for thee to dwell in, in the Sanctuary, O Lord, which thy hands have established" (Ex. 15:17). Later, we learn:

> And the Lord spake unto Moses, saying,
>
> Speak unto the children of Israel, that they bring me an offering: of every man that giveth it willingly with his heart ye shall take my offering.
>
> And this is the offering which ye shall take of them; gold, and silver, and brass,
>
> And blue, and purple, and scarlet, and fine linen, and goats' hair,
>
> And rams' skins dyed red, and badgers' skins, and shittim wood,
>
> Oil for the light, spices for anointing oil, and for sweet incense,
>
> Onyx stones, and stones to be set in the ephod, and in the breastplate.
>
> And let them make me a sanctuary; that I may dwell among them.
>
> *According to all that I shew thee, after the pattern of the tabernacle,* and the pattern of all the instruments thereof, even so shall ye make it. . . .
>
> *And look that thou make them after their pattern, which was shewed thee in the mount.* (Ex. 25:1–9, 40, emphasis added.)

Apparently, the earthly tabernacle is to replicate the heavenly tent and its furniture and personnel, enabling the children of Israel to participate in heavenly ceremonies. That Moses saw the heavenly temple at the top of Mount Sinai is confirmed by Paul in his letter to the Hebrews, an idea already present in Judaism at the time. Several references to the heavenly temple and throne are found also in the book of Psalms (see Ps. 11:4; 102:19; 150:1). In all likelihood, both Micaiah (see 1 Kgs. 22:19) and Ezekiel (see Ezek. 1, 10) also saw the heavenly sanctuary.

This idea of an earthly copy is not a first-century Platonic philosophical abstraction; for Paul, the sanctuary in heaven is real, and Christ is really present as the High Priest. Paul argues the point to its logical conclusion:

> But now hath [Jesus Christ] obtained a more excellent ministry, by how much also he is the mediator of a better covenant, which was established upon better promises.

For if that first covenant had been faultless, then should no place have been sought for the second.

For finding fault with them, he saith, Behold, the days come, saith the Lord, when I will make a new covenant with the house of Israel and with the house of Judah:

Not according to the covenant that I made with their fathers in the day when I took them by the hand to lead them out of the land of Egypt; because they continued not in my covenant, and I regarded them not, saith the Lord.

For this is the covenant that I will make with the house of Israel after those days, saith the Lord; I will put my laws into their mind, and write them in their hearts: and I will be to them a God, and they shall be to me a people. (Heb. 8:6–10.)

Paul argues that the covenant made with ancient Israel is done away in Christ. He continues:

And they shall not teach every man his neighbour, and every man his brother, saying, Know the Lord: for all shall know me, from the least to the greatest.

For I will be merciful to their unrighteousness, and their sins and their iniquities will I remember no more.

In that he saith, A new covenant, he hath made the first old. Now that which decayeth and waxeth old is ready to vanish away. (Heb. 8:11–13.)

Hebrews 9 continues the author's discussion as he begins to describe the Mosaic tabernacle (cf. Ex. 25–26):

Then verily the first covenant had also ordinances of divine service, and a worldly sanctuary.

For there was a tabernacle made; the first, wherein was the candlestick, and the table, and the shewbread; which is called the sanctuary.

And after the second veil, the tabernacle which is called the Holiest of all;

Which had the golden censer, and the ark of the covenant overlaid round about with gold, wherein was the golden pot that had manna, and Aaron's rod that budded, and the tables of the covenant;

And over it the cherubims of glory shadowing the mercyseat; of which *we cannot now speak particularly.* (Heb. 9:1–5, emphasis added.)

As has been described earlier, the ancient tabernacle was divided into three parts—first, the outer courtyard; second, the Holy Place; and third, the Holy of Holies. The Holy Place and the Holy of Holies were both within the tent proper but were divided by the inner veil. Here, Paul talks about two tabernacles, by which he must be referring to the two divisions within the tent of meeting. Paul refrains from giving us a detailed interpretation of the meaning of the holy instruments, saying, "We cannot now speak particularly," because he had no time for such detailed interpretations and because they were too sacred to discuss. Instead, he concentrates upon just one feature of the early tabernacle—its arrangement in the form of an outer room and an inner room (first tabernacle and second tabernacle).

The discussion of the sanctuary is, in reality, the historical background for the doctrinal point of the letter. He continues the discussion of the place of Christ as the true High Priest:

> Now when these things were thus ordained, the priests went always into the first tabernacle [Holy Place], accomplishing the service of God.
>
> But into the second [Holy of Holies] went the high priest alone once every year, not without blood, which he offered for himself, and for the errors of the people:
>
> The Holy Ghost this signifying, that *the way into the holiest of all was not yet made manifest, while as the first tabernacle was yet standing:*
>
> Which was a figure for the time then present, in which were offered both gifts and sacrifices, that could not make him that did the service perfect, as pertaining to the conscience;
>
> Which stood only in meats and drinks, and divers washings, and carnal ordinances, imposed on them until the time of reformation. (Heb. 9:6–10, emphasis added.)

The way into the inner sanctuary, or, as Paul describes it, "the holiest of all," was not made known at the time when the ancient tabernacle stood. The goal, Paul argues, of temple worship was access to God. The fact that only the high priest could enter that part of the tabernacle that represented the presence of God, which he reminds the Saints was only the earthly counterpart of God's heavenly abode, showed that the goal had not been attained in ancient Israelite temple worship.

Now, let us understand the main point of his analysis:

> But Christ being come an high priest of good things to come, *by a greater and more perfect tabernacle* [heavenly temple], *not made with hands, that is to say, not of this building;*
> Neither by the blood of goats and calves, but by his own blood he entered in once into the holy place [the abode of God], having obtained eternal redemption for us.
> For if the blood of bulls and of goats, and the ashes of an heifer sprinkling the unclean, sanctifieth to the purifying of the flesh:
> How much more shall the blood of Christ, who through the eternal Spirit offered himself without spot to God, purge your conscience from dead works to serve the living God? (Heb. 9: 11–14, emphasis added.)

Christ is "the mediator of the new testament, that by means of death, for the redemption of the transgressions that were under the first testament, they which are called might receive the promise of eternal inheritance" (Heb. 9:15). The eternal inheritance is ultimately access to God in his heavenly temple.

And just as the early tabernacle was purified by blood, so the heavenly temple was purified by blood, "that the patterns of things in the heavens should be purified with these; but the heavenly things themselves with better sacrifices than these. For Christ is not entered into the *holy places made with hands,* which are the figures of the true; but into heaven itself, now to appear in the presence of God for us." (Heb. 9:23–24, emphasis added.)

Paul does not argue that ancient temple worship was useless. It did at least restore external purity because the ordinances were only "patterns" of things to come. He limits the efficacy of the sacrifices performed in the ancient tabernacle to a cleansing from defilements caused by the violation of ritual laws, such as the dietary proscriptions outlined in Leviticus 11 and Numbers 6. Christ's sacrifice, on the other hand, had power to clean the inward person. "How much more shall the blood of Christ, who through the eternal Spirit offered himself without spot to God, *purge your conscience* from dead works to serve the living God?" (Heb. 9:14, emphasis added.) In the end, the sacrifices and ordinances of the ancient tabernacle were not meaningless; they presupposed better sacrifices through Christ.

The risen Christ passed through the heavenly tabernacle into the highest heaven, the abode of God, the counterpart of the inner tabernacle, the Holy of Holies (see Heb. 4:14, 9:24). Paul argues that just as the high priest had the right to enter the Holy of Holies on the Day of Atonement because he bore the blood of the sacrificial animals, so Christ's life offered in sacrifice gives him the right to access the heavenly sanctuary.

For the author of the book of Hebrews, the heavenly sanctuary always existed, but the heavenly sacrifice, not eternally present, entered into the eternal order at a determined point of time. Finally, Paul makes one last allusion to Old Testament temple worship: "So Christ was once offered to bear the sins of many; and unto them that look for him shall he appear the second time without sin unto salvation" (Heb. 9:28). When he returns at the Second Coming, the appearance of Jesus will be like that of the high priest coming out of the Holy of Holies on the Day of Atonement.

The Shadow of Things to Come (Heb. 10)

Paul continues: "For the law having a *shadow* of good things to come, and not the very image of the things, can never with those sacrifices which they offered year by year continually make the comers thereunto perfect" (Heb. 10:1, emphasis added). He continues to argue that if the Mosaic sacrifices were sufficient to wipe away sin, they would not have been repeated (see Heb. 10:2–9). "By the which will we are sanctified through the offering of the body of Jesus Christ *once for all*," he boldly declares (Heb.

10:10, emphasis added). This Jesus has entered into the heavenly temple and sits on the "right hand of God" (Heb. 10:12)—which in all likelihood represents the same imagery found in the book of Revelation where Jesus says that he overcame and sat down on his Father's throne (see Rev. 3:21; cf. Heb. 12:2).

The law, the Mosaic ordinances and commandments, does not lead to salvation—they are only a "shadow of good things to come." This is shown by the fact that it provided for repeated sacrifices. In contrast, Christ's sacrifice is once for all and, therefore, self-validating.

A Journey Back to God (Heb. 11)

Paul gives several examples of faith from the Hebrew scriptures. Abraham, and the men and women who exercised similar faith, "looked for a city which hath foundations, whose builder and maker is God" (Heb. 11:10). The city is the New Jerusalem (see Rev. 21). "These all died in faith," Paul contends, "not having received the promises, but having seen them afar off, and were persuaded of them, and embraced them, and confessed that they were strangers and pilgrims on the earth" (Heb. 11:13). This was a hopeful pilgrimage toward the city of God—that is, into God's presence (see Heb. 13:14).

The Church of the Firstborn and Sacrifices of Praise (Heb. 12–13)

Paul now moves on to discuss those who enter the heavenly temple to worship God and the Son. "For they [the fathers of our flesh] verily for a few days chastened us after their own pleasure; but he for our profit, that we might be partakers of his *holiness*" (Heb. 12:10, emphasis added). The idea of holiness is bound up in ancient temple worship and symbolism. "For I am the Lord your God," Jehovah declared to the Israelites, to whom he had revealed his ordinances for the tabernacle; "ye shall therefore sanctify yourselves, and ye shall be holy; for I am holy" (Lev. 11:44).

The blessing that follows from righteousness and holiness is seeing the face of the Lord (see Heb. 12:14). For "ye are come unto mount Sion, and unto the city of the living God, the heavenly Jerusalem, and to an innumerable company of angels, to the general assembly and church of the firstborn, *which are written in heaven,* and to God the Judge of all, and to the spirits of just men made perfect" (Heb. 12:22–23, emphasis added). The early Saints approached "Mount Zion," not Mount Sinai. This was none other than the capital city of the promised land.

Zechariah had promised that when the Lord became king, Jerusalem would remain aloft upon its site as a city without a curse (see Zech. 14:9–11; cf. Rev. 22:3). In Ezekiel's vision of the restored temple (see Ezek. 40–48), he saw the glory of the Lord entering the temple (see Ezek. 43:6–7, 9). The Saints' names are listed in the book of life, a membership roll of the elect that God keeps (see Rev. 3:5). Paul already addresses the Hebrew Saints as "holy brethren" (Heb. 3:1); now they receive additional honorific titles of "firstborn," those "written in heaven," the "righteous," the "just" ones.

The picture of the "innumerable company" gathered at Jerusalem on the Day of Atonement reminds us of the perfection that takes place because of the atoning blood of Jesus. Entering the eternal Holy of Holies—the very presence of God and his angels as symbolized in the ancient tabernacle and temple by the ark of the covenant with its cherubim—is made possible by a mediator. Jesus, the great High Priest, had acted as the "mediator of the new covenant," bringing as a sin offering his own "blood of sprinkling" (Heb. 12:24).

In this scene, those who had received the benefits of Christ's atonement joined the throng of those Saints gathered at Mount Zion. In this case, Jesus' death is characterized as a priestly sacrifice, similar to that offered in the temple on the Day of Atonement. For that reason, it was necessary for Jesus to have been a "priest-king," not just the Davidic Messiah.

Paul, on one last occasion, uses the symbolism of ancient temple worship to illustrate his point. In Hebrews 13, we find "altar," "tabernacle," "blood," "High Priest," and "sanctify" as metaphors to recall the Saints to their heritage. Instead of sacrifices of beasts and fowls, Paul states: "Let us offer the sacrifice of praise to God continually, that is, the fruit of our lips giving thanks to his name . . . for with such sacrifices God is well pleased" (Heb. 13:15–16). This is reminiscent of the early disciples who returned to Jerusalem after the Lord's resurrection with "great joy: and [who] were continually in the temple, praising and blessing God" (Luke 24:52–53).

In summary, the author of the book of Hebrews discusses the temple and the Mosaic ordinances and interprets them in light of the coming of Christ. Use of typology is evident throughout the text. Typology is, according to one biblical scholar, the "practice in the New Testament and the early church whereby a person or a series of events occurring in the Old Testament is interpreted as a type or foreshadowing of some person (almost invariably Christ) or feature in the Christian dispensation."[4] The heavenly temple—city of God—is the goal of the Saints' earthly pilgrimage and the final refuge and resting place we seek.

According to the book of Hebrews, there was a heavenly temple that was the prototype for the tabernacle and the temple at Jerusalem (see Heb. 8:1–5). Notice the use of the word *figure* in the King James Version here in Hebrews 9:9. The Greek could be translated as "similitude" (see also Heb. 9:12, 24).

Men and women may worship anywhere, especially where the ark is located, such as the temple in Jerusalem. The Lord customarily dwells in his heavenly sanctuary, yet he will hear and respond to the faithful. On special occasions, he visits his people in an earthly representation of the heavenly temple. Possibly Moses saw the true *tabnit,* that is, the heavenly sanctuary. This served as the model for all subsequent replicas, the tabernacle and Solomon's temple. Though man-made temples last for only a period of time, there is no doubt that the heavenly temple still exists. Heavenly temples are built to last forever.

Paul is not the only New Testament writer to discuss the heavenly temple. In fact, a much fuller description of the heavenly temple is found in the Revelation of John, where the backdrop for much of the vision is the heavenly sanctuary.

NINE

The Body-as-Temple and the Temple-Church

Know ye not that ye are the temple of God, and that the Spirit of God dwelleth in you?

—1 Corinthians 3:16

Ye also, as lively [living] stones, are built up a spiritual house.

—1 Peter 2:5

We naturally think of the ancient Mosaic tabernacle, the Jerusalem temple that succeeded it, the temples of the Greco-Roman world, and the heavenly temple when the word *temple* is mentioned in connection with the New Testament. Yet the authors of the New Testament speak of at least two other temples: the body-as-temple and the spiritual temple—the Church.

The Body-as-Temple (1 Cor. 3 and 6)

In writing to the Saints in Corinth, Paul refers to the body-as-temple, an allusion to something Jesus had stated earlier:

◄ Herod's construction in the Temple Mount area used local limestone. Some of the cornerstones weighed forty tons and sometimes more. For Jesus, Peter, and Paul, the impressive physical aspects of the temple became metaphors to teach spiritual truths to the early Saints.

Then answered the Jews and said unto him, What sign shewest thou unto us, seeing that thou doest these things?

Jesus answered and said unto them, Destroy this temple, and in three days I will raise it up.

Then said the Jews, Forty and six years was this temple in building, and wilt thou rear it up in three days?

But he spake of the temple of his body. (John 2:18–21.)

The Corinthian Saints were also temples of God and, as such, were holy. "Know ye not," Paul informs them, "that ye are the temple of God, and that the Spirit of God dwelleth in you?" (1 Cor. 3:16.) Earlier, Paul states, "For we are labourers together with God: ye are God's husbandry, ye are God's building" (1 Cor. 3:9). While Paul's reference here to the members' being the temple of God uses the plural "ye" and therefore has application to the body of the Church, Paul also alludes to the individual member as part of the temple building and therefore as a temple as well.

Just as the earthly sanctuary of God could be defiled by unholy and wicked people (see Isa. 1), so likewise the temple-body could be defiled: "If any man defile the temple of God, him shall God destroy; for the temple of God is holy, which temple ye are" (1 Cor. 3:17).

Defilement of the temple-body comes in many ways. In 1 Corinthians 3, Paul states: "For ye are yet carnal: for whereas there is among you envying, and strife, and divisions, are ye not carnal, and walk as men?" (1 Cor. 3:3.) The divisions among the Saints are, of course, uppermost in his mind.

For while one saith, I am of Paul; and another, I am of Apollos; are ye not carnal?

Who then is Paul, and who is Apollos, but ministers by whom ye believed, even as the Lord gave to every man?

I have planted, Apollos watered; but God gave the increase.

So then neither is he that planteth any thing, neither he that watereth; but God that giveth the increase. (1 Cor. 3:4–7.)

Again, in 1 Corinthians 6, Paul states:

What? know ye not that your body is the temple of the Holy Ghost which is in you, which ye have of God, and ye are not your own?

For ye are bought with a price: therefore glorify God in your body, and in your spirit, which are God's. (1 Cor. 6:19–20.)

Here the precise allusion to the individual body-as-temple is clear.

Jesus, his disciples, and the authors of the New Testament were concerned about the defilement of the temple-body. The temple at Jerusalem and its place in early Christian scripture (our present-day Old Testament) became a vehicle to help the early Saints understand their own divine potential as temples of the Holy Spirit.

The Church as a Temple (1 Pet. 2:5–8)

Peter also speaks of another temple—the spiritual temple, that is, the Church. "Ye also, as lively [living] stones, are built up a spiritual house," writes Peter to the early New Testament Saints,[1]

an holy priesthood, to offer up spiritual sacrifices, acceptable to God by Jesus Christ.

Wherefore also it is contained in the scripture, Behold, I lay in Sion a chief corner stone, elect, precious: and he that believeth on him shall not be confounded [disappointed or ashamed].

Unto you therefore which believe he is precious: but unto them which be disobedient, the stone which the builders disallowed, the same is made the head of the corner,

And a stone of stumbling, and a rock of offence, even to them which stumble at the word, being disobedient: whereunto also they were appointed. (1 Pet. 2:5–8.)[2]

The metaphor of "living stones" suggests another image that had wide currency among the early Saints—the new Church was a spiritual temple, or, as Peter states, "a spiritual house." The Saints were then like the ancient masonry of the temple of

Jesus proclaimed that he was the true chief cornerstone.
The Apostle Peter, while paraphrasing Isaiah, taught
that Jesus was a stone both to the faithful and to those
who rejected the gospel message. To the righteous, he
is "a chief corner stone, elect, precious," but to the
wicked, he is "a stone of stumbling, and a rock of
offence." (1 Pet. 2:6–8.)

Jerusalem, "spiritual living stones." The sacrifices offered in it by
this new community of believers were "spiritual sacrifices." Yet
Christ was the "chief corner stone" in the spiritual temple.

Of course, Peter's words echo those of the Master. Jesus'
promise to build a temple "made without hands" (Mark 14:58)
is in reality a promise to build the Church (see Matt. 16:18).
This saying is well attested in the Gospels (see Mark 15:29 and
parallels; cf. John 2:19; Matt. 16:18).

When the witness in the trial had failed to report the messianic claim correctly, the high priest directed the decisive question to Jesus: "Art thou the Christ, the Son of the Blessed?" (Mark 14:61.) The ancient prophecy of Nathan stands behind this question and explains the messianic implications of the temple saying of Jesus. The son promised to David by Nathan will build a house for God (see 2 Sam. 7:13). This is the "temple made without hands" as promised by Jesus. It will be a "sanctuary of man," as the temple which the hands of God will build. Jesus called this temple his church. That is why he could confirm the confession of Peter, "Thou art the Christ, the Son of the living God" (Matt. 16:16), by the announcement to build his church (see Matt. 16:18).

This church, the new temple made without hands, consists of people who want to return to the Lord. This is revealed by the time span of three days, which most probably points to Hosea 6:2: the one of Israel who repents will be "raised" by God on "the third day." Matthew 16:18 is dependent on Isaiah 28:16; God will lay a sure foundation and a precious cornerstone on Mount Zion. This reminds us of the massive cornerstones of the temple and the prophetic scriptures which refer to this architectural feature (see Zech. 4:7; Ps. 118:22–23; and Peter's own statement in 1 Pet. 2:6).

In speaking of the foundation walls of the temple enclosure, Josephus mentions stones that measured 40 cubits. Elsewhere he speaks of the temple building proper as built of stones 25 or even 45 cubits in length. In fact the stones in the first seven courses in the western wall are very large: many are 15 feet long and 3 to 4 feet high; at the southwestern corner there are stones 40 feet long, 3 feet high, and 8 feet thick, estimated to weigh about 50 tons apiece. Typical of the work of Herod the Great, these are smooth-faced blocks, drafted with margins on their faces, and they are fitted together with such precision that no cement or mortar of any kind is used.

Paul also stated that the Lord's church, or "household of God," has a distinctive architecture: it is "built upon the foundation of the apostles and the prophets, Jesus Christ himself being

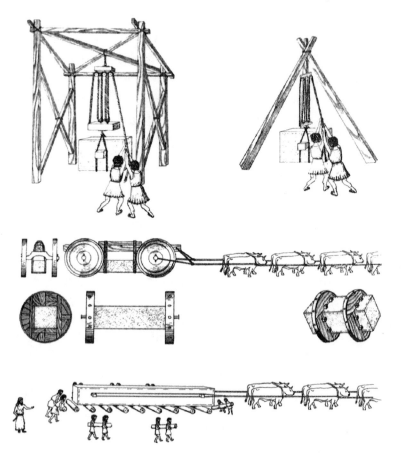

During the building of Herod's temple, some one thousand wagons were used to haul the small and medium stones to the temple site. The largest stones, however, were brought to the temple with a team of oxen. The impressive stones were placed on wooden rollers to ease the movement to the building site some two miles away.

the chief corner stone" (Eph. 2:19–20), which the nation of Israel had rejected as predicted in Isaiah 28 and Psalm 118. Paul's idea of a "household of God . . . fitly framed together" (see Eph. 2:19, 21) is also referred to in 1 Corinthians 12, where Paul argues that the Church is composed of many members who work together harmoniously and thus united become one body (see 1 Cor. 12:12, 21–24).

Paul continues in Ephesians 4: "From whom the whole body

fitly joined together and compacted by that which every joint supplieth, according to the effectual working in the measure of every part, maketh increase of the body unto the edifying of itself in love" (Eph. 4:16). When thus fitly joined together, the household of God grows "unto an holy temple in the Lord" (Eph. 2:21) and becomes the "habitation of God through the Spirit" (Eph. 2:22).

It is of interest that Paul uses this same image of the temple-Church in his discussion of the "falling away," or apostasy, in 2 Thessalonians 2:3–4. The context here clearly indicates that the temple in which Satan, the "man of sin," sits is the Church, now left desolate through the rebellion of faithless members. Just as Jesus had predicted that the physical temple (the Jerusalem temple) would be left desolate because of rebellion (see Matt. 23:38), Paul predicts that the spiritual temple (the temple-Church) would also be left desolate because of apostasy.

A Kingdom of Priests (1 Pet. 2)

Peter's insights into the position of the early Saints has wider implications for redemptive history and is also tied to another important Old Testament precedent.

Peter states categorically that the Saints of God are "a chosen generation, a royal priesthood, an holy nation, a peculiar people" (1 Pet. 2:9). This is an obvious allusion to the words of the Lord to Moses in Exodus 19; and, as is the case with the book of Revelation, Peter has in mind something majestic. Exodus 19 sets the stage for our discussion:

> And Moses went up unto God, and the Lord called unto him out of the mountain, saying, Thus shalt thou say to the house of Jacob, and tell the children of Israel;
>
> Ye have seen what I did unto the Egyptians, and how I bare you on eagles' wings, and brought you unto myself.
>
> Now therefore, if ye will obey my voice indeed, and keep my covenant, then ye shall be *a peculiar treasure* unto me above all people: for all the earth is mine:

And ye shall be unto me *a kingdom of priests,* and *an holy nation.* These are the words which thou shalt speak unto the children of Israel. (Ex. 19:3–6, emphasis added.)

Peter understood the individual transforming power of Christ's atoning sacrifice in the lives of those who accepted him as Lord and Messiah (see, for example, Acts 2:37–40). Yet here in 1 Peter he articulates a much broader application of Old Testament ideology. Peter writes to the early Saints as the high priest might have written to the nation of Israel—the Saints constituted a "nation" just as ancient Israel did. Indeed, the early Saints replaced covenant Israel as God's own people; and yet they were not a totally new society, without a past. They were the continuation of God's work among the nations of the earth. They were "chosen" from among other nations as a special kind of "kingdom," with the divine task of offering a unique "priestly" service to God.

Of course, all these ideas were present in the Hebrew scriptures that Peter and the Saints used during their ministry. The fundamental scriptural text for this vision was, of course, the material found in Exodus. Exodus 19 begins the most majestic section in the whole book of Exodus. The theme of this section is a consummate vision, playing a role of decisive importance in Israel's history and, in fact, in the history of humanity as a whole.

The children of Israel have been liberated by God's "outstretched hand" from Egyptian servitude. The scripture, already noted, states in part: "Now therefore, if ye will obey my voice indeed, and keep my covenant, then ye shall be *a peculiar treasure* unto me above all people: for all the earth is mine: and ye shall be unto me *a kingdom of priests,* and *an holy nation*" (Ex. 19:5–6, emphasis added).

The conclusion of this passage is in reality a proposal—Israel should make a covenant and become a chosen people, "a people of special possession" on condition that they accept certain obligations and responsibilities. All their firstborn were intended to be priests, not just the Levites. In the New Testament setting,

Peter applies this kingdom theme to the new Christians, redeemed by Christ's blood.

A *peculiar* people in both the New Testament Greek and the Old Testament Hebrew does not mean strange and does not refer to a "dress code" or a "peculiar" belief system, but *peculiar* is the King James Version's equivalent to "purchased or preserved" or "special possession or property."[3]

Israel, both ancient and the New Testament Saints to whom Peter wrote, were purchased by blood from slavery. During the days of Pharaoh, the children of Israel were in heavy bondage; and, through the slaying of the firstborn Egyptians, they were liberated. In New Testament times, all humanity were in a state of spiritual bondage. God's Firstborn Son shed his own blood to "purchase" each person from Satan and death, thus allowing God to again create a new nation that would serve him faithfully as their king.

Exodus 19 and 1 Peter 2 are, therefore, remarkable chapters in the Bible. In the first place, they discuss the creation of Israel as a social, political, and economic nation—separate from all other nations. The founding of a "new nation-kingdom" is a singular event. Although this event is even more transcendent than the mere emergence of a new country among the nations of the earth, this was a remarkable beginning. Unlike that of other nations (both in the Old and New Testament worlds), Israel's history did not begin with a mortal king—their king, their lawgiver, and their savior was God Almighty—not a human being.

The promise to those people standing at the foot of Mount Sinai and also to the Saints of the New Testament period and to us of the latter days could be paraphrased as follows: "Now, if you will obey me fully and keep my covenant, then out of all nations you will be my treasured possession. Although the whole earth is mine, you will be for me a kingdom of priests and a holy nation." (See Ex. 19 and 1 Pet. 2.)

The covenant between God and Israel at Mount Sinai and in the New Testament is the outgrowth and extension of the Lord's covenant with Adam and Eve, Enoch, Noah, Abraham and Sarah, Isaac, and Jacob. It is renewed at Sinai and renewed again

Herod's builders solved the problem of how to hoist huge ashlars onto a rising wall. The stones, in fact, did not have to be lifted from below but were actually lowered into place from above. The sixteen-foot-thick walls of the Temple Mount were basically retaining walls, built to retain the high pressure of fill that was dumped between the previous platform and the new Temple Mount wall.

in the New Testament. Participation in the divine blessing is conditioned on obedience added to faith. To be a "chosen people" can mean several things. First, to be a chosen people is to be a "people belonging to God." Second, it is to "choose God"; anyone who chooses God is "chosen."

To be a "kingdom of priests" is to constitute the Lord's kingdom (the people who acknowledge him as their king), and priests are to be wholly consecrated to his service. God's people, both individually and collectively, are to be "set apart" to do his will.

By audible consent, the people promised to obey the terms of the covenant. In Exodus, we read: "And all the people answered together, and said, All that the Lord hath spoken we will do" (Ex. 19:8).

So these ancient passages from the sacred scriptures find fulfillment in the new community of Saints in the first century; but, paradoxically, this new nation was largely composed of men, women, and children who, being Gentiles, had long been regarded by the Jews as automatically disqualified from playing any such role in history. Yet even this paradox could be illuminated from the Hebrew scriptures. Hosea, in his vivid representation of the infidelity of the chosen people, had talked of Israel's being called by God "Not my people," and of the possibility that, when it repented, "Not my people" would once more be called "My people" (see Hosea 1–2). The Gentiles, who had always seemingly been "Not my people," were now, through Christ's at-one-ment, a "chosen generation, a royal priesthood, an holy nation, a peculiar people" (1 Pet. 2:9).

The application is complete—bondage, redemption, and the establishment of a new kingdom, a "kingdom of priests." Like the New Testament Saints, we as new Israel—a purchased people—"should shew forth the praises of him who hath called [us] out of darkness into his marvellous light: which in time past were not a people, but are now the people of God: which had not obtained mercy, but now have obtained mercy" (1 Pet. 2: 9–10).

AND SHOWED ME THAT GREAT CITY,
THE HOLY JERUSALEM, DESCENDING
OUT OF HEAVEN FROM GOD, HAVING
THE GLORY OF GOD.

TEN

Promises to the Faithful in John's Revelation

*Unto him that loved us, and washed us from our sins in his
own blood,*
And hath made us kings and priests unto God and his
Father; to him be glory and dominion for ever and ever.
—Revelation 1:5–6

The New Testament ends with the awe-inspiring "Revelation
of Jesus Christ" given to John on the Isle of Patmos (see Rev. 1:1,
9). In this context, the Greek word *apokalypsis* (revelation) expresses the idea that God, through Jesus Christ, his servant
John, and this book, will reveal mysteries about heaven and
earth—past, present, and future.

Kings and Priests (Rev. 1:5–6)

John introduces his revelation to the seven churches through
a series of statements to remind them of their position—

◄ John saw the heavenly New Jerusalem in vision while imprisoned on the Isle
of Patmos for his testimony of Jesus Christ. If the earthly temple was a sacred
and holy place, the heavenly temple was the place of holiness par excellence.
It was a temple made by God—not human hands—a temple without walls, because God's own presence fills heaven, and the temple is, by definition, a
counterpart of the place where God dwells in all his glory.

statements that John knew they would understand: ". . . and from Jesus Christ, who is the faithful witness, and the first begotten of the dead, and the prince of the kings of the earth. Unto him that loved us, and washed us from our sins in his own blood, and hath made us *kings and priests* unto God and his Father; to him be glory and dominion forever and ever. Amen." (Rev. 1:5–6, emphasis added.)

John is making an allusion to Exodus 19, which states that Israel "shall be unto me a *kingdom of priests,* and an holy nation" (Ex. 19:6, emphasis added; see also Isa. 61:6; Rev. 5:10; 1 Pet. 2:9). John asserts that redemption through Jesus Christ involves liberation from bondage and slavery, which is the point of Exodus 19:6 as well.

In this context, John encourages the early Christian Saints to keep faith in the face of trial and persecution. It is Jesus as the lamb in ancient temple worship and symbolism that stands as the witness of God's covenant and promises, to which John will allude and which John hopes the Saints will recall as they experience the harsh realities of discipleship. In powerful imagery and sometimes moving temple language, John reveals the eternal promises made by the Lord to his faithful followers.

John expresses the dignity the Saints receive through the titles *basileia* (kingdom) and *hiereis* (priests), which were in ancient times the symbols of those who were bearers of political power and sacral authority. These words and other similar phrases found in Revelation may have been intended to be understood only by those who were initiated and familiar with their special meaning.

The purpose for ancient Israel's exodus from Egypt was similar to the "exodus" of the New Testament Saints from spiritual Egypt or Babylon—the sanctification of a people so the kingdom of God could be established on earth. During the Mosaic period, the formation of the kingdom of Israel was brought about by the intervention of God in history as the Lord stretched out his arm against the Egyptians. The children of Israel were brought into the wilderness on "eagles' wings" and came unto the Lord in his desert sanctuary (see Ex. 19:4).

Anciently, the priests represented the people as they approached the Lord in the tabernacle and later in the temple at Jerusalem. The high priest wore two onyx stones on his shoulders with Israel's names as well as the breastplate. The high priest also represented Christ, as we have reviewed in our discussion of the book of Hebrews. As with many symbols, there are often multiple intrepretations. In this case, however, we want to emphasize the role of the priest as representing the children of Israel.

These priests were washed and anointed, wore "holy garments," and were set apart for their sacred duties (see Ex. 28–29). The allusions to Old Testament temple ritual and dress are abundant throughout the book of Revelation.[1]

John uses a wealth of symbols and symbolic language to help the Saints of the first century place their hope and confidence in the Lord. Without any concern for possible misunderstanding on their part, John employs an impressive number of images: colors and numbers; animal figures; stars and the elements of the cosmos; the plant and pastoral world centered around the tree of life; the world of the heavenly temple and angels; and, for our discussion, symbols drawn directly from the religious language of Old Testament temple worship.

The book of Revelation is notoriously difficult to interpret, and it is an impossible book to interpret completely. At first, we may feel that Revelation contains too many symbols and images and that it may almost be impossible to see the forest for the trees. It all appears too complicated and too confusing; we get the impression of entering a real labyrinth. We can feel that once we have entered, we may never get out. For many Latter-day Saints, the mere presence of rich, symbolic imagery dissuades them from entering. This attitude, of course, is a pity, because the Lord is a master at employing rich symbolism to help us understand his plan. Our purpose here is to review those images and symbols in John's Revelation that relate to the ancient temple.

The Revelation of John is full of images relating to the temple. That the author of the book of Revelation is extraordinarily interested with the temple can be shown from a brief vocabulary count; John gives *naos* (temple) no less than a third of its forty-five New Testament uses.[2] *Naos* in Revelation has three applications: the earthly temple, the heavenly temple, and the temple of the world to come.

Jesus as the High Priest (Rev. 1:12–18)

The book of Revelation opens with Christ (the High Priest) walking among the lampstands of the temple, such as those found in Solomon's temple, which signify the divine presence of God in the temple at Jerusalem.

> And I [John] turned to see the voice that spake with me. And being turned, I saw seven golden candlesticks [see Ex. 25:31];
> And in the midst of the seven candlesticks one like unto the Son of man, clothed with a garment down to the foot, and girt about the paps with a golden girdle.
> His head and his hairs were white like wool, as white as snow; and his eyes were as a flame of fire;
> And his feet like unto fine brass, as if they burned in a furnace; and his voice as the sound of many waters. (Rev. 1:12–15.)

The menorah—also referred to as the golden, pure, or holy candlestick (lampstand)—is a prominent feature of the ancient tabernacle and the temple in Jerusalem (see 2 Chr. 13:2; Lev. 24:4; and, in the Apocrypha, Sir. 26:17). Light and lamps, of course, played a significant role in the temple celebration of the Feast of Tabernacles, both in the massive lampstand in the Court of the Women (standing some 86 feet high) and in the dancing with torches before the lampstand. The celebration of this feast lasted seven days and nights. Four huge lampstands, fitted out with wicks made from the worn-out garments of the temple priests, illumined the entire temple area. Under them, the celebrants danced a torch dance to the accompaniment of flute playing, and the Levites chanted the Psalms of Ascent (Ps. 120–34), one each on the fifteen steps that led down from the Court of the Israelites to the Court of the Women. It lasted most of the night for each of the seven days.

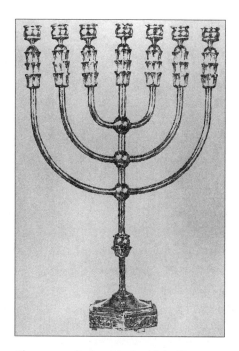

The menorah stood in the Holy Place and represented the light of God as one approached the Holy of Holies—the very abode of God.

But perhaps more in line with John's vision is the inspection of the *menorah* in the temple with which the festive daily offering would begin, the priest trimming those lamps still alight and rekindling those whose flames had gone out. There could hardly be a more apt description of the messages that Christ (the great High Priest) sends to the churches.

John's description of Christ's dress is the same as that in the Greek Old Testament (Septuagint) for the dress of the high priest serving in the ancient tabernacle (see Ex. 28:4; 29:5; and Dan. 10:5).[3] Also, the combination of king and priest is shown in the description of the golden girdle, or clasped belt, worn just under the armpits, which anciently was a symbol of royal office (see, in the Apocrypha, 1 Macc. 10:89; 11:58).

Promises to the Faithful (Rev. 2–3)

The faithful receive several distinctive promises from the Lord. These promises reinforce John's previous assurance: "Blessed is he that readeth, and they that hear the words of this prophecy, and keep those things which are written therein" (Rev. 1:3). Although discussion of this material is usually divided into seven separate sections, we have chosen to divide the promises into fifteen specific assurances. However, because these promises are interconnected, the division is artificial. The promises are described in the second and third chapters of Revelation and are loaded with allusions to temple worship.

The Lord, through John, speaks directly to the Christian Saints in seven locations: Ephesus (see Rev. 2:1–7); Smyrna (see Rev. 2:8–11); Pergamos (see Rev. 2:12–17); Thyatira (see Rev. 2:18–29); Sardis (see Rev. 3:1–6); Philadelphia (see Rev. 3:7–13); and Laodicea (see Rev. 3:14–22). It seems clear that as John addresses the individual message to the various churches, the promises made are for the faithful no matter where they live, as is evidenced by the plural "churches" at the end of each letter (see, for example, Rev. 2:11).

John introduces the promises to those who overcome in a formula, "He that hath an ear, let him hear" (see Rev. 2:7, 11, 17). This formula is a red flag to warn these early Saints and the modern reader to take note of what is being said. The phrase is a significant statement that introduces or follows immediately a promised blessing from the Lord. The phrase also reminds us of certain passages in the Gospels (see Mark 4:9, 23; 17:16; Matt. 11:15; 13:9, 43; Luke 8:8; 14:35).

Although John identifies the Spirit as the speaker here, it is the risen Christ who promises the Saints specific blessings. Along with this specific promise, the Saints are warned to be "faithful unto death," since, for them, the alternatives are not simply death or survival. Through faithfulness, they can have life in the full sense which that word has in the Gospel of John (see John 10:10; 11:25). Even if this involves the ultimate cost of discipleship on earth, the Saints are safe from that "second death," which (as in Rev. 20:14) means the final condemnation passed at the Judgment on those who, because of their unrepentant lives, have lost their claim to share in the life of the age to come. This caution does not overshadow the glorious promises given by Christ to the faithful:

1. "I give to eat of the tree of life" (Rev. 2:7).
2. "I will give thee a crown of life" (Rev. 2:10).
3. "[He] shall not be hurt of the second death" (Rev. 2:11).
4. "To him . . . will I give to eat of the hidden manna" (Rev. 2:17).
5. "[I] will give him a white stone" (Rev. 2:17).
6. "And he shall rule them with a rod of iron" (Rev. 2:27).
7. "And I will give him the morning star" (Rev. 2:28).
8. "The same shall be clothed in white raiment" (Rev. 3:5).
9. "I will not blot out his name out of the book of life" (Rev. 3:5).
10. "I will confess his name before my Father" (Rev. 3:5).
11. "Him . . . will I make a pillar in the temple of my God" (Rev. 3:12).
12. "I will write upon him the name of my God" (Rev. 3:12).
13. "Buy of me gold . . . ; and white raiment . . . ; and anoint thine eyes" (Rev. 3:18).
14. "I will come in to him, and will sup with him" (Rev. 3:20).
15. "To him . . . will I grant to sit with me in my throne" (Rev. 3:21).

Most of the promises to the faithful are prefaced by the phrase "He that overcometh" (see, for example, Rev. 2:7, 11, 17, 26; 3:5, 12, 21). To overcome, or to conquer, is to prevail in battle or in an athletic contest. In John's writings, it symbolizes the goal of prevailing in the battle against the demonic kingdom. Although the Saints have been transferred to the kingdom of God and freed from their sins and the kingdom of Satan (see Rev. 1:5, 9), God's kingdom (the Church) is under attack by Satan and his allies. In this case, it includes the concrete representation of that kingdom, the Roman Empire. But the risen Christ, through the commissioning formulas presented here, promises to those who "conquer" through their endurance and perseverance specific rewards. In this case, these blessings relate to Old Testament temple motifs.

First Promise: The Tree of Life (Rev. 2:7). The first promise given to the early Christian Saints, "I give to eat of the tree of life" (Rev. 2:7), alludes to the tree of life that was in the midst of the Garden of Eden (see Gen. 2:8–9). The Garden of Eden is also a powerful image of promise. In parallel with "the garden of the Lord," Eden appears in Isaiah 51:3 as a metaphor for the renewal of the land of Israel after the Babylonian exile. Again, in Ezekiel 36:35 and Revelation 22:2–3, the garden motif is used to describe the eternal Eden.

There are numerous indications that the ancient temple represented paradise. According to Genesis 2, Eden was the garden of the Lord, a place of trees, rivers, and cherubim. When Adam and Eve were cast out, cherubim and a flaming sword were placed to guard the gate.

The prophet Ezekiel used these same symbols and motifs to portray the temple. In chapter 40 of Ezekiel, the prophet describes a temple built on a high mountain, whose courtyard walls are decorated with palm trees (see Ezek. 40:31). In chapter 41, the interior of the temple is decorated with palm trees and cherubim (see Ezek. 41:17ff), and from the temple flows a river that brings fertility to all the land around it (see Ezek. 47:1–12). In anticipation of the description of the New Jerusalem, which will contain the tree of life (see Rev. 22:2), the Saints are promised salvation within the New Jerusalem or temple of God.

During the first century, when Herod's temple stood, those who entered the Temple Mount and the priests who entered the special rooms of the temple itself were confronted with the lampstands. The Jewish *menorah* ("candlestick" in the King James Version) was a stylized representation of the tree of life. The seven branches of the menorah (seven being a sacred and significant number) were the branches of the tree of life. Thus, the tree of life in the midst of the garden was represented in the midst of the temple; and the promise of partaking of its fruit in a future day was implied.

Jewish tradition anticipated that the tree of life would reappear in the end times, the Messianic Era. Some pseudepigraphical sources (noncanonical writings from 200 B.C. to A.D. 200) state that the eventual role of the Levite priests is to officially remove the threatening sword that will allow the righteous to eat from the tree of life.[4] Joseph Smith also taught that the Levitical priests will offer anew in the temple an "offering in righteousness" (D&C 13:1; 84:31; 124:39).

Second Promise: A Crown of Life (Rev. 2:10). The next promise, "I will give thee a crown of life" (Rev. 2:10), is in reality a promise of a "laurel" (Greek *stephanos*).[5] Here in Revelation 2, it is primarily the award for athletic prowess and skill. The Greeks viewed it as the primary symbol of accomplishment and victory.

The political crown (Greek *diadema*) is used for the first time on the head of the dragon (see Rev. 12:3), then on the beast (see Rev. 13:1), and finally, John sees "many crowns" on the head of the Savior (Rev. 19:12). These are the only times *diadema* appears; every other reference to "crowns" should be read as "laurels."

In the vision, laurels may also refer to both eternal life and/or political victory or the forces of evil (see Rev. 12:3; 13:1; 19:12). As stated earlier in Revelation 1, the Saints could become kings and priests, denoting the two-fold nature of political and sacral authority in the hands of those worthy (see Rev. 1:6). The title of priest-king is not surprising because, in antiquity, politics and religion were closely interrelated.[6] It is exemplified in the vision of the twenty-four elders:

> And immediately I was in the spirit: and, behold, a throne was set in heaven, and one sat on the throne.
>
> And he that sat was to look upon like a jasper and a sardine stone: and there was a rainbow round about the throne, in sight like unto an emerald.

And round about the throne were four and twenty seats: and upon the seats I saw four and twenty elders sitting, clothed in white raiment; and they had on their heads *crowns of gold.* (Rev. 4:2–4, emphasis added.)

The political authority as kings would give them "power over the nations" (Rev. 2:26). Along with the references to crowns, emphasizing the kingship of the Saints under Christ, Revelation contains the Lord's statement: "To him that overcometh will I grant to sit with me in my throne, even as I also overcame, and am set down with my Father in his throne" (Rev. 3:21). The hope of the Saints was that the God of Israel would again intervene in history and that the "kingdoms of this world [would] become the kingdoms of [the] Lord, and of his Christ; and he shall reign for ever and ever" (Rev. 11:15).

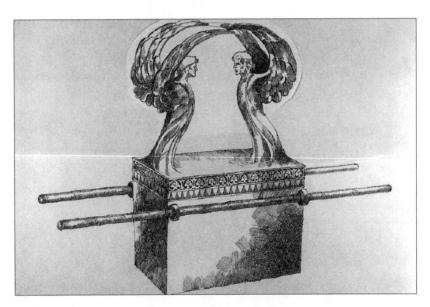

The ark of the covenant in the ancient tabernacle represented the heavenly throne of God, who sat between the cherubim. This throne was also known as the mercy seat, which was daubed with blood on the Day of Atonement, signifying that God covered the sins of Israel. The throne of God plays a significant role in John's vision, not only as the seat of power but also as a sign of overcoming the world through the blood of the Lamb.

The promised crown may also refer to a Jewish tradition. According to a rabbinic source, when the Israelites accepted the covenant at Sinai and were made a "kingdom of priests," they received two crowns. The crowns were snatched away by "destroying angels" when the children of Israel removed them. In the Messianic Age, the tradition states, the Lord would restore the crowns to those faithful.[7] This promise alludes to Isaiah 35: "And the ransomed of the Lord shall return, and come to Zion with songs and everlasting joy upon their heads: they shall obtain joy and gladness, and sorrow and sighing shall flee away" (Isa. 35:10, emphasis added).

Throughout the vision, the (golden) crown is worn by those of a high rank, by the twenty-four elders (see Rev. 4:4, 10), also by the Son of Man (see Rev. 14:14), who, however, in Revelation 19 wears the real headdress of the ruler—the *diadema* (see Rev. 19:14)—which may indicate his special role as "King of kings" (Rev. 17:14) and "King of saints" (Rev. 15:3).

Third Promise: Not Hurt by Second Death (Rev. 2:11). The Spirit spoke to the early Christian Saints at Ephesus: "He that overcometh shall not be hurt of the second death" (Rev. 2:11). This phrase, "second death," occurs four times in Revelation but does not appear elsewhere in the New Testament. Later, John testifies, "Blessed and holy is he that hath part in the first resurrection: on such the second death hath no power, but they shall be priests of God and of Christ, and shall reign with him a thousand years" (Rev. 20:6).

John likens the second death to being cast into the lake of fire, into which the devil, the beast, the false prophet, death, and hell are thrown (see Rev. 20:14; 21:8). An Aramaic translation of Isaiah (known as a *Targum*—a translation of the Hebrew text into the vernacular language used by Jews in Roman Palestine during the first century) states, "You shall leave your name to my chosen for an oath, and the Lord God will slay you with the second death; but his servants, the righteous, he will call by a different name" (*Targum* Isa. 65:15).[8] The relationship to a name will be discussed below.

Fourth Promise: The Hidden Manna (Rev. 2:17). The promise to those faithful at Pergamos, the very seat of Satan (see Rev. 2:13), refers to the food supplied by God to the people of Israel in the wilderness (see Ex. 16). "To him that overcometh will I give to eat of the hidden manna," which naturally we assume will also be the food of the elect in heaven (Rev. 2:17). Manna is also called, poetically, "corn of the heaven" (Ps. 78:24). The hidden manna is in contrast to the unclean food of the Balaamites (see Rev. 2:14). A common belief during this period of Jewish history was that the gift of manna would be repeated in the Messianic Age (see, in the Apocrypha, 2 Baruch 29:8, for example; cf. John 6:47–51).

Fifth Promise: A White Stone (Rev. 2:17). Associated with the promise of hidden manna is, "[I] will give him a white stone, and in the stone a new name written, which no man knoweth saving he that receiveth it" (Rev. 2:17). White (like "light" and "brightness") is a frequent symbol for good in John's vision (see Rev. 1:14; 3:5; 7:9; 19:14; 20:11). This enigmatic stone, however, has been difficult for scholars to explain. The Latter-day Saints have Joseph Smith's statement to help place this promise in context. Of course, it is a temple context.

> Then the white stone mentioned in Revelation 2:17, will become a Urim and Thummim to each individual who receives one, whereby things pertaining to a higher order of kingdoms will be made known;
> And a white stone is given to each of those who come into the celestial kingdom, whereon is a new name written, which no man knoweth save he that receiveth it. The new name is the key word. (D&C 130:10–11.)

In all likelihood, the white stone in John's Revelation is also known as the "Urim and Thummim," as discussed in several biblical passages (see Ex. 28:30; 1 Sam. 28:6). The Urim and Thummim may also have had a function in the first-century Church and would thus be recognizable to the early Saints.

The biblical Urim and Thummim were sacred instruments by which the mind and will of the Lord in relation to particular situations were ascertained. The prophet or priest initiated the communication as he laid before the Lord a question couched in precise words and expected an answer, or decision, in like manner, usually in the form of "yes" or "no." An example of such usage is found in 1 Samual 23:9–12 and 30:7–8.

The Lord has already promised the Saints he would make them "kings and priests," but now he may be expanding their roles to include that of "prophets," as the Urim and Thummim were used primarily by the ancient prophets of Israel. Thus, the honorific titles of prophet, priest, and king are bestowed upon the faithful (see Rev. 19:10 for additional comments regarding the spirit of prophecy).

In the New Testament period, casting lots was a means of ascertaining the Lord's will (see Acts 1:26). The story of the choosing of Matthias to replace the fallen Judas may reflect the Old Testament use of the Urim and Thummim because, in some cases, the term *lot* is used in the Greek Old Testament where it could have been the Urim and Thummim. The principle remains the same: the Lord determines the outcome.

In the book of Revelation, the Saints receive a promise from the Lord that all of them will have their own Urim and Thummim with a new name written on it. This account may also be an allusion to Isaiah 62: "And the Gentiles shall see thy righteousness, and all kings thy glory: and thou shalt be called by a new name, which the mouth of the Lord shall name. Thou shalt also be a crown of glory in the hand of the Lord, and a royal diadem in the hand of thy God." (Isa. 62:2–3.) Throughout the Bible, names are full of meaning.

In ancient Israel, the name of a person, place, or thing was somehow connected to and descriptive of its status. This naming process is reflected in those stories where an individual's name is changed in recognition of a changed status. Examples include Jacob's name being changed to Israel after his encounter with a divine being (see Gen. 32:22–32); Abram's name being changed to Abraham and Sarai's to Sarah after the institution of the covenant (see Gen. 17:1–8); Simon's name being changed to Cephas by Jesus in the context of receiving the keys of the kingdom (see Matt. 16:17–18); and Saul's name being changed to Paul as he began his missionary activities (see Acts 13:9, 13).

In other instances, a name change or the assumption of an additional name by individuals occurred when they assumed the role of king in Israel, as when Mattaniah was renamed Zedekiah (see 2 Kgs. 24:17). Through faithfulness, the early Christian Saints were promised a "new name" that reflects a new position or status with Christ in the world to come.

Sixth Promise: A Rod of Iron (Rev. 2:27). "And he that overcometh, and keepeth my works unto the end, to him will I give power over the nations: and he shall rule them with a rod of iron; as the vessels of a potter shall they be broken to shivers: even as I received of my Father" (Rev. 2:26–27). The "rod of iron" can be translated as "iron scepter" (see New International Version, Rev. 2:27). This promise makes more sense in light of Psalm 2:

> Why do the heathen rage, and the people imagine a vain thing?
> The kings of the earth set themselves, and the rulers take counsel together, against the Lord, and against his anointed, saying,
> Let us break their bands asunder, and cast away their cords from us. . . .
> Yet have I set my king upon my holy hill of Zion.
> I will declare the decree: the Lord hath said unto me, Thou art my Son; this day have I begotten thee. . . .
> Thou shalt break them with a *rod of iron;* thou shalt dash them in pieces like a potter's vessel. (Ps. 2:1–3, 6–7, 9, emphasis added.)

The scepter is a tangible symbol of authority received from Christ's Father. This promise of power and authority is shared with Christ and legitimized by both the Father and the Son to the faithful. The faithful Saints are promised a blessing like that mentioned in Psalm 2, which also is a messianic prophecy that had its ultimate fulfillment in the life of Jesus. Nevertheless, the Saints receive the same promises—including being the "anointed" of the Lord; being set as a king in the temple, the holy hill of Zion being the symbolic representation; being "adopted" into the family of God, thus becoming his "son"; and, finally, receiving a royal scepter.

John again distinguishes the rule of God from that of man when John utilizes a scepter instead of a sword (which we might have expected). This use demonstrates the difference between the kingdom of God and the kingdom of the devil (Rome as the concrete example in the latter case). Because the sword is the symbol of Roman authority, the scepter is the symbol of the shepherd who leads his people. In Greek, *poimainein,* which is generally translated "to rule," can also be translated "to shepherd."[9] Thus, Christ's rule is like that of a shepherd, not a tyrant.

Seventh Promise: The Morning Star (Rev. 2:28). Another promise to the faithful connected with the scepter is, "And I will give him the morning star" (Rev. 2:28). The identity of the morning star is revealed only at the end of the book (see Rev. 22:16; see also 2 Pet. 1:19), and it is Jesus himself. It may further imply that one who receives the "morning star" is made like the morning star: the faithful will be glorified (cf. Dan 12:3; Matt. 13:43; 1 Cor. 15:40–44).

Eighth Promise: White Raiment (Rev. 3:4–5). Those who had not "defiled their garments . . . shall walk with me in white . . . [and] shall be clothed in white raiment" (Rev. 3:4–5). Defiling one's garments, literally soiling the garments, is a general symbol of sinfulness (see Zech. 3:3–5). On the other hand, remaining clean signifies the continued blessed state of the righteous and is a description of the redeemed of God (see Rev. 3:18; 6:11; 7:9, 13; cf. 4:4; 19:14). White also represents victory as well as purity.

Anciently, only the tribe of Levi was given "holy garments" (see Ex. 28:1–3); but now, through Christ, all are made "priests" (Rev. 1:6)—as predicted in Exodus 19, "a kingdom of priests" (Ex. 19:6).

In the book of Revelation, the righteous who suffered under Roman rule, which was exploitative, destructive, and dehumanizing, would eventually come "out of great tribulation" to "have washed their robes, and made them white in the blood of the Lamb" (Rev. 7:14). This is reminiscent of the other biblical paradox, "Come now, and let us reason together, saith the Lord: though your sins be as scarlet, they shall be as white as snow; though they be red like crimson, they shall be as wool" (Isa. 1:18). That which seems impossible to mankind is not to God. The Lord added another allusion to the temple clothing of the priests: "And white robes were given unto every one of them; and it was said unto them, that they should rest yet for a little season, until their fellowservants also and their brethren, that should be killed as they were, should be fulfilled" (Rev. 6:11).

The dominant symbolic meaning of the color white, as already mentioned, during the early empire followed that of the Republic: victory. The Septuagint uses it in this sense, but as with other symbols, John utilizes both the Jewish and non-Jewish aspects of the symbol. The white, therefore, complements and highlights the crown (laurel), both symbols of absolute victory gained through perseverance and the blood of the Lamb which made the garments white (purity *and* victory).

Ninth Promise: Book of Life (Rev. 3:5). "I will not blot out his name out of the book of life" (Rev. 3:5). This symbolic phrase, "book of life," is similar to other terms the scripture associates with the phrase "of life": tree, bread, water, fountain, river, path, word, and crown. In each case, God is the source and giver of this life, which is more than the years we know between birth and death.

A divine ledger is first mentioned in Exodus 32:32–33. It was, in effect, a listing of all the citizens of the new kingdom. To have one's name erased from this book indicates loss of citizenship (see Rev. 13:8; 17:8; 20:12, 15; 21:27; Philip. 4:3). The book also represents the roster of names of those who will survive the manifestation of God's wrath at the end of time (see Mal. 3:16 to 4:3). John's vision also describes such a book:

And I saw the dead, small and great, stand before God; and the books were opened: and another book was opened, which is the book of life: and the dead were judged out of those things where were written in the books, according to their works.

And the sea gave up the dead which were in it; and death and hell delivered up the dead which were in them: and they were judged every man according to their works.

And death and hell were cast into the lake of fire. This is the second death.

And whosoever was not found written in the book of life was cast into the lake of fire. (Rev. 20:12–15.)

The list of those who will enter the New Jerusalem is also located in a similar book (see Rev. 21:27).

Tenth Promise: Confess His Name (Rev. 3:5). The Lord says of him whose name is found in the book of life, "But I will confess his name before my Father, and before his angels" (Rev. 3:5). Even then, having one's name on the roll meant nothing unless Jesus acknowledged it. This is a clear allusion to another saying of Jesus in Matthew: "Whosoever therefore shall confess me before men, him will I confess also before my Father which is in heaven. But whosoever shall deny me before men, him will I also deny before my Father which is in heaven." (Matt. 10:32–33.)

Eleventh Promise: Pillar in the Temple (Rev. 3:12). Another blessing for faithfulness expressed in Old Testament temple language is, "Him that overcometh will I make a pillar in the temple of my God, and he shall go no more out" (Rev. 3:12). The righteous, according to Hebrew scripture, have always "loved the habitation of [the Lord's] house, and the place where [his] honour dwelleth" (Ps. 26:8). The Psalmist recorded, "One thing have I desired of the Lord, that will I seek after; that I may dwell in the house of the Lord all the days of my life" (Ps. 27:4). Anciently, that was possible only for a select few; but, as John understood, through Christ all "that overcometh will I make a pillar in the temple of my God, and he shall go no more out" (Rev. 3:12).

This promise may allude to a promise found in Exodus 15: "Thou shalt bring them in, and *plant them in the mountain of thine inheritance,* in the place, O Lord, which thou hast made for thee to dwell in, in the Sanctuary, O Lord, which thy hands have established" (Ex. 15:17, emphasis added).

Paul's reference in Galatians to James, Cephas, and John as "pillars" may also suggest a connection between the faithful and the temple (see Gal. 2:9). The word is most frequently used in the Greek Old Testament known as the Septuagint, or LXX, in reference to the supports of the tabernacle and pillars of the temple (see 1 Kgs. 7:15–22; 2 Chr. 3:15–17), named Jachin and Boaz, which evidently had a covenant significance (see 2 Kgs. 23:3; 2 Chr. 34:31). Likely, the reference in Galatians is to the three as "pillars in the temple," as John reveals.

Twelfth Promise: The Name of God (Rev. 3:12). Along with the promise that the faithful person will become a "pillar" in the temple, Jesus states: "And I will write upon him the name of my God, . . . and I will write upon him my new name" (Rev. 3:12). The description of these individuals is also recorded in Revelation 22: "And there shall be no more curse: but the throne of God and the Lamb shall be in it; and his servants shall serve him: and they shall see his face; and *his name shall be in their foreheads*" (Rev. 22:3–4, emphasis added).

In ancient times, criminals were banished from the presence of the king (see 2 Sam. 14:24); here, the faithful are promised they will see the face of the Lord. Associated with worshiping God and seeing his face is the notion that God's name will be on the foreheads of the redeemed as a sign of protection, deliverance, and possession (see also Rev. 7:3; 9:4; 14:1).

We may see a reference to the ancient Jewish practice of binding God's name to the forehead in daily prayers through the use of the *tefillin.*[10] At the time of Jesus, it was customary for Jewish males to attach leather thongs to the upper arm and to the forehead. Fastened to the straps were the *tefillin* (Greek "guardians" or phylacteries in the New Testament), which normally were rectangular in shape and contained tiny slips of parchment inscribed with short portions of the Bible—including the *Shema,* which states, in part, "Hear, O Israel: The Lord our God is one Lord" (see Deut. 6:4–9). This custom was based on the commandment of the Lord to remember him (see Deut. 6:6, 8), and the archaeological evidence in Jewish Palestine suggests a widespread use of these religious symbols.

The *tefillah* (the single box) worn on the forehead had the letter *shin* on each side, while the strap holding it was tied in a knot in the shape of the letter *daleth.* Also, the *tefillah* worn on the arm was tied on with a knot in the shape of the letter *yod.* Together these letters form the divine name *Shaddai,* a word often translated "Almighty." This combination of letters may have signified that the bearer belonged to the Lord. A close connection between the use of the symbolic *tefillin* and the mark of the Lord's name mentioned in Revelation seems reasonable. Yet, the allusion in Revelation appears to refer more concretely to the ceremonial crown of the high priest (in fact, the use of the *tefillin* may also have this as its basis and may represent the same idea).

The allusion to the mitre of the high priest, who had the name of God written on the gold band of his cap, seems appropriate:

> And thou shalt make a plate of pure gold, and grave upon it, like the engravings of a signet, HOLINESS TO THE LORD.
> And thou shalt put it on a blue lace, that it may be upon the mitre [turban or cap]; upon the forefront of the mitre it shall be.
> And it shall be upon Aaron's forehead, that Aaron may bear [atone for] the iniquity of the holy things, which the children of Israel shall hallow in all their holy gifts; and it shall be always upon his forehead, that they may be accepted before the Lord. (Ex. 28:36–38.)[11]

John's allusion to having God's name written on the foreheads of the faithful thus implies that all the righteous now enjoy the blessings that the priests did. They bear the name of God and stand in his presence, a privilege once denied to all save the high priest on the Day of Atonement.

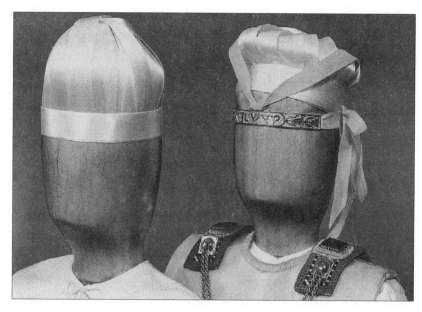

The priest of the ancient temple wore a cap and special robe. The high priest's clothing had added features, including a special gold band with the phrase "Holiness to the Lord" inscribed thereon. John uses this imagery to depict the status of the early Christian Saints who belonged to the Lord.

It also relates to the allusion mentioned in Ezekiel 9, in which an angel clothed in linen is instructed to go through the city of Jerusalem and put God's mark upon the foreheads of the faithful (see Ezek. 9:4). In the verses that follow we learn that destroyers will come and pass through the city after the angel and smite and slay anyone without the mark. Ezekiel's vision is nothing less than a time of ultimate judgment commanded by the Lord. Here the mark is of protective significance.

More important, however, having God's name or mark on their foreheads designates them as God's own possession—as is the case in Exodus 19:6 and 1 Peter 2:9, where the idea is presented that the righteous are God's own special treasure or possession (see footnotes keyed to these verses in the LDS edition for the Hebrew and Greek meanings of *peculiar*). Thus the special blessing of having God's name marked on the forehead refers to possession, protection, and deliverance.

Thirteenth Promise: Gold, White Raiment, and Ointment (Rev. 3:18). To the Saints in Laodicea, a city famous for its wealth, wool, and medical school, the Lord promises: "I counsel thee to buy of me gold tried in the fire, that thou mayest be rich; and white raiment, that thou mayest be clothed, and that the shame of thy nakedness do not appear; and anoint thine eyes with eyesalve [ointment], that thou mayest see" (Rev. 3:18).

The "gold tried in the fire" is an allusion to the Old Testament metaphor of the testing of precious metals. As it relates to ancient temple worship, it is an important concept. The experience of being in the presence of the Lord evokes in mortals a sense of impurity and sin (see Ps. 90; Isa. 6). Anciently, the gate ceremony at the temple (see Ps. 24) was intended to prevent anyone from approaching the Lord in the temple unworthily, for then, far from receiving the blessings of the Lord promised to those who enter his house, an unworthy person would be struck with a curse.

The Psalmist states, "The Lord is in his holy temple, the Lord's throne is in heaven: his eyes behold, *his eyelids try,* the children of men. *The Lord trieth [tests] the righteous.*" (Ps. 11:4–5, emphasis added.) The Hebrew word employed in this text actually denotes the purifying of metals—smelting. The process serves the purpose not only of testing but also of refining and working metal. The testing represents the purification necessary to approach God in the holy sanctuary. The experience of God and Christ as consuming fire can purge Saints from all their dross.

The smelting process also includes the use of water. Fire and water are among the most important elements of ritual purification in the Old Testament (see Num. 31:23; cf. Ps. 26:6). Again, the Psalmist states: "For thou, O God, has proved us: thou hast tried us, as silver is tried" (Ps. 66:10). This, of course, is the context of this promise in Revelation 3:18.

The white raiment may be contrasted with the black wool for which Laodicea was renowned (these woollen cloaks were called *laodicia*). Yet the clothing of the priests in the Jerusalem temple and the congregation in the heavenly temple may also be implied here as John has already done earlier (see Rev. 3:4–5). A tradition among the Samaritans that was also part of their liturgy for the eve of the Day of Atonement was to note that the Gentiles (the ungodly) will be raised naked, whereas the righteous will rise again with the clothes in which they were buried.[12]

The Lord draws a similar parallel between wickedness and nakedness when he says, "Because thou sayest, I am rich, and increased with goods, and have need of nothing; and knowest not that thou art wretched, and miserable, and poor, and blind, and naked" (Rev. 3:17). In Judaism, from the first century onward, the dead were buried in white linen clothes with the hope of being raised in white raiment. Isaiah spoke of the Messianic Age: "I will greatly rejoice in the Lord, my soul shall be joyful in my God; for he hath clothed me with the garments of salvation, he hath covered me with the robe of righteousness" (Isa. 61:10).

White was predominantly reserved for priestly vestments in the Old Testament and was the basic color of the ancient temple generally. In fact, the symbolism of color in ancient Israel was predominantly white, completely excluding black. By the first century, Rabbinic Judaism, and Jews in general, displayed a great fondness for white clothes. They were worn on joyous occasions or feast days and were regarded as a mark of distinction. White also denoted purity, and so even white linen clothes were specially washed. In the New Testament, including the book of Revelation, white is mentioned almost always in eschatological and apocalyptic contexts or as the heavenly color.

The whiteness of the garment promised by the Lord is of a heavenly color (see Rev. 1:14; 2:17; 6:2; 14:14; 19:11, 14; 20:11). The book of Revelation designation of white clothing demonstrates membership in the heavenly congregation. It may also signify the gift of eternal life in fellowship with the exalted Christ before the throne of God (see Rev. 3:4; 7:15ff). In this sense, whiteness signifies that they who are changed are made like him (cf. 1 Cor. 15:51; Philip. 3:21; 1 John 3:32). Whiteness is so strongly emphasized that the white clothes are a gift—they cannot be personal clothes but are a gift from Christ.

The promise of white is shown by most of the passages in the New Testament by the Greek word *leukos,* found in Revelation.[13] This color is effectively contrasted in Revelation 19 with the obstrusive and bloody finery of the great harlot (see Rev. 17:4; 18:16). "And to her [the Lamb's wife, that is, the faithful] was granted that she should be arrayed in fine linen, clean and white: for the fine linen is the righteousness of saints" (Rev. 19:8).

Laodicea had a famous medical school near Men-Karou, where Phrygian powdered stone (combined with oil) was used for eye salve. The combination of white clothing and anointing is also alluded to in Ecclesiastes. "Let thy garments be always white; and let thy head lack no ointment" (Eccl. 9:8). The Lord declared through Ezekiel, referring to his birth: "Then washed I thee with water; yea, I thoroughly washed away thy blood from thee, and I anointed thee with oil. I clothed thee also with broidered work, . . . and I girded thee about with fine linen." (Ezek. 16:9–10.)

Naturally, when we think of purifying by water and fire, anointing, and clothing in sacred clothing, the story of Aaron in the book of Exodus looms before us:

> And Aaron and his sons thou shalt bring unto the door of the tabernacle of the congregation, and shalt wash them with water.
>
> And thou shalt take the garments, and put upon Aaron the coat [tunic], and the robe of the ephod, and the ephod, and the breastplate, and gird him with the curious [or skillfully woven] girdle of the ephod:
>
> And thou shalt put the mitre [turban] upon his head, and put the holy crown upon the mitre.
>
> Then shalt thou take the anointing oil, and pour it upon his head, and anoint him. (Ex. 29:4–7.)

Moses was then commanded to do the same to Aaron's sons, except they were simply clothed in a white robe, an apron or sash, and the turban or cap, instead of the special clothing of the high priest.

To anoint—that is, to touch or smear a person with oil—is

associated with holiness in ancient Israel in several important ways. Objects are anointed as a sign of their dedication to the Lord, such as Jacob's pillar at Bethel (see Gen. 28:18). The book of Exodus itself prescribes the anointing of the tabernacle and its furnishing, especially the altar (see Ex. 29:36; 30:22–29; 40:9–11). With the institution of kingship in Israel, anointing the king rather than coronation was the ceremony in which the king took office under the hand of the prophet (see 1 Kgs. 1:39). And, as has already been discussed, the anointing of the priests set them apart for God's service in the temple. Several prophets were also anointed in their callings (see 1 Kgs. 19:6; Ps. 105:15).

As anointing symbolized the special responsibility and relationship to God of king, priest, and prophet, so the language might be used of anyone thought to stand in a similar position. In fact, the Jews expected one so anointed to come as their promised redeemer. The Hebrew word *Mashiyach* means "anointed." The English equivalent, *Messiah,* derives from the verb *mashah,* meaning "to anoint."[14] The Greek New Testament equivalent is *christo,* or Christ in the King James Version.

Closely related to the idea of washing, anointing, and robing is that of crowning with the blessings of salvation, as the early Saints in Laodicea have been told.

Fourteenth Promise: The Messianic Feast (Rev. 3:20). The Risen One states to the faithful, "Behold, I stand at the door, and knock: if any hear my voice, and open the door, I will come in to him, and will sup with him, and he with me" (Rev. 3:20). The marriage feast spoken of by Jesus when he was ministering among the people (see Mark 13; Matt. 24; and Luke 12) is related to this particular promise.

The heavenly feast promised here is already anticipated by the Saints through the administration of the sacrament, a meal which not only reminds us of past events but also points us forward to another meal in the Messianic Age (see, for example, D&C 27:4–14).

The Old Testament temple imagery is clear. The ancient priest entered the tabernacle to partake of the shewbread—liter-

The table of shewbread stood in the Holy Place. It represented, on one level, the great messianic banquet promised to the faithful. Dining with the Lord, as during the Last Supper, is a covenantal experience. The twelve loaves represented the tribes of Israel.

ally, the bread of the presence. It consisted of twelve loaves of unleavened bread. Its location just on the north side in front of the veil of the temple demonstrates the proximity of the Lord, and that proximity renders the bread holy. It also symbolizes the covenant between the Lord and his people Israel. When the high priest disposed of the bread each week, he gave it to the priests, who in turn ate the bread within the temple complex.[15]

Christ promises the faithful Saints, who are priests unto God, that they will be with him in the heavenly temple near the throne of God and will partake of the heavenly banquet, like the priests of old. Later in the vision, John gives this description:

> Let us be glad and rejoice, and give honour to him: for the marriage of the Lamb is come, and his wife hath made herself ready.
>
> And to her was granted that she should be arrayed in fine linen, clean and white: for the fine linen is the righteousness of saints.

And he saith unto me, Write, Blessed are they which are called unto the marriage supper of the Lamb. And he saith unto me, These are the true sayings of God. (Rev. 19:7–9.)

This vision of the messianic banquet and the earlier promise of partaking of the heavenly manna (see Rev. 2:17) are to be contrasted with the invitation to the "supper of the great God," where the word *flesh* is stressed five times (see Rev. 19:17–18).

Ancient meal customs were regarded in different ways than is common in the modern Western world. To the ancients, sharing a meal was imbued with ritual meaning and often signified the most solemn and intimate of social relationships. The primary social event for these people was eating a meal together. It created a tie or bond among the participants, which, in turn, created an obligation toward each other. The idea of social bonding at the meal was especially symbolized with the specific action of sharing food together. For those Saints living in the first century, this imagery had a powerful effect regarding the covenant nature of their relationship with the risen Christ.

Fifteenth Promise: A Throne (Rev. 3:21). The fifteenth and final promise noted in this section is, "To him that overcometh will I grant to sit with me in my throne, even as I also overcame, and am set down with my Father in his throne" (Rev. 3:21). The last promise ends with the customary "He that hath an ear, let him hear what the Spirit saith unto the churches" (Rev. 3:22).

Those who overcome will sit with the Lord on his throne as Jesus also conquered and sat down with the Father on his throne. The throne is a symbol of God's authority (occurring more than forty times in Revelation alone). The enthronement of Jesus alongside God is a striking image of their equality (see Rev. 1:14, 15, 17). In the Messianic Age (the Millennium) those who recognize Christ's authority will share God's rule over the new creation (see Rev. 2:26–27; 5:10; 22:5). Sharing the throne of glory is a powerful image, and it prepares us for a smooth transition into Revelation 4, the vision of the heavenly Holy of Holies, where the throne of God is located.

The Throne of God and the Twenty-four Elders (Rev. 4–5)

Revelation 4 and 5 are a composite of many elements, but among these are the elements from ancient temple worship and the celebration of certain holy festivals that centered on the temple. Many of these components center on the throne of God (see Rev. 4:2–3) and the figures of the twenty-four elders (see Rev. 4:4–6). John recalls: "After this I looked, and, behold, a door was opened in heaven: and the first voice which I heard was *as it were of a trumpet talking with me;* which said, Come up hither, and I will shew thee things which must be hereafter. And immediately I was in the spirit: and, behold, a throne was set in heaven, and one sat on the throne." (Rev. 4:1–2, emphasis added.)

What seems apparent at this point is that John has been invited to enter the celestial Holy of Holies: "Come up hither." Like ascending the stairs of the earthly temple, John is required to ascend into the heavenly Holy of Holies. John makes other explicit references to the heavenly temple as in the case here (see also Rev. 7:15; 14:15–17; 15:5–8; 16:17). Now that he has entered the sacred throne room (the throne is the center of activity for much of the book of Revelation), he is allowed to see many things.

The first element of this particular section is God seated upon a throne (the mercy seat of the ancient ark represented the throne): "And immediately I was in the spirit: and, behold, a throne was set in heaven, and one sat on the throne. And he that sat was to look upon like a jasper [red, yellow, or green stone] and a sardine [a deep red] stone: and there was a rainbow round about the throne, in sight like unto an emerald." (Rev. 4:2–3.)

The second is the twenty-four elders: "And round about the throne were four and twenty seats: and upon the seats I saw four and twenty elders sitting, *clothed in white raiment;* and they had *on their heads crowns of gold.* And out of the throne *proceeded lightnings and thunderings and voices:* and there were seven *lamps of fire burning before the throne,* which are the seven Spirits of God. And before the throne there was a sea of glass like unto crystal: and in the midst of the throne, and round about the throne, were four beasts full of eyes before and behind." (Rev. 4:4–6, emphasis added.)

The vision continues: "And when those beasts give glory and honour and thanks to him that sat on the throne, who liveth for ever and ever, the four and twenty elders fall down before him that sat on the throne, and worship him that liveth for ever and ever, and cast their crowns before the throne, saying, Thou art worthy, O Lord, to receive glory and honour and power" (Rev. 4:9–11).

The number of the twenty-four elders is especially reminiscent of the twenty-four courses of priests who rotated in weekly temple service and whose presence in the temple had a certain representative dimension. Although only one course was responsible each week for temple service, all twenty-four courses were in attendance at the Feast of Tabernacles (as well as the other pilgrimage feasts).

The Mishnah describes the distinctive activities of the Feast of Tabernacles, revealing several details about what the feast may have been like during the first century while the temple still stood.

> At the close of the first Festival-day of the Feast they went down to the Court of the Women. . . . There were golden candlesticks . . . set alight, and there was not a courtyard in Jerusalem that did not reflect the light of the Beth ha-She'ubah. Men of piety and good works used to dance before them with burning torches in their hands, singing songs and praises. And countless Levites [played] on harps, lyres, cymbals and trumpets and instruments of music, on the fifteen steps leading down from the Court of the Israelites to the Court of the Women, corresponding to the Fifteen Songs of Ascents in the Psalms. . . . They blew never less than twenty-one blasts in the Temple.[16]

Each elder in John's vision has a crown, like the crowns of leaves worn in the procession around the altar during the Feast of Tabernacles. Of course, the altar is a symbol of God's throne and is the place where human-divine contact is made or where it could be established.

The lightnings, thunderings, and voices are reminiscent of the trumpet blast heard throughout the Temple Mount during the celebration of the feasts. The sounding of trumpets, of course, has a symbolic meaning. In some cases, the soundings are associated with the vision of God. At such visions, the blast of the trumpet does not simply announce God's coming. In some cases, the sound of trumpets probably denotes the inexpressible voice of God. This seems to be the case in Exodus: "And when the voice of the trumpet sounded long, and waxed louder and louder, Moses spake, and God answered him by a voice" (Ex. 19:19). Another passage from the writings of Moses confirms such an interpretation: "These words the Lord spake unto all your assembly in the mount out of the midst of the fire, of the cloud, and of the thick darkness, with a great voice" (Deut. 5:22).

Both in Revelation 1 and in this chapter (Rev. 4), John hears a voice "as it were of a trumpet" (see Rev. 1:10; 4:1). In all likelihood, the loudness and the indescribability of the tone is the point of John's description. The light, noise, and voice all find their corresponding elements within the setting of the Feast of Tabernacles.

The prostration of the twenty-four elders might have more than one symbolic meaning. The priests of the temple (dressed in the white priestly robes and the caps or turbans—representing a "kingdom of priests") prostrated themselves, along with the people, when the divine name (KJV Jehovah) was pronounced on Yom Kippur—the Day of Atonement—with the acclamation, "Blessed be the name of the glory of his kingdom forever and ever!"[17]

The vision found in Revelation 5 will be discussed later, but it is part of this vision of the elders. In Revelation 6, John reveals his vision of the opening of the six seals—a review of prophetic history. It is a vision of death, hunger, disease, and destruction. The vision also includes a scene of the faithful dead who had been slain "for the word of God, and for the testimony which they held" (Rev. 6:9). Disturbances in the earth and sky dominate the scene of destruction and hopelessness of the wicked. The scene shifts rapidly to an interlude—a relief from the awful vision of human destruction and wickedness—to a view of heaven and those saved through the blood of the Lamb.

The One Hundred Forty-four Thousand (Rev. 7)

Something arresting and suggestive is always associated with a great crowd. The language of the Feast of Tabernacles and the Day of Atonement is part of the vision of the great multitude in Revelation 7:

> And after these things I saw four angels standing on the four corners of the earth, holding the four winds of the earth, that the wind would not blow on the earth, nor on the sea, nor on any tree.
>
> And I saw another angel ascending from the east, having the seal of the living God: and he cried with a loud voice to the four angels, to whom it was given to hurt the earth and the sea,
>
> Saying, Hurt not the earth, neither the sea, nor the trees, till we have sealed the servants of our God in their foreheads.
>
> And I heard the number of them which were sealed: and there were sealed an hundred and forty and four thousand of all the tribes of the children of Israel. (Rev. 7:1–4.)

Then John describes the sealing of twelve thousand from each tribe (see Rev. 7:5–8). "After this," the seer writes, "I beheld, and, lo, a great multitude, which no man could number, of all nations, and kindreds, and people, and tongues, stood before the throne, and before the Lamb, clothed with white robes, and palms in their hands" (Rev. 7:9). The song of the righteous is joined by a heavenly choir, who fall on their faces to worship the Lord. The numberless multitude "cried with a loud voice, saying, Salvation to our God which sitteth upon the throne, and unto the Lamb. And all the angels stood round about the throne, and about the elders and the four beasts, and fell before the throne on their faces, and worshipped God, saying, Amen:

Blessing, and glory, and wisdom, and thanksgiving, and honour, and power, and might, be unto our God for ever and ever. Amen." (Rev. 7:10–12.)

The language describing the multitude reminds us of the description of the multitude at Jerusalem on Pentecost (see Acts 2:5–11). The white garment is both a Jewish festive dress and the clothing of the priests in the temple. The palms in their hands in all likelihood represent several concepts. The date palm was one of the most characteristic and important trees in the Near East. It provided not only shade in the desert but also food and drink (*honey,* mentioned in many biblical texts, refers to the drink made from the date palm; cf. Rev. 10:9, for example). In the book of Psalms, the righteous "shall flourish like the palm tree" in the house of the Lord (Ps. 92:12). The frequent occurrence of the palm tree carved in relief on the walls, doors, doorjambs, and other parts of Solomon's temple is noted in the biblical record (see 1 Kgs. 6:29, 32, 35; 7:36); and the temple seen by Ezekiel (see references above) suggests more than mere decorative coincidence. As already noted, the palm tree is associated with the tree of life; and the leaves are associated with victory and celebration.

In the New Testament, Jesus was greeted by disciples waving palm fronds during his triumphal entry into Jerusalem (see John 12:13)—obviously recalling what the Jews had done earlier for Simon, son of Mattathias, the founder of the independent Jewish state nearly 170 years before as he entered Jerusalem following the defeat of Israel's enemy: "On the twenty-third day of the second month, in the one hundred seventy-first year, [the date is equivalent to 3 June 141 B.C.], the Jews entered it [the citadel on the Temple Mount at Jerusalem] with praise and palm branches, and with harps and cymbals and stringed instruments, and with hymns and songs, because a great enemy had been crushed and removed from Israel" (New Revised Standard Version Bible, Apocrypha, 1 Maccabees 13:51; cf. 2 Maccabees 10:7).

The book of 1 Maccabees describes the struggles of the Jews as they sought independence from the Greco-Macedonian Seleucid kings from 166 to 135 B.C. This symbol of praise and victory was a powerful image. John's vision of the righteous in heaven, clothed in white, with crowns on their heads and palms in their hands, signifies the ultimate triumph of the Lamb against all enemies.

As the vision continues, one of the elders asks John a question, "What are these which are arrayed in white robes? and whence came they?" (Rev. 7:13.) In answering his own question, the elder says, "These are they which came out of great tribulation and have washed their robes, and made them white in the blood of the Lamb. Therefore are they before the throne of God, and serve him day and night in his temple: and he that sitteth on the throne shall dwell among them. They shall hunger no more, neither thirst any more; neither shall the sun light on them, nor any heat. For the Lamb which is in the midst of the throne shall feed them, and shall lead them unto living fountains of waters: and God shall wipe away all tears from their eyes." (Rev. 7:14–17.)

John saw that, unlike the present Roman rule, which was only the concrete representation of the demonic power's dominion, a more humanized world through Christ would be created through his establishment of a "kingdom of priests" where there would be no more pain and sufferings of this present world. "They shall hunger no more, neither thirst any more; neither shall the sun light on them, nor any heat. For the Lamb which is in the midst of the throne shall feed them, and shall lead them unto living fountains of waters: and God shall wipe away all tears from their eyes." (Rev. 7:16–17.)

The allusion again to the temple theme in Psalm 121 seems obvious and plays a role in understanding John's vision:

> I will lift up mine eyes unto the hills [the temple], from whence cometh my help.
> My help cometh from the Lord, which made heaven and earth.
> He will not suffer thy foot to be moved: he that keepeth thee will not slumber.
> Behold, he that keepeth Israel shall neither slumber nor sleep.

The Lord is thy keeper: the Lord is thy shade upon thy right hand.

The sun shall not smite thee by day, nor the moon by night.

The Lord shall preserve thee from all evil: he shall preserve thy soul.

The Lord shall preserve thy going out and thy coming in from this time forth, and even for evermore. (Ps. 121:1–8.)

In our day, Joseph Smith asked the Lord some questions regarding the one hundred forty-four thousand seen by John. Joseph says: "We are to understand that those who are sealed are high priests, ordained unto the holy order of God, to administer the everlasting gospel; for they are they who are ordained out of every nation, kindred, tongue, and people, by the angels to whom is given power over the nations of the earth, to bring as many as will come to the church of the Firstborn" (D&C 77:11).

The Altar of Incense (Rev. 8:3–5)

In Revelation 8, John records, "And another angel came and stood at *the altar,* having a golden censer; and there was given unto him much *incense,* that he should *offer it with the prayers of all saints* upon the golden altar which was before the throne" (Rev. 8:3, emphasis added). John has already made reference to the altar and the incense in Revelation 5. There, as well as here, he associates the ancient tabernacle's altar of incense smoke with the "prayers of saints" (Rev. 5:8).

This altar was placed before the veil of the temple in the Holy Place. The priest, such as Zacharias, brought a small shovel (KJV "spoon") full of a specially mixed resinous material to the altar and poured it over the glowing coals. The smoke from the burning coals in a pan on the altar blended with the incense. This act (of the smoke rising to heaven) symbolized the prayers of the children of Israel, who stood outside praying vocally and with uplifted hands in the outer court at the moment the priest stood before the altar and the veil. Thirteen ingredients made up the incense, which had been gathered from the sea, the desert,

The altar of incense stood before the veil of the Holy of Holies. The daily burning of incense on this altar represented the prayers of the righteous that accompanied temple worship (see Ps. 141:2).

and the fertile country land, symbolizing the extent of the Lord's creation brought together to praise him.

Behind the veil, at the time of Solomon, was the physical symbol of God's presence: the ark of the covenant. The righteous knew that he was not only a silent listener but also, at times, an articulate speaker—for example, where the angel states, "Thy prayer is heard" (Luke 1:13). "Let my prayer be set forth before thee," wrote the Psalmist, "as incense; and the lifting up of my hands" (Ps. 141:2). John's vision in Revelation 8 continues: "And the smoke of the incense, which came with the prayers of the saints, ascended up before God out of the angel's hand" (Rev. 8:4).

Both Revelation 5 and 8 describe worship in heaven and the relationship of the earthly altar to its heavenly counterpart.

Holy Trumpets (Rev. 8:6–13)

John begins his description of the Revelation by saying, "I John, who also am your brother, and companion in tribulation, and in the kingdom and patience of Jesus Christ, was in the isle that is called Patmos, for the word of God, and for the testimony of Jesus Christ. I was in the Spirit on the Lord's day, and heard behind me a great voice, as of a trumpet." (Rev. 1:9–10.)

Trumpets played an important role in ancient Israel, especially in the temple. The command to make trumpets and the instructions for their use were given by the Lord to Moses (see Num. 10:1–10; cf. 2 Chr. 13:12–14). They were used in summoning the congregation (the people), the breaking of camp, sounding the alarm in time of war, and celebrating the holy festivals, including Sabbath day observance. Originally, the trumpet was not so much a musical instrument as an alarm. Later, it became a priestly instrument sounded during temple service.

At Herod's temple during the first century, trumpets were used to signal the beginning of the Sabbath day and other festivals—in a way signaling the separation of the holy from the common. Trumpets, as we have already noted, played a significant role in ancient Israel and at the temple. They heralded the glory of God (see Ex. 19:16, 19) and victory against the enemy (see Josh. 6:6) and were used in temple worship (see Lev. 25:9). As the Psalmist noted, "With trumpets and sound of cornet make a joyful noise before the Lord, the King" (Ps. 98:6).

The New Temple (Rev. 11)

At one point during the vision, John was commanded to "rise, and measure the temple of God, and the altar, and them that worship therein" (Rev. 11:1). When Solomon's temple was destroyed in 587 B.C., both Ezekiel and Zechariah received visions of measurements being taken for a new temple to replace the one destroyed. It was a symbolic assurance that God would not abandon Israel and that the temple would be replaced so the Lord could dwell among his people again. Shortly before John received his vision, the Jerusalem temple had been destroyed. Now John, like Ezekiel and Zechariah before him, is given the assignment to measure the heavenly temple.

At the end of the period seen in vision, John states, "And the temple of God was opened in heaven, and there was seen in his temple the ark of his testament: and there were lightnings, and voices, and thunderings, and an earthquake, and great hail" (Rev. 11:19). That this is a temple in heaven is made clear by this vision.

The Heavenly Temple (Rev. 15)

Again, John looks toward heaven and says:

> And after that I looked, and, behold, the temple of the *tabernacle of the testimony* in heaven was opened:
> And the seven angels came out of the temple, having the seven plagues, clothed in pure and white linen, and having their breasts girded with golden girdles.
> And one of the four beasts gave unto the seven angels seven golden vials full of the wrath of God, who liveth for ever and ever.
> And the temple was filled with smoke from the glory of God, and from his power; and no man was able to enter into the temple, till the seven plagues of the seven angels were fulfilled. (Rev. 15:5–8, emphasis added.)

Besides Acts 7:44, this is the only reference to the ancient tabernacle as the "tent of witness" (see Ex. 33:7). Again, drawing on the images of the Old Testament tabernacle and temple, John describes the angels as wearing the clothing of the priests and high priests. The girdles may refer to the special golden sash worn by the high priest (see also Rev. 1:13).

The heavenly temple is "filled with smoke from the glory of God," which reminds us of the dedication of the temple by Solomon: "And it came to pass, when the priests were come out of the holy place, that the cloud filled the house of the Lord, so that the priests could not stand to minister because of the cloud: for the glory of the Lord had filled the house of the Lord. Then spake Solomon, The Lord said that he would dwell in the thick darkness." (1 Kgs. 8:10–12.)

The cloud represented the very presence of the Lord in the

temple. John's vision testifies that God is indeed in his heavenly temple, of which the earthly temple is only a type and shadow.

The Holy City and Its Temple (Rev. 21–22)

This glorious vision of John ends with a view of the earth in its eternal glory—a new heaven and a new earth. John saw and described "the holy city, new Jerusalem, coming down from God out of heaven" (see Rev. 21:1–2). The earthly temple will continue to operate during the Millennium, as is so dramatically illustrated in Ezekiel and in John's own vision of the Millennium. The temple will continue to serve as a reminder of the heavenly temple.

John's Revelation gives further exceptional insight about the temple following the end of the Millennium, when a "new heaven and a new earth" are created, in which the heavenly city descends from heaven to earth, at which time the Father himself will dwell on the earth with those worthy to be there with him.

The city will be the temple of God, where his eternal presence will dwell, just as the *Shekinah* (symbol of God's presence) of God came over the tabernacle in the wilderness (see Rev. 21:11; Ex. 29:45 and 40:34–38). The Lord God and the Lamb will be the eternal temple of the New Jerusalem (see Rev. 21:22). And, in that city, all the faithful, ten thousand times ten thousand, shall see "his face" while he sits upon the eternal throne of David (see Rev. 22:3–4).

In Revelation 21–22, the whole city is not only the temple but also the Holy of Holies. The twelve stones of its foundation correspond to the stones on the high priestly breastplace (reverse order from the description in Ex. 28, however). The most important identification of this city as the bride of the Lamb shows it to be none other than the people of God, shining in a new relationship that fulfills all hope.

The stream of water in Revelation 22 is associated with the end of Ezekiel's vision; there it shows that the divine glory has resumed residence on Zion and that the blessings are flowing out from his presence. More directly related to our present discussion, however, is Zechariah 14:6–21. The river of living water flows from Jerusalem, and the Lord will reign over all the earth without rival. Jerusalem will be exalted and secured, and mention is made of three gates. After a description of the fate of the nations, Zechariah mentions that all surviving people will go up to Jerusalem to worship the Lord as King and to celebrate the Feast of Tabernacles. If they do not go to the temple, there will be no rain; and they will be afflicted with a plague.

The miraculous fountain in Revelation, the last element added to the description of the holy city, is a climax taken from images based on the enthronement of the Lord. In Revelation, it fulfills the same function as in Joel, Zechariah, and Ezekiel—it is the sign that the basic concept of the temple is fulfilled in all its richness: the Lord reigning as triumphant King, enthroned forever in his house. By this painting of the image with such broad strokes and daring hues, John shows that all other temples have been incomplete by comparison, just as the complete sovereignty of God and the Lamb will only be seen in the full effect when the New Jerusalem is established.

The book of Revelation ends with the dramatic announcement that God and the Lamb are a temple: "And I saw no temple therein: for the Lord God Almighty and the Lamb are the temple of it" (Rev. 21:22). This announcement recalls Ezekiel's statement that the Lord would be "as a little sanctuary" to the scattered tribes of Israel "in the countries where they shall come" (Ezek. 11:16). The Lord is, in fact, a "refuge and [a] fortress" for the righteous (Ps. 91:2).

While the earth stands in its present state and during the Millennium, the temple on earth is but a dim shadow of the heavenly temple. In that day, however, there will be no temple; the need of it will have simply disappeared with the presence on the renewed earth of the Son and the Father himself.

The Message of Revelation (Rev. 5)

In conclusion, the book of Revelation is best understood by those who have been initiated into the mysteries of the kingdom. John chooses language that is pregnant with meaning to those who are familiar with temple worship. During a time of severe trials and persecutions, John gives the early Saints hope and a vision of a day when they will sing a new song.

The "new song" sung by the twenty-four elders affirms the worthiness of the risen Christ to take dominion of the earth for a thousand years. The Lamb's worthiness is based on the fact that he can and does open the sealed book:

> And I saw in the right hand of him that sat on the throne a book written within and on the backside, sealed with seven seals.
> And I saw a strong angel proclaiming with a loud voice, Who is worthy to open the book, and to loose the seals thereof?
> And no man in heaven, nor in earth, neither under the earth, was able to open the book, neither to look thereon.
> And I wept much, because no man was found worthy to open and to read the book, neither to look thereon. (Rev. 5:1–4.)

At this point, one of the elders speaks: "Weep not: behold, the Lion of the tribe of Juda, the Root of David, hath prevailed to open the book, and to loose the seven seals thereof" (Rev. 5:5). Then John writes:

> And I beheld, and, lo, in the midst of the throne and of the four beasts, and in the midst of the elders, stood a Lamb as it had been slain, having seven horns and seven eyes, which are the seven Spirits of God sent forth into all the earth.
> And he came and took the book out of the right hand of him that sat upon the throne.
> And when he had taken the book, the four beasts and four and twenty elders fell down before the Lamb, having every one of them harps, and golden vials full of odours, which are the prayers of saints. (Rev. 5:6–8.)

These elders and beasts begin praising God and the Lamb by singing: "Thou art worthy to take the book, and to open the seals thereof: for thou wast slain, and has redeemed us to God by thy blood out of every kindred, and tongue, and people, and nation; and hast made us unto our God kings and priests: and we shall reign on the earth" (Rev. 5:9–10). John knows that the twenty-four elders are simply representative of those saved from every "kindred, and tongue, and people, and nation," because he continues:

> And I beheld, and I heard the voice of many angels round about the throne and the beasts and the elders: and the number of them was ten thousand times ten thousand, and thousands of thousands;
>
> Saying with a loud voice, Worthy is the Lamb that was slain to receive power, and riches, and wisdom, and strength, and honour, and glory, and blessing.
>
> And every creature which is in heaven, and on the earth, and under the earth, and such as are in the sea, and all that are in them, heard I saying, Blessing, and honour, and glory, and power, be unto him that sitteth upon the throne, and unto the Lamb for ever and ever.
>
> And the four beasts said, Amen. And the four and twenty elders fell down and worshipped him that liveth for ever and ever. (Rev. 5:11–14.)

The reasons given in the above verses for the Lamb's worthiness to be both King of kings and Lord of lords is threefold:

First, the Lamb is worthy because he was "slain" (see Rev. 5:9). The verb *sphazein* (to slaughter) refers to the violent death of the Lamb and probably alludes to the slaughtering of the Passover lamb.[18] This image evokes the memory of ancient Israel's exodus and liberation from Egypt.

Second, the Lamb is worthy because he has purchased (KJV "redeemed") a people for God from every tribe, tongue, people, and nation with his blood (see Rev. 5:9). The Lamb is pictured as a purchasing agent for God and has traveled throughout the whole earth to purchase a people for God. The price that is paid is his blood. This metaphoric language is used to emphasize the high value of the purchased ones as well as the infinite and eternal nature of Christ's atonement. The verb *agorazein* (to purchase or redeem) is a secular as well as a religious term.[19] It denotes a commercial transaction, as is also evident in Revelation

3:18 and 13:17. In this case, it probably refers to a slave market because people are the objects of the purchase. This is also true of the use of the word in Revelation 7, where one hundred forty-four thousand are purchased from every nation.

The third and final reason for the worthiness of the Lamb is that he "hast made us unto our God kings and priests" (Rev. 5:10). Just as according to Roman law the freed prisoners of war were brought back home and reintegrated into their own nation, so here it is said that the purchased ones are "kings and priests." John thus depicts redemption and salvation in economic language and political imagery and understands it as an event analogous to the liberation of Israel from the slavery of Egypt (see Ex. 19). The Lord commanded ancient Israel to establish the tabernacle among the people. Through the tabernacle and its ordinances, Israel could be made holy—consecrated to the Lord. Ancient Israel constituted the Lord's kingdom on earth—a people who acknowledged him as their King, and like the Levitical priests, they were to be wholly consecrated to his service. As God's people, both individually and collectively, they were "set apart" to do his will.

To become holy, consecrated, and set apart is the key theme of the "holiness code" of Leviticus. "For I am the Lord that bringeth you up out of the land of Egypt, to be your God: ye shall therefore be holy, for I am holy" (Lev. 11:45). Each individual and as a "new" nation, a holy nation, Israel was to express holiness in every aspect of life, to the extent that all of life could have a certain sacred quality. Because of who the Lord is and what he has done, his people must dedicate themselves fully to him.

Just as ancient Israel had once entered the promised land, the Saints will now enter the eternal promised land and "reign on earth" with Christ as the King and Lord over his people (see Rev. 19:16). The images of a *new* Israel, a *new* exodus, a *new* Jerusalem, a *new* temple, a *new* heaven, a *new* earth, and a *new* Eden are a major theme throughout the book:

> And he shewed me a pure river of water of life, clear as crystal, proceeding out of the throne of God and of the Lamb.

In the midst of the street of it, and on either side of the river, was there the tree of life, which bare twelve manner of fruits, and yielded her fruit every month: and the leaves of the tree were for the healing of the nations.

And there shall be no more curse: but the throne of God and of the Lamb shall be in it; and his servants shall serve him:

And they shall see his face; and his name shall be in their foreheads." (Rev. 22:1–4.)

Central to the Passover feast was the sacrificial lamb "without blemish, a male of the first year" (Ex. 12:5). Thousands of such lambs were brought to the Temple Mount to be slaughtered each year. The Lamb also plays a critical role in the book of Revelation. Twenty-nine of the thirty-four references to a lamb in the New Testament are found in the Revelation, where Jesus is portrayed as a "Lamb as it had been slain" (Rev. 5:6). John's vision closes as he sees "a pure river of water of life, clear as crystal, proceeding out of the throne of God and of the Lamb. In the midst of the street of it, and on either side of the river, was there the tree of life, which bare twelve manner of fruits, and yielded her fruit every month: and the leaves of the tree were for the healing of the nations. And there shall be no more curse: but the throne of God and of the Lamb shall be in it; and his servants shall serve him: and they shall see his face; and his name shall be in their foreheads. And there shall be no night there; and they need no candle, neither light of the sun; for the Lord God giveth them light: and they shall reign for ever and ever." (Rev. 22:1–5.)

The book of Revelation ends with its echoes of the beginning (Genesis). With the tree of life restored and with no more curse, the climax is a fitting one to the whole Bible story.

At the beginning of his Revelation, John states: "Blessed is he that readeth, and they that hear the words of this prophecy, and keep those things which are written therein" (Rev. 1:3). The promises to the faithful, expressed in terms of ancient temple imagery, are for all those who "readeth" and "hear" them, but most important, for those who "keep those things which are written therein." If they do read, hear, and keep, they are "called, and chosen, and faithful" (Rev. 17:14).

My House

It is written, My house shall be called the house of prayer.
—*Matthew 21:13*

The four Gospels indicate that Jesus "taught daily in the temple" when in Jerusalem (see Luke 19:47). He spoke of the temple as "my Father's house" in the Gospel of John (John 2:16) as he began his mortal ministry. But, on another occasion, he spoke of the temple as "my house" (see Matt. 21:13; Mark 11:17; Luke 19:46). From the expression "my Father's house" at the beginning of his mission to the personal "my house" as he closed his mission, Jesus may have been suggesting that he had received all things from the Father, including his temple.

Temple worship and symbolism play an important role in the New Testament. The Gospel writers discuss Jesus' activities at the Jerusalem temple during his mortal ministry. An understanding of temple construction and the place of temple worship and symbolism in ancient Israel helps us appreciate the rich and significant experiences of the Master as he walked the sacred

---

◄ When Jesus came to Jerusalem he spent much of his time in the temple teaching about the kingdom of God. Not only did he take possession of his Father's house, but he claimed that he was one with the Father, since he was doing the Father's will. The temple, therefore, became the Savior's house also.

precincts of the holy temple. It seems clear that on his last visit to the temple he came as God's Son, sent by his Father to sacrifice himself for mankind, so that each person could return to the Father.

For the early Christian Saints, the temple was a visual reminder that the Lord dwelt in their midst. The gospel they preached in the courts of the temple taught that the purpose of life was to return home to our Father's house, the true temple. To live with him, we must become like him—holy as he is holy. Holiness was taught in the ancient temple through a series of rites, ordinances, and symbols. Three prominent symbols are water, Spirit, and blood. The temple sacrifices under the law of Moses especially emphasized the atonement of the Lamb of God, which had not yet occurred (see Moses 5:6–7).

The process of becoming holy is doctrinally known as sanctification and is a rebirth that occurs through water, Spirit, and blood. The Lord taught his children how to become holy through the use of sacred space and time. This process was accomplished not only in everyday activities within the community and the home but also, more important, through temple worship.

Rising above the main section of the city of Jerusalem, the temple stood on the mountain of the Lord. As the people approached the Temple Mount, spiritually and physically, they ascended to God's house. This site had been sanctified through sacred events in the past, beginning with Abraham's offering of Isaac in similitude of the Savior and including the temples of Solomon and of Zerubbabel.

Before entering the sacred ground of the temple the people washed themselves with water, they removed the shoes from their feet, and they often dressed in white. To enter the court of the temple, they had to be in a state of ritual purity and personal worthiness. Under the law of Moses, the priest had to enter the sanctuary itself on behalf of the people. Through the Melchizedek Priesthood, under the higher law revealed by Christ and restored in our day, all individuals are able to enter the temple and represent themselves as they approach the veil. Sacred space was only one division taught under the law of Moses.

The priests stood on the roof of the temple and announced by a trumpet blast the approach of the Sabbath day and, on the next evening, its close. The Mishnah, when discussing the trumpet blasts required on various occasions, also mentions the three blasts proclaiming the separation of the holy (the Sabbath) from the common (the rest of the week). This consecrated one day out of seven to the Lord. Through their thoughts and actions on this holy day, people were able to commune with God. Other religious holidays, such as Passover, also helped the children of Israel dedicate special time to the Lord—in this way recalling his great acts in the past and his promises in the future.

Later, the Lord's disciples continued praising God in the holy temple, which also became the focus of their missionary activities in Jerusalem. As the Church continued to increase in size and spread throughout the Greco-Roman world, missionaries came in contact with pagan temples of the day. Not only did these magnificent and ever-present structures stand near the major crossroads of the Roman Empire and in remote sites but also their presence and meaning in society played a role in proclaiming Jesus' name to the Gentiles. Eventually, the Jerusalem temple was destroyed, fulfilling Jesus' own words.

Ancient temple symbolism went beyond the physical sanctuary in Jerusalem and was applied to other things. Both Jesus and Paul spoke of the temple-body; Peter spoke of the spiritual temple, even the Church; and the author of the book of Hebrews spoke of the heavenly temple built without hands.

According to the Epistle to the Hebrews, Jesus was the blameless High Priest. He had no need to offer daily sacrifices for his own sins and for those of his people, "for this he did once, when he offered up himself" (Heb. 7:27). Paul's message is reflected in the sayings of Jesus, such as those found in Mark 10:45 and 14:24; the Son of Man gives his life as "a ransom for many."

For this reason the disciples were promised that they would "see heaven open, and the angels of God ascending and descending upon the Son of man" (John 1:51). The Son of Man, the Word of God, is the true place of atonement and therefore the "Beth-el" of the Messianic Age and of the new covenant. He is the divine Word who dwelled among humanity; through him the glory of God became manifest (see John 1:14). His body is the temple, destroyed by humans but raised again within three days (see John 2:19–21). By giving his life Jesus carried away the sins of the world (John 1:29), and through his death and resurrection the worship in spirit and in truth was made possible (John 4:23–24).

As the New Testament period came to a close, the early Christian Saints looked toward God during a period of great persecution and trials. Although in the book of Revelation John does not explicitly cite any Old Testament passages, he does employ the symbols and images of ancient temple worship. John wove out of these materials a brilliant tapestry proclaiming the events of the new order established through the Lamb. In his vision of heaven, John the Revelator described the New Jerusalem for these Saints in an effort to focus their attention toward the Lord and give them hope of a better day. "And I saw no temple therein," John states, "for the Lord God Almighty and the Lamb are the temple of it" (Rev. 21:22).

The New Testament portrays the temple in its true light as it discusses the reality of man's struggle to understand how to worship God. It portrays righteous men and women who came to "appear before the Lord," and those who did not understand that to be holy was more than just performing temple ritual. From the beginning, it seems, people have attempted to communicate with God at the highest point of earth, which touched the lowest point of heaven, the very gates of heaven. Later, the Lord commanded the children of Israel to build "cosmic mountains" where he could reveal himself.

Anciently, the high priest represented all the children of Israel as he entered into the Holy of Holies of the temple once a year (see Ex. 28:9–30). But for the New Testament Saints, Christ had become the High Priest; and he entered into the eternal Holy of Holies and now made it possible for all to approach the veil and meet God (see Heb. 8–9).

Through the sacrifice of Christ Jesus, the Saints have been liberated from spiritual bondage as he has "washed us" (set us

Ancient and modern temples focus on the life and mission of Jesus Christ through sacred symbols. The New Testament authors wrote about the temple of Herod (made with hands); they also taught us that Jesus was a temple and that each individual is a temple. Modern revelations through Joseph Smith affirm these same truths and go beyond them by showing that the atonement of Christ really links together the man-made temple, Jesus as a temple, and each of us as a temple in a way often missed by students of the New Testament. The At-one-ment is the central reality of the temple. Through modern temple worship, as was the case for those who lived in the New Testament era, we raise our hands and hearts to praise the Lord in his holy house.

free), according to Revelation 1:6. And, as a result, the Saints now sing a new song, saying: "Thou art worthy . . . : for thou wast slain [slaughtered], and hast redeemed [ransomed/purchased] us to God [a people for God] by thy blood out of every kindred, and tongue, and people, and nation; and hast made us unto our God kings and priests [a kingdom of priests]: and we shall reign on the earth" (Rev. 5:9–10). The scene portrayed by John echoes that of an ancient slave market. Jesus buys the slaves (the Christians) with a high price—his own precious blood—not the blood of the firstborn Egyptian as he had done when the children of Israel were in bondage, but with his own blood, the Firstborn Son of God.

Our appreciation for the messages of the New Testament is enhanced with a study of ancient temples, temple worship, and temple symbolism. They are significant in and of themselves, but for the Latter-day Saint community—a temple-building people—these stories and expressions from the New Testament can have a modern application, especially as we attend and worship in modern temples. Christ, the atoning one, is the focus of all temple worship, ancient or modern. And so it is that we too have been commanded to worship God and his Christ in temples made with hands:

> Therefore, verily I say unto you, my friends, call your solemn assembly, as I have commanded you.
> And as all have not faith, seek ye diligently and teach one another words of wisdom; yea, seek ye out of the best books words of wisdom; seek learning, even by study and also by faith.
> Organize yourselves; prepare every needful thing; and establish a house, even a house of prayer, a house of fasting, a house of faith, a house of learning, a house of glory, a house of order, a house of God;
> That your incomings may be in the name of the Lord; that your outgoings may be in the name of the Lord; that all your salutations may be in the name of the Lord, with uplifted hands unto the Most High. (D&C 88:117–20.)

Through faith on the Lord Jesus Christ and obedience to his holy ordinances, every man and every woman can enter the temple and stand before God with uplifted hands and proclaim this is "my Father's house."

Notes

Publication details for sources cited in the notes that follow are given in the Bibliography.

Prologue: My Father's House

1. The entire Temple Mount was twice as large as the monumental Forum Romanum built by Trajan, and three and a half times more extensive than the combined temples of Jupiter and Astarte-Venus at Baalbek. The retaining walls themselves towered more than 80 feet above the roadways going around its perimeter and reached over 50 feet below street level in their foundation courses. This was truly an awesome structure.

2. This verse is part of the Hallel, or "Praise," a name given to a group of Psalms (113–18) recited by Jews at the great feasts; Psalm 136 was known as the "great Hallel"; for more information, see "Hallel," LDS Bible Dictionary, p. 698.

3. Babylonian Talmud *Sukkot.* 51b; see *Hebrew-English Edition of the Babylonian Talmud*, vol. 7.

4. The synoptic Gospels (Matthew, Mark, and Luke) talk about a cleansing of the temple during Jesus' last week of activity in Jerusalem, but John also notes that a cleansing occurred at the beginning of his ministry.

5. See Meyers and Meyers, *Zechariah 9–14*, pp. 489–90.

6. See, for example, Herzog, Aharoni, and Rainey, "Arad: An Ancient Israelite Fortress with a Temple to Yahweh," pp. 16–35. Even

when the temple was abandoned during the religious reforms by either King Josiah or King Hezekiah, the incense altars were reverently laid on their sides and were covered with earth.

Chapter 1. The Temple as the Pathway to Eternal Life

1. See Donald W. Parry, "Ritual Anointing," pp. 279–81.
2. See Joseph Smith, *Teachings,* pp. 264, 266.
3. See ibid., p. 314.

Chapter 2. The Temples of Ancient Israel

1. Haran (Abr. 2:6–13); Jershon (Abr. 2:17); plain of Moreh (Abr. 2:18; Gen. 12:6–7); east of Bethel (Abr. 2:20; Gen. 12:8; 13:3, 4); plain of Mamre (Gen. 13:18); Beer-sheba (Gen. 21:33); and Moriah (Gen. 22:9–14).

2. Josephus, *Jewish War* 6.438; see Loeb Classical Library *Josephus* 3:502–3.

3. Joseph Smith, *Teachings,* p. 181.

4. See Haran, *Temples and Temple-Service,* p. 26.

5. The most recent work calculates the cubit used for the measurement of the temple as 20.7 inches to the cubit; see Patrich, "Reconstructing the Magnificent Temple Herod Build," pp. 18–19. For a concise discussion of biblical measurements, see Barkay, "Measurements in the Bible," p. 37.

6. In Hebrew, juxtaposing a singular noun, "holy," with its plural form, "holies," is a way of making a superlative—literally "holy of holies" but meaning "the most holy place."

7. Joseph Smith, *History of the Church* 2:428.

8. See Haran, *Temples and Temple-Service,* pp. 26–42.

9. For a description of the interior of Solomon's temple with its furnishings and their possible symbolic value, see Hurowitz, "Inside Solomon's Temple," pp. 24–37, 50.

10. See Hurowitz, "Inside Solomon's Temple," p. 33. Hurowitz cites Meyers, "Jachin and Boaz in Religious and Political Perspective," pp. 167–78. Meyers's essay was reprinted in Madsen, ed., *The Temple in Antiquity,* pp. 135–50.

11. Some scholars, based on other Near Eastern models, believe

the name of each pillar represented a significant word of a dynastic inscription. Thus, Jachin may be the Hebrew word *hakin,* "to establish," from an inscription like Ps. 89:4, "Thy seed will I establish [*'akin*] forever." and perhaps Boaz, Hebrew *be'oz,* "in the strength of," comes from an inscription to Ps. 21:1, "The king shall joy in thy strength [*be'oz*]." Both of these would remind Israel of the divinely ordained kingship which the Lord established with David as a type of the Messiah. See Scott, "Jachin and Boaz," pp. 780–81.

12. Letter of Aristeas, 83–120; see *The Old Testament Pseudepigrapha* 2:7–34. This text is dated anywhere from 250 B.C. to A.D. 100, but it is most likely from the period before Herod replaced Zerubbabel's temple with his own building.

13. Excellent descriptions based on these sources can be found in Safrai and Avi-Yonah, "Temple," pp. 961–69; Ritmeyer, "Reconstructing Herod's Temple Mount in Jerusalem," pp. 23–42; and Ogden, "Jesus and the Temple," pp. 12–19.

14. Reports of these excavations written for the non-specialist include Mazar, *The Mountain of the Lord,* and Ben-Dov, *In the Shadow of the Temple.*

15. Josephus, *Antiquities* 15.380; see Loeb Classical Library *Josephus* 8:184–85.

16. See Meyers, "Temple, Jerusalem," pp. 364–65.

17. Babylonian Talmud *Sukkah* 51b; see *Hebrew-English Edition of the Babylonian Talmud,* vol. 7.

18. Josephus, *Jewish War* 5.222–23; see Loeb Classical Library *Josephus* 3:268–69.

19. See Josephus, *Antiquities* 20.219; see Loeb Classical Library *Josephus* 9:504–5.

20. The Ritmeyers measure the length of the walls as follows: the north wall 1,035 feet, the south wall 912 feet, the west wall 1,590 feet, and the east wall 1,536 feet; see Ritmeyer, "Reconstructing Herod's Temple Mount in Jerusalem," p. 27.

21. The Ritmeyers document the archaeological evidence for the gates so far discovered; see Ritmeyer, "Reconstructing Herod's Temple Mount in Jerusalem," pp. 23–42.

22. Josephus, *Antiquities* 15.418; see Loeb Classical Library *Josephus* 8:202–3.

23. Josephus, *Jewish War* 5.208; see Loeb Classical Library *Josephus* 3:262–63.

24. Mishnah *Middot* 4.7; see *The Mishnah,* p. 597.

25. Mishnah *Middot* 4.7; see *The Mishnah,* p. 597.

26. Josephus, *Antiquities* 15.395; see Loeb Classical Library *Josephus* 8:190–91.

27. Josephus, *Jewish War* 5.210; see Loeb Classical Library *Josephus* 3:264–65.

28. Josephus, *Jewish War* 5.212–14; see Loeb Classical Library *Josephus* 3:264–65.

29. Josephus, *Jewish War* 5.216–18; see Loeb Classical Library *Josephus* 3:266–67.

30. Mishnah *Yoma* 5.1; see *The Mishnah,* p. 167.

31. Ibid.

32. Tosefta *Yoma* 4.6; see Ginzberg, *Legends of the Jews* 5:14–15.

33. For a concise survey of this period, see Robinson, "The Setting of the Gospels," pp. 10–37.

34. See Craig A. Evans, "Opposition to the Temple: Jesus and the Dead Sea Scrolls," in Charlesworth, ed., *Jesus and the Dead Sea Scrolls,* pp. 235–53.

35. Josephus, *Antiquities* 17.250–68, 295; see Loeb Classical Library *Josephus* 8:488–97, 508–9.

36. Josephus, *Antiquities* 18.55–62; see Loeb Classical Library *Josephus* 9:42–47.

37. This teaching is attributed to Rabbi Yohanan ben Zakkai, one of the prominent Jewish leaders after the destruction of the temple. "Once as Rabban Yohanan ben Zakkai was coming out of Jerusalem, Rabbi Joshua followed him, and beheld the Temple in ruins. 'Woe unto us,' Rabbi Joshua cried, 'that this place, the place where the iniquities of Israel were atoned for, is laid waste.' 'My son,' Rabban Yohanan said to him, 'be not grieved. We have another atonement as effective as this. And what is it? It is acts of lovingkindness, as it is said, "For I desire mercy, not sacrifice" (Hos. 6:6).' " (Cited in Neusner, ed., *The Life of Torah,* pp. 72–73.)

Chapter 3. Temple Worship at the Time of Christ

1. Mishnah *Berakoth* 9.5; see *The Mishnah,* p. 10.

2. Josephus, *Jewish War* 2.1; see Loeb Classical Library *Josephus* 2:322–23.

3. Josephus, *Antiquities* 20.216–18; see Loeb Classical Library *Josephus* 9:502–5.

4. Joseph Smith, *Lectures on Faith* 6:7; see Lundwall, comp., *A Compilation Containing the Lectures on Faith,* p. 58.

5. The Hebrew word *minhah* means simply "gift" or "offering." The offerings described in the various scriptural passages all consist of cakes made from the flour of various grains and oil; see *A Hebrew and English Lexicon of the Old Testament,* p. 585.

6. The Mishnaic tractates containing descriptions of the temple ritual include *Tamid* ("the daily whole offering"), *Middot* ("measurements" of the temple), *Yoma* (the "Day of Atonement"), *Pesahim* ("the Feast of Passover"), and *Sukkah* ("the Feast of Tabernacles"). A useful summary of this information can be found in Safrai, "Temple: Ritual," pp. 970–83.

Chapter 4. Luke and the Presence of God in the Temple

1. For example, there is a similar story of the priest Hyrcanus found in Josephus, *Antiquities* 13.282–83; see Loeb Classical Library *Josephus* 7:368–71.

2. Josephus, *Against Apion* 2.103–4; see Loeb Classical Library *Josephus* 1:332–35.

3. Josephus, *Jewish War* 5.222–23; see Loeb Classical Library *Josephus* 3:268–69. The archaeological work in Jerusalem since 1968 demonstrates that the descriptions of the temple were not exaggerated by first-century witnesses like Josephus; see Finegan, *The Archeology of the New Testament,* pp. 194–97.

4. Josephus, *Antiquities* 5.348–51; see Loeb Classical Library *Josephus* 5:156–57.

5. The Joseph Smith Translation (JST) clarifies this interchange: "And they were hearing him, and asking him questions" (JST, Luke 2:46).

6. See, for example, *The NRSV-NIV: Parallel New Testament in Greek and English,* p. 169.

7. See Fitzmeyer, *The Gospel According to Luke* 1:443.

8. See *A Greek-English Lexicon of the New Testament,* p. 734.

9. Josephus, *Antiquities* 15.412–13; see Loeb Classical Library *Josephus* 8:198–201.

10. See *Treasures of the Holy Land,* pp. 210–21.

11. For a list of additional information revealed through modern revelation regarding this event, see "Transfiguration, Mount of," LDS

Bible Dictionary, p. 786. The Prophet Joseph Smith added some details to what happened on the mount; see Ehat and Cook, comps. and eds., *The Words of Joseph Smith,* pp. 9, 246.

12. See *A Grammatical Analysis of the Greek New Testament,* p. 214.

13. The Joseph Smith Translation adds to the story, indicating that John the Baptist may also have been present (see JST, Matt. 17:10–14).

14. See Baltzer, "The Meaning of the Temple in the Lucan Writings," pp. 263–77.

15. Josephus, *Antiquities* 14.105–12; see Loeb Classical Library *Josephus* 7:502–5. Also, Josephus, *Against Apion* 2.184–86, 193–98; see Loeb Classical Library *Josephus* 1:366–69, 370–73.

16. Josephus, *Antiquities* 20.206–7; see Loeb Classical Library *Josephus* 10:110–11.

17. 2 Baruch 10:18; see *The Old Testament Pseudepigrapha* 1:624.

18. See *The Aramaic Bible: Targum Jonathan,* p. 13.

19. Mishnah *Kerithoth* 1.7; see *The Mishnah,* p. 564.

20. See, for example, Mishnah *Shekalim* 4.3–4; see *The Mishnah,* pp. 157–58.

21. Mishnah *Shekalim* 6.5; see *The Mishnah,* p. 159.

22. Josephus, *Jewish War* 6.251; see Loeb Classical Library *Josephus* 3:448–49.

23. Josephus, *Antiquities* 15.413; see Loeb Classical Library *Josephus* 8:200–201.

24. Josephus, *Antiquities* 15.415–18; see Loeb Classical Library *Josephus* 8:200–203.

25. Josephus, *Antiquities* 15.411; see Loeb Classical Library *Josephus* 8:198–99.

Chapter 5. The Early Church and the Temple in Acts

1. See Nibley, "The Forty-day Mission of Christ," "Christian Envy of the Temple"; both republished in *Mormonism and Early Christianity,* pp. 10–44, 391–434.

2. See *A Greek-English Lexicon of the New Testament,* p. 850.

3. See Corbo, *The House of Saint Peter at Capernaum,* p. 44.

4. See Hunt, *Holy Land Pilgrimage,* p. 2.

5. Joseph Smith Diary, 11 June 1843; see Ehat and Cook, comps. and eds., *The Words of Joseph Smith,* p. 211.

6. Originally, the Qumran community consisted of priests who

had been expelled from—or had left—the temple in Jerusalem. These priests were led into the Judean wilderness by a man they called the "Teacher of Righteousness." Later, new members not of the priestly families joined this group. See Charlesworth, ed., *Jesus and the Dead Sea Scrolls,* pp. xxxiii–xxxiv.

7. For a fuller discussion of these three arguments, see Weinert, "Luke, Stephen, and the Temple in Luke-Acts," pp. 88–90.

8. Ibid., pp. 89–90.

9. See Behm, "Thuo," pp. 182–83.

10. See "Nike," in *The Oxford Classical Dictionary,* p. 735.

11. See *Pausanias's Description of Greece,* p. 157.

Chapter 6. Jesus and the Temple in the Gospel of John

1. The connection between the narratives of John and the Jewish festivals is explored in depth by Guilding, *The Fourth Gospel and Jewish Worship.* The connection between the narratives and the temple has been more recently discussed at length by Brown, *The Gospel According to John.*

2. The word for "tabernacle" in Greek is the noun *skene,* from the same verb as "dwelt," *skenein,* in John 1:14; see *A Greek-English Lexicon of the New Testament,* p. 762.

3. See Brown, *The Gospel According to John* 1:206.

4. Josephus, *Antiquities* 11.321–47; see Loeb Classical Library *Josephus* 6:468–83.

5. See Waltke, "Samaritan Pentateuch," p. 938.

6. See Brown, *The Gospel According to John* 1:326–27.

7. Mishnah *Sukkah* 5.1; see *The Mishnah,* p. 179.

8. Mishnah *Sukkah* 5.2, 3; see *The Mishnah,* p. 179.

9. See Isaiah 58: "And the Lord shall guide thee continually, and satisfy thy soul in drought, and make fat thy bones: and thou shalt be like a watered garden, and like a spring of water, whose waters fail not" (Isa. 58:11); or Proverbs 18: "The words of a man's mouth are as deep waters, and the wellspring of wisdom as a flowing brook" (Prov. 18:4). See Brown, *The Gospel According to John* 1:321–22 for a fuller discussion.

10. See Brown, *The Gospel According to John* 1:322–23.

11. For a more complete discussion, see Brown, *The Gospel According to John* 1:206.

12. The books of Maccabees are from the Apocrypha and contain some valuable historical data for the period 175–135 B.C.; see "Maccabees," LDS Bible Dictionary, p. 727.

13. See Brown, *The Gospel According to John* 1:404–5.

14. Josephus, *Jewish War* 5.185; see Loeb Classical Library *Josephus* 3:254–55. Also, Josephus, *Antiquities* 20.221; see Loeb Classical Library *Josephus* 9:506–7.

15. Joseph Smith, *Teachings*, pp. 150–51.

Chapter 7. Matthew and the Destruction of the Temple

1. Josephus, *Jewish War* 2.258–63; 6.285–88; 7.437–42; *Antiquities* 20.167–72; see Loeb Classical Library *Josephus* 2:422–25; 3:458–61, 626–29; and 9:478–81.

2. Eusebius, *Ecclesiastical History* 3.5.4; see *Eusebius: The History of the Church from Christ to Constantine,* p. 111.

3. Josephus, *Jewish War* 6.252–53, 271–73, 275–76; see Loeb Classical Library *Josephus* 3:448–49, 454–55, 456–57.

Chapter 8. The Temple Made Without Hands in Hebrews

1. See Thomas, "Hebrews: To Ascend the Holy Mount," pp. 479–91.

2. See *A Grammatical Analysis of the Greek New Testament,* p. 669.

3. See Freedman, "Temple Without Hands," pp. 21–30, and Parry and Parry, "The Temple in Heaven," pp. 515–32.

4. Hanson, "Typology," pp. 783–84.

Chapter 9. The Temple-Body and the Temple-Church

1. See McKinlay, "Temple Imagery in the Epistles of Peter," pp. 492–514.

2. For the bracketed words, see footnotes in the LDS Edition of the King James Bible.

3. For Hebrew and Greek meanings of *peculiar,* see footnotes for individual instances in the LDS Edition of the King James Bible.

Chapter 10. Promises to the Faithful in John's Revelation

1. See Riley, "Temple Imagery and the Book of Revelation," pp. 81–102.

2. See *A Greek-English Lexicon of the New Testament,* p. 535.

3. See "Septuagint," LDS Bible Dictionary, p. 771.

4. See "Pseudepigrapha," LDS Bible Dictionary, p. 755; and *Testament of Levi* 18:9–12 in *The Old Testament Pseudepigrapha* 2:795.

5. See *A Greek-English Lexicon of the New Testament,* pp. 774–75.

6. See Fiorenza, *The Book of Revelation,* p. 68.

7. Babylonian Talmud *Shabbath* 88a; see *Hebrew-English Edition of the Babylonian Talmud,* vol. 3.

8. *Targum Isaiah* 65:15; see *The Aramaic Bible: The Isaiah Targum.*

9. See *A Greek-English Lexicon of the New Testament,* p. 690.

10. For more information regarding *tefillin,* see "Phylacteries," LDS Bible Dictionary, p. 751.

11. For bracketed words, see footnotes in the LDS Edition of the King James Bible.

12. See Oepke, "Gumnos," p. 774.

13. See *A Greek-English Lexicon of the New Testament,* p. 473.

14. See Holzapfel, "The 'Hidden' Messiah," pp. 80–95.

15. Exceptions were made; see, for example, 1 Samuel 21:6.

16. Mishnah *Sukkah* 5.1–5; see *The Mishnah,* pp. 179–80.

17. Mishnah *Yoma* 6.2; see *The Mishnah,* p. 169.

18. See *A Grammatical Analysis of the Greek New Testament,* p. 750.

19. See *A Greek-English Lexicon of the New Testament,* pp. 12–13.

Bibliography

1. Editions and Translations Cited or Quoted

Ancient Bible Editions

The Aramaic Bible: The Isaiah Targum. Edited by Bruce D. Chilton. Wilmington, Delaware: Michael Glazier, Inc., 1987.

The Aramaic Bible: Targum Jonathan of the Former Prophets. Edited by D. J. Harrington and A. J. Saldarini. Wilmington, Delaware: Michael Glazier, Inc., 1987.

The Greek New Testament. Edited by Kurt Aland, Matthew Black, Carlo M. Martini, Bruce M. Metzger, and Allen Wikgreen. New York: American Bible Society, 1975.

The Interlinear Greek-English New Testament. Edited by Alfred Marshall. London: Samuel Bagster and Sons Limited, 1972.

The Septuagint with Apocrypha: Greek and English. Translated by Sir Lancelot C. L. Brenton. 1851. Reprint. Grand Rapids, Michigan: Zondervan Publishing House, 1975.

Modern Bible Editions

The Holy Bible. LDS Edition of the King James Version of the Bible. Salt Lake City: The Church of Jesus Christ of Latter-day Saints, 1979.

The Holy Scriptures: Inspired Version. Independence, Missouri: Herald Publishing House, 1974.

The New Oxford Annotated Bible with the Apocrypha: New Revised Standard Version. New York: Oxford University Press, 1991.

The New Oxford Annotated Bible with the Apocrypha: Revised Standard
   Version. New York: Oxford University Press, 1977.
The NIV Study Bible: New International Version. Edited by Kenneth
   Barker. Grand Rapids, Michigan: Zondervan Bible Publishers, 1985.
The NRSV-NIV: Parallel New Testament in Greek and English. Edited by
   Alfred Marshall. Grand Rapids, Michigan: Zondervan Bible
   Publishers, 1990.

The Dead Sea Scrolls

The Dead Sea Scriptures. Translated by Theodor H. Gaster. New York:
   Anchor Books, 1976.
The Temple Scroll. Edited by Yigael Yadin. 3 vols. Jerusalem: The Israel
   Exploration Society, 1983.

Rabbinic Literature

Hebrew-English Edition of the Babylonian Talmud. Edited by I. Epstein.
   25 vols. London: Soncino Press, 1989.
The Mishnah: Translated from the Hebrew with Introduction and Brief
   Explanatory Notes. Translated by Herbert Danby. Oxford: The
   Clarendon Press, 1933.

Other Jewish Literature and Texts

Josephus: The Life, Against Apion, Jewish Wars, and Antiquities. The Loeb
   Classical Library. Translated by J. St. J. Thackeray, Ralph Marcus,
   and Louis H. Feldman. 10 vols. Cambridge, Mass.: Harvard
   University Press, 1925–65.
The Old Testament Pseudepigrapha. Edited by James H. Charlesworth. 2
   vols. Garden City, New York: Doubleday & Company, Inc.,
   1983–85.

Other Ancient Sources

Eusebius: The History of the Church from Christ to Constantine. Translated
   by G. A. Williamson. Minneapolis, Minn.: Augsburg Publishing
   House, 1965.
Pausanias's Description of Greece. Translated by J. G. Frazer. New York:
   Biblio and Tannen, 1965.

2. Reference Works Cited or Quoted

The Anchor Bible Dictionary. Edited by David Noel Freedman. 6 vols. New York: Doubleday, 1992.

A Grammatical Analysis of the Greek New Testament. Edited by Max Zerwick and Mary Grosvenor. Rome: Biblical Institute Press, 1981.

A Greek-English Lexicon of the New Testament and Other Early Christian Literature. Edited by Walter Bauer, William F. Arndt, and Wilbur F. Gingrich. Chicago: The University of Chicago Press, 1957.

A Hebrew and English Lexicon of the Old Testament. Edited by Francis Brown, S. R. Driver, and Charles A. Briggs. Oxford: The Clarendon Press, 1951.

Horizontal Harmony of the Four Gospels in Parallel Columns. Edited by Thomas M. Mumford. Salt Lake City: Deseret Book Co., 1979.

An Intermediate Greek-English Lexicon. Edited by Liddell and Scott. Oxford: Clarendon Press, 1975.

The Joseph Smith Translation of the Four Gospels: A Harmony. Edited by Steven J. Hite and Julie Melville Hite. Orem, Utah: S & J Publishing, 1989.

The Oxford Classical Dictionary. Edited by N.G.L. Hammond and H. H. Schullard. Oxford: Clarendon Press, 1976.

The Oxford Companion to the Bible. Edited by Bruce M. Metzger and Michael D. Coogan. New York: Oxford University Press, 1993.

Synopse der drei ersten Evangelien/Synopsis of the First Three Gospels with the Addition of the Johannine Parallels. Edited by Albert Huck. Tunbingen, W. Germany: J.C.B. Mohr (Paul Siebeck), 1981.

Theological Dictionary of the New Testament. Edited by Gerhard Kittel. 10 vols. Grand Rapids, Michigan: Wm. B. Eerdmans Publishing Company, 1982.

3. General

Baltzer, K. "The Meaning of the Temple in the Lucan Writings." *Harvard Theological Review* 58 (1965): 263–77.

Barkay, Gabriel. "Measurements in the Bible." *Biblical Archaeology Review* 12 (March/April 1986): 37.

Behm, Johannes. "Thuo." In *Theological Dictionary of the New Testament,* edited by Gerhard Kittel, 10 vols., 3:182–3. Grand Rapids, Michigan: Wm. B. Eerdmans Publishing Company, 1965.

Ben-Dov, Meir. *In the Shadow of the Temple.* Jerusalem: Keter Publishing House, 1982.

Brown, Raymond E. *The Gospel According to John.* The Anchor Bible 29, 29A, 2 vols. Garden City, New York: Doubleday, 1966, 1970.

Bruce, F. F. *The Acts of the Apostles: Greek Text with Introduction and Commentary.* Grand Rapids, Michigan: Wm. B. Eerdmans Publishing Company, 1990.

Charlesworth, James H., ed. *Jesus and the Dead Sea Scrolls.* Garden City, New York: Doubleday, 1992.

Corbo, V. *The House of Saint Peter at Capernaum: A Preliminary Report.* Jerusalem: Franciscan Print Press, 1972.

Dunn, James D. G. *The Parting of the Ways Between Christianity and Judaism and Their Significance for the Character of Christianity.* Philadelphia: Trinity Press International, 1991.

Ehat, Andrew F., and Lyndon W. Cook, comps. and eds. *The Words of Joseph Smith: The Contemporary Accounts of the Nauvoo Discourses of the Prophet Joseph.* Provo: Religious Studies Center, Brigham Young University, 1980.

Eppstein, Victor. "The Historicity of the Gospel Account of the Cleansing of the Temple." *Zeitschrift für die neutestamentliche wissenschaft und die kunde der älteren kirche* 55 (1964): 42–58.

Evans, Craig A. "Jesus' Action in the Temple: Cleansing or Portent of Destruction?" *The Catholic Biblical Quarterly* 51 (April 1989): 237–70.

Finegan, Jack. *The Archeology of the New Testament: The Life of Jesus and the Beginning of the Early Church.* Rev. ed. Princeton, New Jersey: Princeton University Press, 1992.

Fiorenza, Elisabeth Schussler. *The Book of Revelation: Justice and Judgment.* Philadelphia: Fortress Press, 1985.

Fitzmeyer, Joseph A. *The Gospel According to Luke.* 2 vols. Garden City, New York: Doubleday & Company, Inc., 1979–85.

Freedman, David Noel. "Temple Without Hands." In *Temples and High Places in Biblical Times,* pp. 21–30. Jerusalem: Hebrew Union College, 1981.

Ginzberg, Louis. *Legends of the Jews.* 7 vols. Philadelphia: Jewish Publication Society, 1937.

Guilding, Aileen. *The Fourth Gospel and Jewish Worship.* Oxford: Clarendon Press, 1960.

Hanson, Anthony Tyrrell. "Typology." In *The Oxford Companion to the*

Bible, edited by Bruce M. Metzger and Michael D. Coogan, pp. 783–84. New York: Oxford University Press, 1993.

Haran, Menahem. *Temples and Temple-Service in Ancient Israel: An Inquiry into Biblical Cult Phenomena and the Historical Setting of the Priestly School.* Winona Lake, Indiana: Eisenbrauns, 1985.

Herzog, Ze'ev, Miriam Aharoni, and Anson F. Rainey. "Arad: An Ancient Israelite Fortress with a Temple to Yahweh." *Biblical Archaeology Review* 13 (March/April 1987): 16–35.

Holzapfel, Richard Neitzel. "The 'Hidden' Messiah." In *A Witness of Jesus Christ: The 1989 Sperry Symposium on the Old Testament,* edited by Richard D. Draper, pp. 80–95. Salt Lake City: Deseret Book Company, 1990.

Hunt, E. D. *Holy Land Pilgrimage in the Later Roman Empire,* A.D. *312–460.* Oxford: The Clarendon Press, 1984.

Hurowitz, Victor. "Inside Solomon's Temple." *Bible Review* 10 (April 1994): 24–37, 50.

Lundwall, N. B., comp. *A Compilation Containing the Lectures on Faith.* Salt Lake City: Bookcraft, n.d.

Madsen, Truman G., ed. *The Temple in Antiquity: Ancient Records and Modern Perspectives.* Provo: Religious Studies Center, Brigham Young University, 1984.

Marshall, I. H. "Church and Temple in the New Testament." *Tyndale Bulletin* 40 (1989): 203–22.

Mazar, Benjamin. *The Mountain of the Lord.* Garden City, New York: Doubleday, 1975.

McConkie, Bruce R. *The Mortal Messiah.* 4 vols. Salt Lake City: Deseret Book Company, 1979–81.

McKinlay, Daniel B. "Temple Imagery in the Epistles of Peter." In *Temples of the Ancient World,* edited by Donald W. Parry, pp. 492–514. Salt Lake City and Provo: Deseret Book Company, and Foundation for Ancient Research and Mormon Studies, 1994.

Meyers, Carol L. "Jachin and Boaz in Religious and Political Perspective." *Catholic Biblical Quarterly* 45 (1983): 167–78.

———. "Temple, Jerusalem." In *Anchor Bible Dictionary,* edited by David Noel Freedman, 6 vols., 6:364–65. Garden City, New York: Doubleday, 1992.

Meyers, Carol L., and Eric M. Meyers. *Zechariah 9–14.* The Anchor Bible 25C. Garden City, New York: Doubleday, 1993.

Neusner, Jacob, ed. *The Life of Torah: Readings in the Jewish Religious*

Experience. The Religious Life of Man Series. Encino, Calif.: Dickenson Publishing Company, 1974.

Nibley, Hugh. "Christian Envy of the Temple." *The Jewish Quarterly Review* 50 (October 1959): 97–123 and (January 1960): 229–40.

————. "The Forty-day Mission of Christ—The Forgotten Heritage." *Vigiliae Christianae* 20 (1966): 1–24.

————. *Mormonism and Early Christianity.* Vol. 4 of *The Collected Works of Hugh Nibley.* Salt Lake City and Provo: Deseret Book Company, and Foundation for Ancient Research and Mormon Studies, 1987.

Oepke, Albrecht. "Gumnos." In *Theological Dictionary of the New Testament,* edited by Gerhard Kittel, 10 vols., 1:774. Grand Rapids, Michigan: Wm. B. Eerdmans Publishing Company, 1964.

Ogden, D. Kelly. *Illustrated Guide to the Model City and to New Testament Jerusalem.* Jerusalem: The Jerusalem Center for Near Eastern Studies, 1990.

————. "Jesus and the Temple." *Ensign* 21 (April 1991): 12–19.

Packer, Boyd K. *The Holy Temple.* Salt Lake City: Bookcraft, 1980.

Parry, Donald W. "Ritual Anointing with Olive Oil in Ancient Israelite Religion." In *The Allegory of the Olive Tree,* edited by Stephen D. Ricks and John W. Welch, pp. 262–89. Salt Lake City and Provo: Deseret Book Company, and Foundation for Ancient Research and Mormon Studies, 1994.

Parry, Donald W., Stephen D. Ricks, and John W. Welch. *Temple Bibliography.* Provo: Foundation for Ancient Research and Mormon Studies.

Parry, Jay A., and Donald W. Parry. "The Temple in Heaven: Its Description and Significance." In *Temples of the Ancient World,* edited by Donald W. Parry, pp. 515–32. Salt Lake City and Provo: Deseret Book Company, and Foundation for Ancient Research and Mormon Studies, 1994.

Patrich, Joseph. "Reconstructing the Magnificent Temple Herod Built." *Bible Review* 4 (October 1988): 18–19.

Riley, William. "Temple Imagery and the Book of Revelation." *Proceedings of the Irish Biblical Association* 6 (1982): 81–102.

Ritmeyer, Kathleen. *A Model of King Herod's Temple in Jerusalem.* Skelton, England: Ritmeyer Archaeological Design, 1993.

Ritmeyer, Kathleen and Leen. *A Model of Herod's Temple.* Skelton, England: Ritmeyer Archaeological Design, 1993.

————. "Reconstructing Herod's Temple Mount in Jerusalem." *Biblical Archaeology Review* 15 (November/December 1989): 23–42.

Robinson, Stephen E. "The Setting of the Gospels." In *Studies in Scripture, Volume 5: The Gospels,* edited by Kent P. Jackson and Robert L. Millet, pp. 10–37. Salt Lake City: Deseret Book Company, 1986.

Safrai, Shmuel. "Temple: Ritual." In *Enclyclopaedia Judaica,* 16 vols., 15:970–83. New York: Macmillan, 1972.

Safrai, Shmuel, and Michael Avi-Yonah. "Temple." In *Encyclopaedia Judaica,* 16 vols., 15:961–69. New York: Macmillan, 1972.

Sanders, E. P. *Paul and Palestinian Judaism.* Philadelphia: Fortress Press, 1977.

Scott, R.B.Y. "Jachin and Boaz." In *Interpreter's Dictionary of the Bible,* 4 vols. and Supplement, 2:780–81. Nashville: Abingdon, 1962.

Smith, Joseph. *History of The Church of Jesus Christ of Latter-day Saints.* Edited by B. H. Roberts. 7 vols. Salt Lake City: The Church of Jesus Christ of Latter-day Saints, 1902–32.

————. *Teachings of the Prophet Joseph Smith.* Selected by Joseph Fielding Smith. Salt Lake City: Deseret Book Company, 1938.

Sylva, Dennis D. "The Temple Curtain and Jesus' Death in the Gospel of Luke." *Journal of Biblical Literature* 105 (June 1986): 239–50.

Thomas, M. Catherine. "Hebrews: To Ascend the Holy Mount." In *Temples of the Ancient World,* edited by Donald W. Parry, pp. 479–91. Salt Lake City and Provo: Deseret Book Company, and Foundation for Ancient Research and Mormon Studies, 1994.

Treasures of the Holy Land: Ancient Art From the Israel Museum. New York: The Metropolitan Museum of Art, 1986.

Waltke, Bruce K. "Samaritan Pentateuch." In *Anchor Bible Dictionary,* edited by David Noel Freedman, 6 vols., 5:938. Garden City, New York: Doubleday, 1992.

Weinert, Francis D. "Luke, Stephen, and the Temple in Luke-Acts." *Biblical Theology Bulletin* 17 (1987): 88–90.

Illustration Credits

Front Cover

Reproduced from "A Model of Herod's Temple Slide Set." Ritmeyer Archaeological Design. Model and slides © 1993 A. W. Garrard. Used by permission.

Back Cover

Reproduced from "A Model of Herod's Temple Slide Set." Ritmeyer Archaeological Design. Model and slides © 1993 A. W. Garrard. Used by permission.

Prologue: My Father's House

Page x   Dennis Lyall. Reproduced from *Jesus and His Times* © 1987. Reader's Digest Association, Inc. Used by permission.

Page 4   Leen Ritmeyer. Ritmeyer Archaeological Design. Used by permission.

Chapter 1. The Temple as the Pathway to Eternal Life

Page 10   Stanley Galli, "Adam and Eve in the Garden" © The

Church of Jesus Christ of Latter-day Saints. Used by permission.

Pages 18–19   Michael Lyon. Courtesy of the authors.

Chapter 2. The Temples of Ancient Israel

Page 20   Paul Calle. Reproduced from *Great People of the Bible and How They Lived* © 1974. Reader's Digest Association, Inc. Used by permission.

Pages 28–29   Michael Lyon. Courtesy of the authors.

Pages 34–35   Michael Lyon. Courtesy of the authors.

Page 45   Palestine Archaeological Museum.

Page 53   Courtesy of Richard T. Nowitz.

Chapter 3. Temple Worship at the Time of Christ

Page 54   James Tissot, "The Multitude in the Temple." Used by permission of The Church of Jesus Christ of Latter-day Saints.

Page 61   Harry Anderson, "Moses Calls Aaron to the Ministry" © The Church of Jesus Christ of Latter-day Saints. Used by permission.

Pages 68–69   Michael Lyon. Courtesy of the authors.

Page 74   Reproduced from "A Model of Herod's Temple Slide Set." Ritmeyer Archaeological Design. Model and slides © 1993 A. W. Garrard. Used by permission.

Chapter 4. Luke and the Presence of God in the Temple

Page 80   James Tissot, "Jesus Sitting in the Midst of the Doctors." Used by permission of The Church of Jesus Christ of Latter-day Saints.

Page 93   *Top:* Israel Museum.
                 Center: Lane Ritmeyer. Ritmeyer Archaeological Design. Used by permission.
                 Bottom: Leen Ritmeyer. Ritmeyer Archaeological Design. Used by permission.

Page 109   James Tissot, "The Widow's Mite." Used by permission of The Church of Jesus Christ of Latter-day Saints.

Page 112   Reproduced from "A Model of Herod's Temple Slide Set." Ritmeyer Archaeological Design. Model and slides © 1993 A. W. Garrard. Used by permission.

Page 116   Walter Rane. Reproduced from *Jesus and His Times* © 1987. Reader's Digest Association, Inc. Used by permission.

Chapter 5. The Early Church and the Temple in Acts

Page 118   Chris Magadini. Reproduced from *After Jesus: The Triumph of Christianity* © 1992. Reader's Digest Association, Inc. Used by permission.

Page 128   The Acropolis of Athens Model. Courtesy of the Royal Ontario Museum, Toronto, Canada.

Page 129   Courtesy of the authors.

Page 132   "Athena Parthenos in Cella." Courtesy of the Royal Ontario Museum, Toronto, Canada.

Page 135   Walter Rane. Reproduced from *Jesus and His Times* ©
                1987. Reader's Digest Association, Inc. Used by per-
                mission.

Page 139   Walter Rane. Reproduced from *After Jesus: The
                Triumph of Christianity* © 1992. Reader's Digest
                Association, Inc. Used by permission.

Chapter 6. Jesus and the Temple in the Gospel of John

Page 140   James Tissot, "The Woman Taken in Adultery." Used
                by permission of The Church of Jesus Christ of
                Latter-day Saints.

Page 156   James Tissot, "But No Man Laid Hands upon Him."
                Used by permission of The Church of Jesus Christ of
                Latter-day Saints.

Chapter 7. Matthew and the Destruction of the Temple

Page 170   Gary E. Smith, "Christ Laments over Jerusalem."
                Courtesy of Gary E. Smith.

Page 178   Courtesy of the authors.

Page 181   George S. Gaadt. Reproduced from *Jesus and His
                Times* © 1987. Reader's Digest Association, Inc.
                Used by permission.

Chapter 8. The Temple Made Without Hands in Hebrews

Page 182   Dennis Lyall. Reproduced from *Jesus and His Times*
                © 1987. Reader's Digest Association, Inc. Used by
                permission.

Chapter 9. The Body-as-Temple and the Temple-Church

Page 194   Paul Calle. Reproduced from *Great People of the Bible and How They Lived* © 1974. Reader's Digest Association, Inc. Used by permission.

Page 198   James Tissot, "The Corner Stone." Used by permission of The Church of Jesus Christ of Latter-day Saints.

Page 200   Leen Ritmeyer. Ritmeyer Archaeological Design. Used by permission

Page 204   Leen Ritmeyer. Ritmeyer Archaeological Design. Used by permission.

Chapter 10. Promises to the Faithful in John's Revelation

Page 206   Michael Lyon. Courtesy of the authors.

Page 211   Ted Henniger, "Menorah" © The Church of Jesus Christ of Latter-day Saints. Used by permission.

Page 216   Ted Henniger, "Ark of the Covenant" © The Church of Jesus Christ of Latter-day Saints. Used by permission.

Page 226   Moshe Levine, "Priest and High Priest." Melechet Hamishkan, Tel Aviv, Israel.

Page 231   Ted Henniger, "Table of Shewbread" © The Church of Jesus Christ of Latter-day Saints. Used by permission.

Page 240   Ted Henniger, "Altar of Incense" © The Church of Jesus Christ of Latter-day Saints. Used by permission.

Page 248   Dennis Lyall. Reproduced from *Jesus and His Times*
                © 1987. Reader's Digest Association, Inc. Used by
                permission.

Epilogue: My House

Page 250   James Tissot, "Jesus Speaking in the Treasury." Used
                by permission of The Church of Jesus Christ of
                Latter-day Saints.

Page 255   "The Tabernacle: A Type for the Temples," CES Slide
                Set K © The Church of Jesus Christ of Latter-day
                Saints. Used by permission.

Index

Page numbers in italics refer to illustrations

— A —

Aaron, blesses the people, 117
  clothed in priestly robes, 229
  set apart, 60
Aaronic Priesthood, had authority
    to conduct temple worship, 56
  held by Levites, 59
  retained by Israelites, 24
Abraham, at sacred places, 21–22
  name changed from Abram, 219
Abrahamic covenant, given to pa-
    triarchs, 21–22
Adam and Eve, given law of sacri-
    fice, 62
  learn plan of redemption, 11–13
Alma, on Melchizedek Priesthood,
    24
Altar of incense, *240*
  and daily sacrifice, 67
  in Herod's temple, 48–49
  in Mosaic tabernacle, 29, 30
  in Solomon's temple, 35, 37
  symbolic of prayer, 83–85,
    239–40
Amulek, on Son of God, 142
Angel, appears to Zacharias, 86

delivers Apostles from prison,
    124
  instructs Apostles to go to
    temple, 125
  marks foreheads of faithful, 226
Angels, in heavenly temple, 242
Anna, witnesses of Christ, 7, 89
Anointing, of faithful, 229–30
  of priests, 60
  related to Holy Ghost, 15–16
Antonia fortress, described, 46
  Jesus condemned at, 113
  Paul at, 136–37
Apostasy, of Israel, 23, 201
Apostles, as foundation stones of
    Church, 199
  filled with Holy Spirit on
    Pentecost, 119
  See also Disciples; Peter; Paul
Ark of the covenant, *216*
  in Mosaic tabernacle, 27, 29,
    30–31
  in Solomon's temple, 35, 37
  missing from Herod's temple, 49
  no longer in Zerubbabel's temple,
    40
  symbol of God's presence, 240

Atonement, and sacrifice, 63
  allows return to presence of God,
    12, 17
  explained, 31
  infinite and eternal, 246–47
  power of, 158
  represented in Passover, 76
  symbolized in Mosaic tabernacle,
    32
  taught through law of Moses, 25

— B —

Baptism, 16
Blessing, daily at temple, 67
Blood, representing cleansing, 32
Body-as-temple, 9, 196–97, 253
Book of life, names of faithful in,
  222–23
Brother of Jared, sees premortal
  Jesus Christ, 13
Burnt offering, described, 63–64,
  66–67

— C —

Cherubim, in Mosaic tabernacle,
  30
Church, as temple, 196, 197–201,
  253
Cleansing, before ascending
  Temple Mount, 57, 252
  from sin, 79
  of disciples, 164–65
  of inner person, 190
  of priests, 27, 66
  ritual, 3, 4, 8
  through blood of Only Begotten,
    15
  through faith and repentance, 15
  to participate in sacred ordi-
    nances, 32
Cleansing of temple, 5–7, 94, 102,
  103–5, 147–48, 174

Clothing, at Temple Mount, 57
  before entering sacred place, 252
  faithful given special, 221–22,
    227–29
  Jesus', at Mount of
    Transfiguration, 95, 97
  of Aaron and sons, 60
  of high priest, 61–62, 211
  of Levites, 60–62
  of priests, 209, 225
  triumphal, 238
Cloud of glory, at Mosaic taber-
    nacle, 32
  at Mount of Transfiguration, 95,
    99
  at second coming of Christ,
    99–100
  at Solomon's temple, 37
Commandments, keeping, 14
Consecration, 60–61
Courts of the temple, described, 5,
    44–47, 57, 70, 87–88
Covenant, Abrahamic, 21–22
  at Mount Sinai, 25
  blessings and cursings, 172–74
  Jesus Christ establishes new, 172,
    186–87
  made in sacred places, 21–22
  represented by ark of the
    covenant, 29
  to become holy people, 201–5
  with David, 33
Covenants, part of temple worship,
    13
Crown, of high priest, 225
  promised to faithful, 215–17
Crucifixion, of Jesus Christ, 113

— D —

David, and sacred places, 33
Day of Atonement, at Mosaic taber-
    nacle, 27, 29
  clothing of high priest for, 62

described, 49, 77–78
high priest enters Holy of Holies
on, 190
represents return to God's presence, 17
sacrifices during, 70
Death (second), faithful will not be
hurt by, 217
Dedicatory prayer, at Kirtland
Temple, 26
at Solomon's temple, 37–38, 79,
127
Degrees of glory, degrees of enjoying presence of God, 58
Deliverance, from bondage, 23, 71,
74, 203
from death, 76
from spiritual bondage, 254
Destruction of Herod's temple, 52,
110–11, 138, 148, 179–81
due to breaking covenant, 173
events leading to, 177–80
foretold by Jesus, 106–7, 134,
171, 176–77
Disciples, in upper room, 120–21
preach and pray in temple, 7, 8,
81, 116–17, 122–23, 183, 253
receive outpouring of Spirit on
Pentecost, 119, 122
Dome of the Rock, 53

— E —

Elders, twenty-four in John's vision,
217, 233–35
Elias (i.e., Elijah), appears at
Mount of Transfiguration, 95,
97–98
Essenes, described, 50
Eternal life, temple prepares for,
11–13
means to live with Eternal
Father, 11
Eusebius, records that Church
members were warned of destruction, 179
Ezekiel, on Lord as sanctuary, 244
sees vision of heavenly temple, 9,
192, 214

— F —

Fall of Adam, brings death, 15
cuts mankind off from presence
of God, 11–12, 17
Feast of the Dedication, Christ's
participation in, 162–63
described, 160–62
Feast of Tabernacles, at dedication
of Solomon's temple, 37
Christ's participation in, 154–60
described, 1, 78, 234
light in, 210
Feast of Weeks. *See* Pentecost
Feasts. *See* Festivals
Festivals, calendar of, 72–73
described, 1, 55, 236–37
noted by John, 145–46
sacrifices during, 70
under law of Moses, 71–73
See also Day of Atonement; Feast
of the Dedication; Feast of
Tabernacles; Passover;
Pentecost; Sabbath
Firstborn, as offering, 86
Forty-day ministry, 120

— G —

Gamaliel, protests high prices of
sacrifices, 104
Garden of Eden, 17, 214
Garden of Gethsemane, 16
Garments. *See* Clothing
Gates of temple, described, 4, 46
Gentiles, and temple worship,
56–57
Glory, 144

in temple, 168
See also Cloud of glory

— H —

Heavenly temple. *See* Temple
    (heavenly)
Herod the Great, 41–43
Herod's temple. *See* Temple of
    Herod
High priest, on Day of Atonement,
    17, 57, 59–60, 77, 184
Holiness, associated with temple
    worship, 3, 56–58, 191
    being set apart to do God's will,
        247
    instruction in, 79
    of ancient Israel, 31–32
    necessary to enter presence of
        God, 14–15
    symbols of, 60
    taught in temple, 252
    through law of Moses, 25
Holy Ghost, as Comforter, 165
    Pentecostal outpouring of, 119
    purifying agent, 15–16
    represented by olive oil, 16
    reveals to Simeon that he will see
        Christ, 88
Holy nation, covenant to become,
    58
    Israel as, 25, 201–5, 208–9
    Saints to become, 208
Holy of Holies, described by Paul,
    188
    entered on Day of Atonement, 77
    in heavenly temple, 233
    in Herod's temple, 47, 49
    in Mosaic tabernacle, 17, 29, 30
    in Solomon's temple, 35, 36, 37
    in Zerubbabel's temple, 40
    symbolizes entering presence of
        God, 184

Holy people. *See* Holy nation
Holy Place, in Herod's temple,
    47–48
    in Mosaic tabernacle, 17, 29, 30
    in Solomon's temple, 35, 36
Hosea, on becoming God's people,
    205
House of the Lord, faithful to al-
    ways dwell in, 223–24
    See also Temple (heavenly)

— I —

Idols, at Sinai, 23
Impurity, under law of Moses, 64
Isaac, renews Abrahamic covenant,
    22
Isaiah, on house of prayer, 105
Israel, covenants with Lord at
    Mount Sinai, 25, 94
    to be holy, 15, 201–2
    worships idols, 35
Israelites, and temple worship,
    56–57

— J —

Jacob, in sacred place, 95–96
    receives Abrahamic covenant, 22
    name changed to Israel, 219
Jeremiah, declares temple is de-
    filed, 147
    foretells destruction of temple,
        174–75
Jerusalem, described, 1–6, 43
    name changed from Salem, 2
    to be restored, 192
Jesus Christ, activities in temple,
    16–17
    authority of, 147–48
    baptized, 92
    before Pilate, 113
    before Sanhedrin, 113, 147–48

cleansing of temple, 5–7, 94,
102, 103–5, 147–48, 174
cornerstone of Church, 199–200
covenant fulfilled in, 33
crucified, 113
establishes new covenant, 172,
186–87
eternal High Priest, 184–86,
188–89, 192, 210–11, 253,
254
feeds five thousand, 152–54
firstborn of Mary, 86
focus of all temple worship,
255–56
foretells destruction of Herod's
temple, 106–7, 110, 171,
176–77
genealogy of, 172
heals on Sabbath, 152
infant in temple, 7, 86–89
infinite sacrifice of, 58, 190–91
the King, 160, 244, 247
Lamb of God, 245–48
laments over Jerusalem, 100,
103, 171, 175–76
like Moses, 155–57
Messiah, 56, 95, 151
observes festivals, 146
passion of, 111
relationship to Father, 163, 166,
168
Samaritan woman and, 149–51
sermon on bread of life, 153–54
Son of God, 152
teaches about renewing
covenant, 155–56
teaches daily in temple, 7, 106,
251
tempted by Satan, 92–94
triumphal entry into Jerusalem,
102–3, 174
types of, 75–76, 77–78, 106–7,
142–68

washes disciples' feet, 164–65
and woman taken in adultery,
157–58
as youth in temple, 7, 89–91
John the Baptist, baptizes Jesus, 92
calls Jesus the Lamb of God, 145
John the Beloved, apocalyptic vision of, 207–49
describes Jesus cleansing the
temple, 6–7
describes New Jerusalem, 254
sees vision of heavenly temple, 9
witnesses mission of Christ,
144–69
Joseph (of Egypt), receives
Abrahamic covenant, 22
Josephus, describes Herod's temple,
42–43, 46–49, 87, 88, 92–94,
111, 112–13, 199
describes destruction of temple,
111, 179–80
describes false prophets, 177
on clothing at Temple Mount, 57
on conflicts between Romans
and Jews, 51
on corruption of priesthood, 104
on Melchizedek, 22
Joy, through obedience, 13
Judgment, Day of, 12

— K —

King Benjamin, learns that God will
dwell among men, 141–42
Kirtland Temple, 26, 32

— L —

Last Supper, 121, 148
initiates new covenant, 172
a Passover meal, 152, 164
Law of Moses, establishes sacred
times, 71–73

given at Mount Sinai, 24–25
points to coming of Christ, 55
instituted series of sacrifices,
    62–63
to direct men to Christ, 15
Levites, held Aaronic Priesthood,
    24
roles in temple worship, 58–62
Light, symbolism, 30
    See also Menorah; Feast of
    Tabernacles
Luke, and temple worship, 81–139

— M —

Maccabees, revolt and rededicate
    temple, 40–41
Manna, promised to faithful, 218
Mary, at temple, 86–88
Matthew, testifies that Christ is
    Messiah, 171
on destruction of temple,
    171–81
Meal offering, described, 64, 67
Melchizedek, and Abraham, 22
prototype of Christ, 184
Melchizedek Priesthood, Abraham's
    ordination to, 22
taken from Israel at Sinai, 23
Menorah, 211
daily lighting of, 66–67
in Herod's temple, 48
in John's revelation, 210–11
in Mosaic tabernacle, 29, 30
in Solomon's temple, 35
symbolic of tree of life, 214
Mercy seat, 216
in Herod's temple, 60
in Mosaic tabernacle, 27, 31
represents throne of God, 233
Messiah, importance of coming of,
    141–42
See also Jesus Christ

Morning star, promised to faithful,
    221
Mortality, as testing period, 11
Moses, and founding of Israel as a
    holy nation, 201–2
appears on Mount of
    Transfiguration, 95, 98
sees God, 13, 23–24
sees heavenly temple, 186
sets apart Aaron, 60
testifies of Christ, 151, 155–57
Mount Hermon, as possible site of
    Transfiguration, 96
Mount of Olives, 2, 100
Mount Sinai, glory of Lord settles
    at, 95
heavenly temple revealed to
    Moses at, 186
Israel covenants with Lord, 25,
    94, 203
mountain of God, 17
place of revelation, 126
site of Lord's instruction to
    Moses, 23
Mountain of God, site of creation
    of Adam and Eve, 17

— N —

Name, faithful to receive God's,
    224–26
faithful to receive new, 218–20
Nephi, on coming of Christ, 55
New Jerusalem, 243, 254
New Testament, as testimony of
    Christ, 7–8

— O —

Obedience, brings one closer to
    God, 14
brings joy, 13
Offerings, brought to temple, 5

See also individual offerings

Olive oil, for light in tabernacle, 30
  represents Holy Ghost, 32
  See also Anointing

Ordinances, eternal, 16
  taken from Israel at Sinai, 23

Overcoming, 213–14

— P —

Parable, of the vineyard, 106, 108
  on prayer, 101–2

Passover, Christ's participation in,
  163–69
  described, 1, 2, 74–76, 90
  during Christ's ministry, 146,
  147–48
  and feeding of five thousand,
  152–54
  and symbols of Christ, 142–43,
  145, 248

Paul, before Sanhedrin, 137
  on body as temple, 196–97
  on Church as temple, 196,
  197–201
  compares worship in pagan and
  divine temples, 129–32
  expelled from temple, 134–36
  receives vision in temple, 136
  sees resurrected Jesus Christ, 13
  teaches of heavenly temple, 183
  worships in temple at Jerusalem,
  132–34

Peace offering, described, 64

Pentecost, celebrates giving of the
  law at Sinai, 122, 151
  described, 64, 119, 122–23
  outpouring of Spirit on, 119
  Paul returns to Jerusalem for,
  132

People of God, becoming, 122

Peter, heals lame man at temple,
  123–24

preaches in temple, 124

Peter, James, and John, on Mount
  of Transfiguration, 95, 99

Pharisees, described, 49–50

Pilate, Pontius, violates Jewish law,
  51
  condemns Jesus, 113

Pinnacle of temple, 92–94, 93

Place of trumpeting, 93, 94

Plan of redemption, to prepare
  people to return to God's presence, 12

Prayer, communicating with God,
  12
  in John's revelation, 239–40
  in sacred places, 97
  parable on, 101–2
  part of temple worship, 13, 79
  represented by incense, 30, 67
  temple as house of, 82, 83–86
  See also Dedicatory prayer

Presence of God, dwelling in,
  11–13
  entering into, 56–58, 79
  leaves temple, 138
  manifest in temple, 9, 82, 86,
  136, 184
  on Mount Sinai, 23
  process to regain, 165–68, 191
  repentance brings one to, 31
  and tabernacle, 25–27
  to be taken away for disobedience, 25

Priests, corruption of, 104–5

Promises, to the faithful, 212–32

Purification, by fire and water, 227
  of Mary, 86
  on Day of Atonement, 77
  See also Cleansing

— Q —

Qumran, library at, 50

— R —

Repentance, 65–66, 101–2
  to enter presence of God, 31
Resurrection, possible through Son
  of God, 152
Robes, of the priesthood, 9
  See also Clothing
Rod of iron, promised to faithful,
  220–21
Romans, conflicts with Jews, 51–52
  an destruction of temple,
  177–81
  in Jerusalem, 5

— S —

Sabbath, as sacred day, 71, 73–74
  healing on, 152
  heralded by trumpets, 93, 241
Sacred meals, Abraham and
  Melchizedek, 22
  messianic feast, 230–32
  peace offering, 64
Sacred places, described, 21–22,
  32–33
  mountains as, 95–97
Sacred times, 70–78
  See also Festivals
Sacrifice, of broken heart, 101
  Christ's infinite, 190–91
  daily, 66–70
  descriptions of types of, 62–70
  as eternal law, 62
  hallmark of temple building, 26
  in Mosaic tabernacle, 27
  in temple, 13
  infinite, 58, 190–91
  offered at sacred places, 21–22
  Savior's, represented by blood,
  16
  types of Christ's, 75–76
Samaritans, 149–50

Sanctification, 15–16
  at Mount Sinai, 23
  See also Holiness
Sanhedrin, hears Christ, 113,
  147–48
  hears Paul, 137
  meeting room on Temple Mount,
  44, 111–13
Scapegoat, on Day of Atonement,
  77–78
Simeon, recognizes Christ, 7,
  88–89
Sin offering, described, 64–65
  Mary's, 86–87
Smith, Joseph, on baptism, 16
  on building Kirtland Temple, 26
  on Melchizedek Priesthood, 23
  on 144,000 high priests, 239
  on place where disciples performed ordinances, 121
  on First and Second Comforters,
  166
  on sacrifice, 62
  sees Lord, 13
Solomon, builds house of God, 33,
  127–28
  gives dedicatory prayer, 37–38,
  79, 127
  prays, 158
Spirit of God. *See* Holy Ghost
Stephen, discourses before
  Sanhedrin, 125–29
Stone. *See* White stone
Stones, compared to Church,
  199–201
Symbols, in temple worship, 16
  See also Jesus Christ

— T —

Tabernacle (Mosaic), 28–29
  described, 26–31, 187–88
  at Mount Sinai, 17

as sacred place, 25–26
Table of shewbread, in Herod's
 temple, 48
 in Mosaic tabernacle, 29, 30
 in Solomon's temple, 35, 36–37
Tablets of the law, in ark of
 covenant, 30
Temple, defined, 44, 82
 as dwelling place of God, 14
 as Father's house, 105
 as focal point of worship, 55
 as house of God, 100
 as house of praise, 101
 as house of prayer, 8, 105, 136
 as sacred space, 56
 and sacrifice, 8
Temple courts. *See* Courts of the
 temple
Temple (heavenly), 183, 184–90
 goal of earthly pilgrimage, 193
 John's vision of, 207, 241–43
 site of messianic feast, 230
Temple Mount, 53, 74
 activities on, 57
 described, 2–5, 44
Temple of Herod, 53, 68–69
 described, 2–3, 5, 8, 42–49
 place for celebrating feasts, 1
 See also Courts of the temple;
  Destruction of Herod's temple;
  Josephus
Temple of Solomon, 34–35
 dedication of, 37–38, 242–43
 described, 33–37
 destruction of, 38
Temple of Zerubbabel, 39–40
Temple Scroll, describes future
 temple, 50
Temple worship, purposes of, 9, 13
 symbols of, 15–17
 at time of Christ, 55–58
Temples, sites other than
 Jerusalem, 8

Thank offerings, described, 70
Throne, promised to faithful, 232
Throne of God, 233–34
Transfiguration, 94–100
Tree of life, 214–15, 249
Trespass offering, described, 65–66
Trumpets, as alarm, 241
Types and shadows, 8
Types of Christ, the bread of life,
 142, 143, 152–54
 Comforter, 142, 165–66
 the good shepherd, 142, 143,
  162–63
 Lamb of God, 142–43, 145, 164
 light of life, 142, 143, 144, 159
 living water, 142, 143, 150–51,
  156–57, 159
 the true vine, 142, 143, 166–68
 the word, 142, 144

— U —

Upper room, as sacred space,
 120–21
Urim and Thummim, 61, 218–19

— V —

Veil, in Mosaic tabernacle, 30
Veil of Herod's temple, 48–49, 184
 rent at time of Crucifixion, 8–9,
  113–16

— W —

Washing, of disciples' feet, 164–65
 of priests, 60
 See also Cleansing; Purification
Western Wall, 53, 107
White stone, promised to faithful,
 218–20
Widow, in temple, 108–10
Worship. *See* Temple worship

— Z —

Zacharias, in temple, 81
　receives revelation in temple,
　　83–86
Zealots, described, 50–51
　revolt against Rome, 177
Zechariah, prophesies of coming of

Messiah, 159–60
　prophesies of millennial temple,
　　147
　sees vision of Jerusalem restored,
　　192
Zerubbabel's temple. *See* Temple of
　Zerubbabel